WHAT PEOPLE ARE SAY

SH*T HAPPENS, MAC
(ALLOW IT!)

It is such a great privilege to write of my love for Carmen Harris and to acknowledge her for the difference she has made in my life. I went to see Carmen on the eve of an emotional storm. I am clear now that I was guided or, you could say, 'sent' to Carmen. It still amazes me how natural it all was, like meeting an old family friend, when we met for the first time – because that is the nature of Carmen, she receives you with pure Love. I had not imagined that this would be the start of my journey of transformation. In that one session she peeled away all the crusty layers of experience that had had me blocked to the point of deep stagnation. From that moment onward my life has been unfolding in the most magical and magnificent of ways. I am clear and without a shadow of a doubt that Carmen is being used as a channel for the greatest good in this world. She has touched my spirit and my life in the most profound way. Her work is so deep that it unfolds over time – not a one-shot-slam-bam thankyou-mam kind of thing. Hers is an immeasurable commitment to greatest potential in all beings; to generosity and to love – simply, she heals. From the depths of my heart I thank you, Carmen, and I pray for your continued ability to touch many more lives as you have touched mine. Love, Peace, Abundance and many Blessings.

Maureen Angela Bryan, Producer, Director, Creator of *Voice Of A Woman*

When you are in trouble and you need help it is very important to find the right person who can support you. But the task is more than just difficult; you can visit ten people and still not find the right one. I am a lucky person. I found Carmen. Her

kindness, spirit, knowledge and understanding of the psychology of people is extraordinary.
Elena Ragozhina, Owner/Publisher, *New Style* Magazine

Carmen's unique perspective on life challenges her readers to think and to re-evaluate their own perceptions and experiences, safe in the knowledge that all will be well!! A rare gift indeed!
Barbara Emile, ex-BBC Executive Producer – BAFTA winner, *Holby City*

Amidst a world dominated by self-interest and exaggerated talents, Carmen is a very rare find. A truly authentic energy healer, she directed my subconscious mind to reveal the core issue that was blocking me, allowing her to clear and heal at the most profound level whilst simultaneously empowering faith in my own ability to find solutions to life's challenges.
Caroline Evans, Founder, Moncrief + founding creative force/Director behind Jigsaw and Hoxton Hotel

Reviews

Carmen Harris, through many insights from her own powerful life story, reveals a soulful path through life's twists and turns and hard knocks to find the quintessential magic of existence. Inspiring and colourful, this book is for anyone who feels they are moving two steps forward and several paces back. If you feel overwhelmed or lost this book will dust you down and inspire you on your merry way.
Steve Nobel, Director of Alternatives, St James's Church, Piccadilly, London (2000–2012), Coach, and Author of *Personal Transitions*

Carmen Harris has produced a gift for the open minded. This book documents the incredible journey of an ordinary single mother who has evolved to become not only an accomplished, inspirational writer but a truly gifted healer. It's a testament to the miracle of life itself, to the magic that can be born of resilience, and to the wonderful experiences that we are afforded when we are brave enough to have the courage of our convictions. You cannot read this book without being moved. You cannot arrive at the end without a transformation of your own. *Sh*t Happens* touches nerves, opens old wounds, yet by the end wraps you up in a blanket of wisdom and guidance. Whether you are religious, spiritual or a seeker with a broad mind – enjoy the ride, bumps and all, and, like the author, end the journey in a remarkable place.

Brenda Emmanus, Broadcaster, Journalist, Art, Fashion & Culture Correspondent

It takes a generosity of spirit to share one's personal failings as well as triumphs so as to help others recognise their own potential. Highlighting her remarkable life experiences, Carmen Harris writes of her belief that being open to the magic of the everyday – whether revealed as synchronicity or coincidence – can miraculously transform perceptions and lead to inner harmony. She also suggests dynamic techniques for dealing with a range of challenges, while reminding us that our dreams contain the truth of who we are: "I believe that we are both the main character and the playwright of our own life story. Consciously or unconsciously, we not only get to choose the part we play, we also select the story that needs telling, and co-author that story with other major and minor role-players (friends, family, authority figures, strangers, acquaintances). We are that powerful, if only we knew it. Another compelling principle we may not be aware of is that for every action we take in life, there is a corresponding reaction. Our thoughts alone amount to action." An inspirational read.

Margaret Busby, OBE

*Sh*t Happens* is a remarkably profound, enjoyable and spiritually valuable book – and Carmen Harris is a wonderful, inspired writer. Her every phrase sparkles with spontaneous, heartfelt wisdom, and echoes deep into a subconscious treasure chest of not just a life, but a dream life profoundly explored. This book is the richly told, moving and inspiring story of how her heartfelt embrace of her dreams since childhood – her nighttime dreams, her unusual no-mind daydreams, and the dreams and aspiration of her heart – led her out of the poverty she grew up with and gradually turned her into a successful television writer and masterful healer. *Sh*t Happens* is also a wise and practical manual for learning how to successfully steer our personal boats through the inevitable storms on the ocean of life, by learning to recognize the magic hidden within every difficult situation we may face. That magic, Harris says, can be revealed and manifested "if we allow it," if we simply learn to notice the blessings disguised within all our failures and times of trouble, and sense the invisible rescuing hand which pulls us out of whatever dark pits we may fall into. Her potentially lifesaving message is one of personal empowerment through awareness of divine synchronicities, of learning to believe in ourselves, in the power of our own thoughts, and the potency of our connection with a universal Source. Although inspiring teachings flow throughout the book, it isn't for a moment preachy; Carmen Harris' wisdom shines through the gems she shares of her own life experiences. Though her story is not all rosy – some of it is a bit nightmarish – the roller coaster ride from wild successes to depressing failures, blazing illuminations and dark nights of the soul is as thoroughly entertaining as you'd expect from the writer of comedic television scripts! Thankfully, it is not only success as a writer she discovered, but spiritual awakening, extraordinary healing powers, and a source of living wisdom we can all benefit from. And she leaves us numerous clues and signposts so that we may follow in her footsteps to find our own dreams fulfilled, our hearts awakened, and our innate capacities for healing fully blossomed. Give yourself a blessing, read *Sh*t Happens* and watch the magic follow in your own life.

Ram Das Batchelder, Author of *Rising in Love: My Wild and Crazy Ride to Here and Now, with Amma, the Hugging Saint*

Carmen Harris has achieved a great deal in her life, overcoming many obstacles to become a successful writer, healer and all round 'good egg'. But what distinguishes her book from others is that she has a unique voice – down to earth, honest, funny. Even though she is fully conversant with all manner of alternative therapies, treatments, philosophies, etc, she can laugh at the slightly 'out there' side of it all – while at the same time communicate a powerful spiritual message from which everyone and anyone could benefit. She knows only too well about the shit that comes everyone's way but, unlike most, she gives you a way of handling it which anyone can follow. This is a book for everyone, whether you are conversant with or an expert in alternative therapies, or someone who has never gone anywhere near that stuff. It is straightforward, kind and honest, and full of insights. It is a great read – I highly recommend it.

Rachel Swann, Producer, ex-Agent – Harry Enfield

Carmen's rare gift is to talk to you in the kind of no-nonsense language that at the same time cuts through the drama and truly empowers. This book is a powerful tool to help her readers connect the dots in their own lives and allow the grace to flood straight back in. This lady is one of life's bright lights, who really walks her talk. Her pulls-no-punches teachings and matter-of-fact wisdom is a testament to that.

Stephen Vasconcellos-Sharpe, Publisher *Global CEO Magazine*

Following the dictum 'Know Thyself', the author embarks on a magnificent journey of self-discovery. Join her on the journey and revel in the magic and the mystery!

Pavel Mikoloski, President of SuperPosition Publicity and former Marketer of the film, *What the #$*! Do We (K)now!?*

Being enlightening whilst maintaining a humorous perspective on life is no easy feat, but Carmen manages to achieve it effortlessly. This book takes you gently by the hand and leads you on an intimate journey from Carmen's first awareness of her healing ability through the fascinating steps she took to hone and understand where this 'gift' comes from, and how we all possess it and can learn to use it in our own lives to create huge shifts in perspective; emotional and physical healing; and to discover and manifest our hearts' desires! I have had countless sessions with Carmen over the years and yet I never cease to be amazed at the transformative power of the work she does. Every single time I have seen her my life has altered in such positive and profound ways that I've been left speechless. I feel extremely blessed to have her as my healer and therapist, and for the privilege of being able to call her 'my mum'.

Naomie Harris, Actress, UK, Hollywood

Sh*t Happens, Magic Follows (*Allow It!*)

A Life of Challenges, Change and Miracles

(includes self-help Allowing Handbook)

Sh*t Happens, Magic Follows (*Allow It!*)

A Life of Challenges, Change and Miracles

(includes self-help Allowing Handbook)

Carmen Harris

BOOKS

Winchester, UK
Washington, USA

First published by O-Books, 2015
O-Books is an imprint of John Hunt Publishing Ltd., Laurel House, Station Approach,
Alresford, Hants, SO24 9JH, UK
office1@jhpbooks.net
www.johnhuntpublishing.com

For distributor details and how to order please visit the 'Ordering' section on our website.

Text copyright: Carmen Harris 2014

ISBN: 978 1 78279 910 8
Library of Congress Control Number: 2014956320

A CIP catalogue record for this book is available from the British Library.

Design: Stuart Davies

Printed and bound by CPI Group (UK) Ltd, Croydon, CR0 4YY, UK

We operate a distinctive and ethical publishing philosophy in all
areas of our business, from our global network of authors to
production and worldwide distribution.

CONTENTS

"The two most important days in your life are the day you were born and the day you find out why."
Mark Twain

There are no wrong turnings, only paths we had not known we were meant to walk.
Guy Gavriel Kay

When I began my journey I had no plan, no map, no idea of how I would travel, so my route was anything but direct. This is not unusual; I'll bet it's the narrative of all our stories. In retracing my steps for the purposes of this book – describing a catalogue of characters, events and stories, some outside the realms of what you might consider 'normal' – you will see me take wrong turns, stumble down blind alleys, retreat, back up on myself, get confused by the signs, consider U-turns, ponder at crossroads, take the exit too soon or too late, and often lose my way and become disheartened. This is the 'stuff' of our everyday, the 'stuff' that challenges our ability to see the magic in the ordinariness of life. But you will notice that there were also times when I stopped, rested, breathed in deeply, smelled the daisies and enjoyed the views. These were the times when I was willing myself to stay open, believing in a force greater than myself... and welcoming magic into my embrace. Having no idea of my journey's end, I would have to trust that every road would not only take me there, but sparkle with this magic – if I allowed it.

This book is a reminder of what you already know.
Carmen Harris

To my readers, critics and improvers:
Barbara Emile
Len Collin
Lyn Corrie
Naomie Harris
Lucy McCarraher
Dr John Nicholson
Steve Nobel
Pam Fraser-Solomon
Rachel Swann
Richard Tharp

Cover illustration by Garth Mule

Introduction

You can't connect the dots looking forwards. You can only connect them looking backwards.
Steve Jobs

Stop what you're doing for a moment. Take stock. Where are you right now? Maybe life is treating you well. Maybe not so well. So, what's going on? Are you unhappy? Confused? In limbo? Wading through the brown stuff? Perhaps for all these reasons the title of this book appealed to you. Perhaps, even despite everything, you're already taking heart. You know that somehow, in time, this state will pass and another (hopefully better) state will take its place. This, after all, is the rhythm of life. We shift in and out of our feelings of love, fear, anger, blame, hope, disappointment, joy, anxiety, sadness, guilt and shame all of the time. Even when it appears that we are stuck, we are, in fact, in motion, moving towards the next big or small event in the varying unfolding dramas of our unique 'story'. On and on until the tide of existence sweeps each and every one of us towards our inevitable end. For, in the words of the late Steve Jobs, *"Death is the destination we all share."*

But my question is this: if we're all heading in the direction of life's Departures Lounge, at what stage in this existence could any of us claim to have encountered Arrivals? When have you ever found yourself crying out loud, "Yes! Yes! *Finally!* I get it! I am fully in the awakened presence of life on this planet! I have *arrived!*"? Surely for that to happen it would require a decisive realisation of our path; a *knowing* that we are fulfilling our highest purpose in treading that path? Scientists may well assure us that we are *this* close to cracking the human genetic code, but are we any nearer to deciphering the code of how to live to our ultimate potential as human beings? Do we even know what that potential looks like? It seems not, when the questions that plague us the most continue to be the ones that keep returning with a dull ring of bewilderment:

Why was I born?
Why am I here?
What's my purpose?
What's my gift?
How can I make a real difference before I die?

If we fully knew the answers to these questions, wouldn't there be an end to the angst, the soul-searching, the turmoil of emotions and sense of personal failure that secretly burrows deep inside each and every one of us? The human condition of *seeking* (that state of eternal wonderment; the quest for an absolute *truth*) would surely dissolve overnight. Long before death, we would have arrived in heaven here on this earth. But we all know that heaven, that infinite, problem-free, peace-and-love fest, does not live at this mortal address. We know, too, that no one, not even the big man, Jesus, could ever hope to depart unscathed from Planet Earth. All of us suffer in some way or other. We wear this chafing human suit, with all of its failings and limitations, as a proviso of pulling on the suit in the first place. It is our reminder of everything that we have forgotten: we are not the suit; we are spiritual beings; we are greatness inside our own skin. So we are told. And indeed, we do in fact catch glimpses all the time of what we could truly become in every area of our existence – the outstanding sportsperson, the scientific genius, the creative prodigy, the remarkable healer, even the model parent. But these superhumans appear to be the exception, held aloft only to mock our own miserable performance. It's a fact of life. Most of us walk through the years in differing degrees of separation not just from one another but from the truth and highest desires of our own selves. The enlightened brigade don't help, preying annoyingly upon our conscience. They tell us that if we were wholly *awake* we would know that we are short of nothing; that only fear and lack of belief (fear in disguise) stands between us and the magic there is to be witnessed, the miracles that could be achieved. So, in order to satisfy our craving for ultimate meaning we turn to our spiritual coaches, seeking rousing reminders, stirring affirmations from the likes of Tony Robbins, Archbishop Desmond Tutu, the Dalai Lama. But in the face of life's hard knocks, we end up returning to the same one-note beseeching: what is it *really* all about? What is my *place* in the order of things? For, when our home is repossessed; when our next meal is nowhere in sight; when our best friend disappoints us; when we face the pain, the fear and uncertainty of ill health; when our children suffer and we are powerless to help them; when our partner betrays us; when we lose our job, our identity, our way of life; when loneliness is all we've ever known; when our cries go unanswered; when our abuser walks free; when our soulmate breathes their last – how could any pithy sentiment hope to shore up our challenged beliefs or bring us any closer to understanding the inner mysteries of life? Yet, still we point to living examples of how we could be; still we search for a way of rising above it all. What other means, what other measures of progressing do we have?

I was often frustrated, felt somewhat cheated, by my father. This was the man who decided from early on that I was bright enough to rise from the ranks of the working classes and become a lawyer. But when teen single-parenthood forced me to take a clerical officer post at the GPO's[1] *Yellow Pages*, and two years later I proudly announced that I had been accepted by London University to study Sociology, my father was appalled. I'll always remember that look, not of pride, not of admiration, but of sheer terror that I might have taken leave of my senses. *"What? You going to leave you good-good job in de*

Post Office?!" Where the father of my dreams was bold and gregarious, mine was not only socially coy but cautious, meticulous, suspicious. Perhaps he had always been like this, for I have heard stories of my mother being the real force behind my father's earlier modestly successful entrepreneurial endeavours in Jamaica. Perhaps it was those frustrating migrant experiences in the UK in adapting to a new reality that extinguished his personal passions, denied any daring dreams of the future.

Watching him consume a plate of food summed up the man. No matter how appetising the offering, each meal was ritualised with an initial sigh that rendered the arrangement in front of him another one of life's testing trials. Next, he would give a churlish little sniff. This seemed to strengthen his resolve before the chore of dissecting each portion on the plate into neat surgical morsels. Once on the tongue, he'd close his eyes to the sound of his masticating dentures, most probably counting each mouthful to a precise number of chews. Sometimes, like a cow ruminating on grassland, he would literally, momentarily, fall asleep over the task until a clean plate was eventually, finally, accomplished. That's not to say he didn't enjoy food, he was an interested grocery shopper and, for a man of his generation, a surprisingly competent cook; but an ingrained apparent joylessness forbade him from wholly indulging in life's abundant pleasures.

I hear my assessment of my father and a part of me cannot help but wince, for is it not true – when we find fault with a parent, our irritation often has more to do with seeing a reflection of our own selves in the lack of their image? I could hold my father accountable for a lot of things. The blame would surely lie in his court for my own lateness in opening up to the world: in realising that it is indeed possible to expand the boundaries of one's 'personal space' without the fear and threat of exposure; that it is more affirming to roll with playful punches than to coil inside and take umbrage; that my authentic self could be found in the wicked joy of my own laughter. These revelations that came about in adulthood were in direct contrast to my younger years when I was accustomed to being hailed as the serious one, the humourless one, the one who lived more naturally in the head than in the world. Not a bad description of my father, as it happens. Though it was painful to admit, my father and I had our similarities.

When he died, some 20 years ago, one of the more useful traits I inherited from him came to the fore. Faced with the double wardrobe of Burton suits, the melamine chest of drawers of neatly pressed dead-man's clothes, and the stack of old documents and paperwork, my siblings blanched. I, however, rolled up both sleeves and relished the opportunity of processing grief through the fastidiousness of creating order. My father would have been proud, even if my determination was being driven by a second, more urgent motive. For, here was my opportunity to examine forensically the man behind the buttoned-up colonial mask; to retrospectively meet my father on equal terms. Halfway through the clear-out, I came across a battered old suitcase that I remembered from my childhood as belonging to my mother. Unopened for quite some time, the lid was coated with a thin film of dust and the metal catch speckled with rust. My excitement mounted, hearing the hinges creak open, inhaling the musty, decades-old nostalgia of the island years. As I rifled through items of my father's clothing, my eyes fell upon a rubber-banded collection of miniature diaries stowed away in the bottom. My heart beat in anticipation. If I failed to understand my father in life, I reasoned, surely now in death his inner being would be revealed to me. I fell upon the task and didn't draw breath until I had examined every single page of the 20 or so diaries dating back to the late 1950s. Disappointment hit me like a heavy door casting its dark shadow before slowly closing on me forever. Each one of the diaries, written in my father's careful cursive style, was an unreflective account of the minutiae of his everyday life: work rotas for the night shift, various doctor's appointments, dates the insurance man called, when the gas meter was due to be emptied or the milkman paid, etc. Whatever heartfelt longings and unrequited desires my father had nursed during his lifetime, he had carried them to the grave as meticulously as he had once cleared a plateful of food.

A decade prior to my father's death, my then boss mentioned that his wife had kept a journal for most of her life, and that its contents could amount to several books. Something about that disclosure struck me as instantly compelling. Before that moment I had never distinguished between a journal and a diary; how the former takes the recording of mundane data and shapes that data with personal reflections; how the very act of journaling declares a person's journey as having value and contribution to the world. It seemed to me an amazing idea, to create a repository for my own great thoughts, my insights, my interpretations of personal situations and passing experiences: those fleeting sparks of inspiration that magically light up our consciousness, begging to be captured before they return to the dark unknown. At the back of my mind there was secret daring, a hopefulness that I might one day turn my own musings into a book.

So I began to apply the art, committing to paper only those events that seemed to illuminate a wider reality or truth. If I recorded eating a meal, its significance would be associated with seeing a news item about the senselessness of starvation in some unfortunate part of the world. If I bumped into an old friend perhaps I would experience an indefinable yearning for the past that cried out to be explored. If I smelled a fragrance it might cause me to reflect on the occasion when that same scent first established a sharp pain in my heart. And so on.

I kept up this journaling for a few decades until I reached a time in my life when there came about an urge to take stock, to look behind, to *'connect the dots backwards'*. All those years of battling valiantly through, of not always comprehending the sensory snowstorm of my life's everyday encounters, of being blinded to any actual progress I was making in the moment. Always two steps forward, several paces back, it appeared. Never as good as the next person ahead of me. Too slow to capture the main prize. Too quick to judge my achievements as poor in relation to others'. I had a strong desire to examine those fragments of feelings, emotions and memories that belonged to the past and, as I searched through my journal, I made a surprise discovery. The dots were actually making sense! Even more gratifying, my existence appeared to be revealing its greater plan. All the while, those confusing, fluttering pieces had been quietly falling into an attractive pattern, forming a solid path both behind and in front of me. I could now see where I had come from, and why most things had to happen the way they had. I could see where I was heading, and was able to grasp a better idea of what the future might possibly hold for me. I could see that every mistake, every mishap, every unrequited desire had been perfectly conceived as an experience that would deliver me *home*.

And this is where I turn to you, dear reader. My aim in writing this book is for you to know that in much the same way as the sun can both burn and heal yet still remain our guiding star, in every bruising skip or painful stumble along life's way there are beautiful experiences and valuable lessons to uncover. I'd like you to realise that whatever your decisions in life, even when it seems unlikely, guidance and acceptance are always there. Every moment, every situation, every regret, every sharp emotion is a reward, and no encounter is ever wasted or showing up by any kind of accident. The best decisions are always made from love but, regardless, life will fall into place no matter what. Whether you choose or refuse to heed life's lessons, the prerogative is always yours. However and wherever you end up is the place where you were always meant to be. You cannot mess up on this journey. When the gift and the magic is in the taking part, absolutely no one fails to Arrive.

Part I

To love a person is to see all of their magic, and to remind them of it when they have forgotten.
Author Unknown

Chapter 1

Dreams

All human beings are dream beings. Dreaming ties all humankind together.
Jack Kerouac

It was the year 1962. I was a skinny, dreamy, thumb-sucking five-year-old, about to leave my homeland with my mother, two brothers and sister. Unusually, we were to travel by plane, the height of privilege in those days. At least, compared to the thousands of other Jamaicans making the same journey by sea, taking up to twenty-two days to reach the shores of the Mother Country. For the past six months, in preparation for our migration, we'd moved from our home in the bustling town of Kingston to live with Aunty Hilda and her family by the sea in Annotto Bay. Now the long-awaited day had finally arrived. Amid the tears, the kisses, and the bosom-heaving farewell hugs, as we embarked on our sleepy night-time journey back towards the capital a whole banana was tucked into each child's hand. I clasped mine and made the decision that I would not eat it. I would save it as a gift for my father, that mysterious figure who had gone ahead of us to that mythical land called England to realise his dream of social and economic self-improvement. His absence had amounted to a lifetime in my young universe. Being just three years old when he'd left our tropical island, I'd virtually forgotten who my father was. When I announced my sacrificial intentions to my brothers and sister and they decided that they too would be saving their banana, my grumpiness was unsurpassed. But I needn't have worried. By the time we reached Palisades Airport, all they had to show for their efforts were three empty skins. Several times on the plane I felt my mother gently

10

prising the yellow fruit out of my grasp, and each time I awoke with a start to tighten my hold. After an eternity of sleepless and sleep-filled hours, our BOAC flight finally landed at Gatwick Airport where, dressed optimistically in flimsy sunny frocks and khaki shorts, my siblings and I stepped on to the tarmac and shivered in the chilly May winds. As we entered the milling terminal building, a tall, caramel-skinned man wearing a brown suit and a felt trilby broke through the crowds and strode confidently towards us. I'd spent many hours dreaming of this exact moment, and now that it had arrived, I froze, unsure of my next move. But as soon as I felt myself rising in the air, swooped into my father's embrace, I remembered to wave the triumph of my gift. My father chuckled aloud. A mixture of pride and joy, it seemed. It didn't for one moment occur to me that it would be at the blackened, oozing mess sticking to my palm.

My friends will tell you, I have a terrible memory – mostly for long-term events. But, of course, there are those images and sensations that embed themselves like a virus in the nervous system. Sometimes the virus will have a conscious presence, either as a recollection to be cherished (the first time I felt the heart-melting warmth of my newborn on my chest), or as a difficult memory (the first time I saw real anger in my father's eyes and feared the sting of a slap). Other times the virus will hide like an invisible echo in the soul, lying near-dormant, till the right trigger catapults the memory into one's awareness, igniting all of one's senses. This banana memory is one that has inhabited my being in full Technicolor for as long as I can remember. I've recalled it so many times you must forgive me for perhaps embellishing it with the sentimental touch of a hero's journey: the silent determination of a dreamy five-year-old travelling 5,000 miles over 24 hours, intent on delivering a soft fruit, uneaten, to a stranger in a strange land – and succeeding.

Though I could not have articulated it then, sucking my thumb was my interface, my high-speed connection, to communicate with my 'other world'. But this 'disgusting' habit wasn't at all appreciated by my parents. They tried every method, from slapping the slimy, shrivelled digit out of my mouth to smearing it with freshly-cut chilli. But nothing would deter me from retreating behind closed doors, burrowing into dark corners, hiding below the safety of the bedclothes, at home, during school, or even behind the flap of my woollen coat whilst walking the streets. Sneaking a suck on my 'pipe' was such a compelling habit, I couldn't imagine living without it. Left in peace I would allow my eyes to roll towards the back of my head and be transported to a place that embraced me like a homecoming; a place that felt like… No-thing. In this space there was no judgement, no anger, no disapproval, no anxiety, no fear, no shame. It just Was. In the end, my parents threw up their hands in defeat. My father rationalised that, as a 'bright' child, my thumb-sucking was most probably aiding my intelligence. He may have had a point. For in that realm of No-thingness, I discovered that I was able to create and manifest a virtual world of anything I desired. Inside this space-time I would paint vivid dreamscapes of shapes and colours that could not be found anywhere on the drab shores of this outer reality where my family of six dovetailed in two cramped rooms. I could fly. I could dive. I could disappear. I could reappear. I had friends. I had comfort. I had laughter. Any quality or concept I desired was mine, in an instant. So, with my parents' new resigned attitude of blind-eye-turning, if not quite tolerance, I continued my ventures into this other plane of existence. The pull was so strong that aged sixteen I was secretly thumb-sucking in between dates with my first boyfriend. And after giving it up in my later teens, shame-faced, I took it up again, albeit briefly, when I became pregnant with my first child.

As an inward-looking immigrant child, I had my fair share of bitter lemons thrown at me by the turbulence of life. My survival technique was to gather up the seeds and grow a sweet-variety lemon tree in my secret Eden of dreams. One early example springs to mind. In those days, trussed up in my seamstress mother's colourful chiffon and organza creations, I wafted around the edges of friendship circles, sensitive to everything and everyone, in a state of perpetual confusion. I was baffled by the unruliness of the playground, the rules of the classroom, wary of the flighty, unpredictable emotions of other children, and slow at deciphering the new cultural codes. In other words, a perfect target. As a consequence, I would find myself involved unwittingly in situations of which I had no idea how they came about. On this particular day, I'd entered the upstairs toilets and encountered a group of whispering girls huddled by the washbasins. My very entrance apparently amounted to a transgression of some unspoken commandment among them. As a result, I was informed that a beating-up was scheduled for next play. During Mr Biffin's class, my ink pen took on a life of its own, scratching emptily at a maths problem that my eyes were barely able to pull into focus. All the while, terror struck at my soul. My heart lurching towards my throat was a constant reminder of my imminent death. There was only one strategy available to me. I withdrew into myself. As if someone had turned a page, a breeze was suddenly refreshing my face. Sunlight was ablaze on my closed eyelids. I found myself bouncing upside-down like a sack of rubber balls on someone's comfortingly broad back. Through that grey-suited fabric I could hear and feel the vibrations of heavy panting. Mr Jones, the head of Robert Blair Primary, was running like the clappers through the Junior playground towards sick bay in the next block, and I was his urgent cargo. I was aware of a hard restriction in my chest, a lack of oxygen reaching my lungs, a trance-like discomfort. But away from the suffocating threat of the classroom, floating in my own fabricated dream world, the struggle to breathe felt more like rapture.

I can't fully remember how the situation resolved itself as the remainder of the story has become misted by the amnesia of time passed. I do know, however, that I did not end up in hospital; and that my mother was called to fetch me. After fleeing her factory workplace in a blind panic, expecting to meet the asphyxiated corpse of her child, her emotions when she saw me could best be described as mixed. There was I, seated outside the Head's office, swinging my legs, contentedly sucking on a boiled sweet – apparently none the worse for having manifested a life-or-death emergency. What's interesting is that prior to that day I had never before experienced an asthma attack; nor have I since.

Fast forward a few decades to the approach of 2013, the much-discussed end of the Mayan calendar. I was walking briskly through the dark winter streets of South London, heading to join a group of people spending the weekend in an impressive converted water tower. Apart from the few accompanied by a friend or partner, we were essentially strangers to one another. What had brought us together was the desire to achieve a Lucid Dream (LD),[2] or Out of Body (OB)[3] Experience. My strong association with the dream state had led me here, seeking a greater understanding of that plane of existence often dismissed as an empty activity of the human brain. Some people scoff that those who take this realm seriously are either deluded or among those preying on the deluded. But I have come to believe that an exploration of the realm of dreams can lead to a real understanding of who we are, and why we are here on this planet. I was among this group of believers, opening the door of 2013 on the eve of Ascension, sharing the conviction that humanity is moving towards a collective shift of consciousness. A kind of divine upgrade that will ultimately transform the human race to a heart-centred awakening. I had a strong desire to be among the awakened.

That lonely, thumb-sucking child with the solemn face (my entire life, builders with their trousers at half-mast would swing like one-armed gorillas off scaff poles to growl reassuringly at me, "Cheer up, luv. It may never 'appen!") had long found her own tribe and was accustomed to hanging out with strangers on her own wavelength. Eager and expectant, shaking off the November chills, our crowd of 16 ranged from the young to the not-so-young, from the professionally employed to the unemployed, male and female. Equipped with pyjamas, duvets, headphones, toothbrushes and eye masks, we were about to share our sleeping habits, bedding down in different parts of a multilevel, multi-bedroom luxury dwelling. The protocol was that we would be woken up several times during the course of the night and our curiously monikered facilitator, Todd Acamesis, employing various tried and tested techniques, would guide us towards the edge of our unconscious. On this plane we might find solutions to problems, understand aspects of our personal identity, and even make contact with those who had passed. During the 48-hour period, I experienced a variety of textbook reactions – from intense all-over-body heat, to heart and hand vibrations, visions of light, and incredible 'out of this world' colours. My biggest breakthrough, though, was connecting with my friend Mark.

Mark was in Intensive Care. After suddenly contracting blood poisoning that had travelled to his brain causing critical inflammation, he'd lapsed into a coma. The unexpected tragedy of someone so larger-than-life had shocked everyone, not least myself. In life, Mark's sole raison d'être, it seemed, was to prank, provoke and bring people together. The time he came to our New Year's Eve celebration is a perfect example of his ebullient character. I'd devised a warm-up to get the party started. The idea was that someone would read out a statement about a particular guest and the rest of the party would have to determine whether the statement was true or false. The statement relating to Mark had left the entire room gasping with disbelief. Surely it had to be false! Mark assured everyone that it was indeed true, and took it upon himself to relay the story in full. Taking up most of the sofa, his trademark cigar between thumb and forefinger, he began doing what he did best, commanding an audience:

He was at a children's birthday party, lounging in conversation with another father and commenting in amusement at the commotion going on around them. The birthday child's present, a puppy only recently bestowed the name Cou-Cou, had mysteriously disappeared. In mid-belly laughter, Mark blanched. He turned urgently to his sofa companion and ordered him, "Don't move!" Then he directed the adults to quickly shoo the children out of the room. When the space was safely cleared, Mark leaned cautiously forward to examine the warm, plump 'cushion' that had been bearing his considerable weight. Mortified, he discovered that Cou-Cou the birthday puppy was no longer! A mad dash to Harrods followed, whereupon 'another' Cou-Cou was purchased before the birthday child could discover the gruesome mishap.

A truly catastrophic incident, but because of Mark's infectious ability to entertain, to this day most of those who were present that evening are still convinced that the 'hilarious story' was just that.

It was as a result of Mark's selfless 'meddling' that I established a close friendship with Nathalie, his young wife, and that both our sons became playmates. I had been lying back in a hospital bed, recovering from the exhaustion and elation of having given birth to my second child. Filling the doorway of the maternity ward with his large frame, I noticed a bespectacled grey-haired man wearing a camel coat and guiding the hand of a small boy. He seemed to be either lost or searching for someone. Little did I know that he had been prowling the wards on the lookout, not for anyone in particular, but for pure mischief. I happened to be the person who first caught his roguish eye.

"Hello!" he boomed, striding towards my bed. "My name's Mark, and this is my son, Adam. What's your name?"

"I... er... my name's Carmen," I replied.

"Beautiful baby," he cooed, peering into my son's cot. "A boy?"

There was some gentle ribbing and friendly banter, most of which I have now forgotten, but I do clearly recall what he said next.

"My wife is back there in the private ward. Her name is Nathalie. We've also just had a son. You two should be friends. I'll introduce you!"

And that was that. In a few minutes, my lasting friendship with Nathalie had been brokered and sealed by this large Jewish man, some ten years his wife's senior.

On that November evening in the Tower, I was still trying to comprehend how a human dynamo of such warmth, vitality and compassion could be struck down into such helpless vulnerability. After turning over and eventually going to sleep, it seemed only a few minutes later that Todd interrupted the group's slumber for a pep talk. We were instructed to now slip on our headphones and listen to isochronic tones that would aid our transition to 'the other side'. For my first experience of the night, I decided that I would focus on connecting with Mark. I was hoping there was some way I could communicate with his subconscious in order to alter his critical condition whilst he lay in his hospital bed. In the half-in-half-out state that ensued, my body was heavy and lifeless whilst my mind was surprisingly alert. Mark's image came to me as I drifted on the outer edges of the dream realms. It was a distressing likeness. I tried to speak to 'him', but 'he' failed to respond. Outside of the group situation, I daresay I would have talked myself out of the 'encounter' being anything other than a fanciful visualisation, a desperate desire to succeed. But during the group feedback, once I gave voice to what I'd seen and heard, the experience developed its own truth.

I knew that I had linked with Mark's 'energy body', and that there was a clear message embedded in the scene I had been a part of. After the workshop I called Nathalie to check up on how she was doing. I had been offering support, visiting the hospital most days to give healing, and generally making myself available as much as I could. During the conversation, I brought up the incident. Nathalie listened openly as I recounted my experience. I asked her what she thought the image might mean (both the image and Nathalie's response contain personal details, so I won't reveal them here). Her interpretation exactly matched mine, reassuringly validating my first Lucid Dreaming experiment.

Sadly, Mark never regained consciousness and died that same week. Though I am not and never have been religious, I do believe that death is not the end. Our true essence is *spirit*: eternal and all-encompassing *oneness* with everyone and everything. We visit this earth in human form on a purposeful journey, to experience the range of emotions through what we call Life. Our *soul*, containing our personality, accompanies our body through each of our lifetimes and is our reminder that pure love is who and what we truly are, and is our portal to spirit. Though Mark was no longer walking this earth, I was confident that there was a way to reach him through his energy body, his soul. What happened a few days later when I attempted a repeat of the LD exercise at home was so shockingly amazing it was only then I was able to grasp the real power of what I had tapped into. Here's an email I wrote to Todd, our facilitator:

Another amazing LD experience! I contacted my late friend, Mark, again. He was looking young and happy – unlike in my workshop LD before his death, when he was looking ill and morose. The image I got was quite bizarre and I convinced myself that I was just 'making it up'. But Mark insisted, "Tell Nathalie (his wife, also my friend); she'll understand!" Anyhow, on waking I was still convinced that I was just being fanciful. Though I entered the experience in my dream diary, I decided against troubling Nathalie with the wacky scenario I'd 'dreamed up'. She had enough on her plate, being newly-widowed. Yesterday my partner and I visited the local farmer's market, held every Sunday. In all the years we have been there we have never before bumped into Nathalie. Yet, who should surprise us by calling out our names from behind!? The three of us strolled together for a bit and after a while I reluctantly brought up my LD. Nathalie smiled quizzically. It didn't ring any bells with her, which confirmed to me that the experience was simply my mind overworking, desperately trying to get into an LD. Anyhow, Nathalie told me that the reason she was at the market was to do some research into what it would entail to have a stall there. Since Mark's death, she'd decided that she needed to look at ways of earning a living. She'd hit upon the idea of selling chicken soup based on her (Jewish) mother-in-law's recipe. We gave our opinions, talked about the branding of the soup, asked some stallholders about rental and procedures, and even discussed the big soup pot that would need to be purchased. Nathalie offered us a lift home, and just as I was about to get out of the car it hit me like a tsunami wave. I yelped like a lunatic. I reminded Nathalie of my LD. Her jaw immediately dropped. In that moment, she finally got it, too! We compared the goose bumps on our arms. What was the clear, spontaneous 'movie' that had come to me several nights previously? A fresh-faced, vivacious Mark racing through a large grey metallic tunnel, chasing after a couple of squawking chickens! Ludicrous, I'd thought. When I 'reasoned' with him that I couldn't possibly relay this image to Nathalie because it was so damn silly and made no sense, that's when he shouted in his characteristically passionate way, "Tell her! Tell her! She'll understand! I promise you!" Nathalie knew instantly that the specific image of chickens was about her soup enterprise.[4] She also clarified something that I hadn't clocked myself, that the 'tunnel' was actually a big metal soup pot! Nathalie had been financially reliant on her husband for their entire married life and, from the other side, Mark, characteris-

tically paternal, would have wanted to communicate his support of her venture and her bid to become independent. Thirty minutes later, Nathalie and I were still talking about it, and I still had goose bumps. The moral? Keep at this LD/OB stuff – even if you think you're faking it! This image came to me at a time when I was getting frustrated at my dismal results since my weekend at the Tower. Another moral: dismiss NOTHING! I truly believe that somewhere, somehow, there's sense/some kind of message embedded in every image that comes to us.

Carmen xx

My single-minded nature has been both my curse and my blessing. Over the years of my development, becoming the person that I am today, its shadow side has expressed itself in acts of stubborn heel-digging, sheer bloody-mindedness, an unwillingness to back down, admit defeat, or to concede forgiveness of either myself or my transgressors. But there is also another side to me. The side that has served me well. Here, I am the dogged Miss Marple, devoted to solving the mystery; the dedicated student of life versed in the art of scratching beneath the surface of what we are accustomed to calling reality. That eternal entity of the latter, which fuelled the grit of that five-year-old seeking the love and approval of her newfound father, has been forever present alongside me, carrying with it an echo, a whisper, deep within my soul. In the beginning it was more of a *felt* resonance than an articulated sound. These days, I hear the words loud and clear: *Our dreams contain the truth and the magic of who we really are.*

I could never have imagined the incredible twists and turns of my life. How its meandering path would have taken me from my island in the Caribbean to a place across the oceans where dreaming would provide my route into earning my living as a writer. That my journey would then lead me to becoming a healer, someone able to transform the mental, emotional, spiritual and physical afflictions of another by using the combined powers of our imagination. I often pinch myself, convinced that it might actually all be just a dream. And how right I am. I dreamed into being the world that surrounds me today. What do I mean by that? By embracing my *dreams*, I let them nourish my *thoughts* with radical *ideas* of who I could *become*; these thoughts strengthened my *beliefs* about what is truly *possible*; and such beliefs gave me the *determination* to pursue certain bold *actions* that, over time, *transformed* the world in which I exist.

When life grinds us down and it's impossible to see a way through, something else is happening to us. Unwittingly, we've allowed ourselves to become locked into rigid routines, strait-jacketed by limiting beliefs, lost in the dense illusion of what we see around us as 'real' life. Trapped in this place of hellish comforts (it's amazing what we put up with, for fear of another hell we don't yet know), we can't imagine how our life could be any different. We crouch in the same tight space and fret about things, but do nothing. Why bother, we ask? When no one is on our side and nothing can be done to solve the problems we face; when we have no idea where the money / the inspiration / the new love / the relief / the solution will come from? These common themes of defeat and powerlessness are the reasons for my decision to write this book. My aim is to bring you hope by revealing that in every unfortunate situation there is also the presence of magic. Like a tightly folded bud, the promise of transformation is poised to burst into a beautiful, undiscovered new flower (new relationship; new job; new path; new choices) the moment we allow it. This miracle of how a life can be trans-formed has been revealed to me, over and over again, and it happens each time I have dared myself... to dream.

In order to witness the magic, first begin by opening up to the wonder that there might just be another way; allow yourself to 'see' the *possibility* of a different situation – even if it is to simply *imagine* the walls of your current circumstances come tumbling down.

It seems a straightforward enough idea, yes? Yet, this altered perception often takes courage. Fear has a habit of rearing up at the merest thought of change, of entering the darkness of the 'unknown'. This kind of envisioning also takes practice. We may be unaccustomed to, resistant to, the notion of our own ability to bring about our own transformation. And, understandably, there are the doubts. The idea that we could influence real change through merely accessing our dreams may come across as wishful or wishy-washy thinking, or just plain naive. "I'm without a job, I have no control over the economy. I didn't *make up* this recession, my situation is *real*," you might be shouting aloud at these words. I hear you. And I can tell you, through my personal experiences, that actual change is kick-started not by doing nothing, not by repeating the same-old same-old, but through the power of visualising, imagining, meditating, dreaming, or even 'daydreaming' something *different* into existence. You may respond by arguing that you are trapped in your present situation precisely because you once believed in a dream, a dream that has since turned sour or let you down. Perhaps you're facing divorce or separation at the end of a long relationship; maybe your adored child has grown up to become a worry or a disappointment; the job you thought was for life has been taken away from you; or it could be that your business has gone under. Regardless, dreams hold the key to starting anew. Dreams are our route into the unconscious and subconscious[5] – the world of our beliefs, behaviours, attitudes and memories that are not in our immediate awareness. This is the realm that drives our imagination, our fantasies, our vision of the future. The power here is phenomenal. Imagine right now:

A big, succulent, juicy, yellow lemon being cut in half
Smell its zesty, citrus aroma
Now, squeeze drops of that sour juice into your mouth
Sense your tongue coming alive with its sharp, acid tang.

Are your taste buds beginning to react? Stirring? Tingling? Mine are. This is an example of how our physical being does not know the difference between what is real and what is in our imagination. It is also a demonstration of how our outer environment (the body, the world) responds to what is in our unconscious. Another example. If you are severely arachnophobic you might shudder or run screaming at the picture of a spider – even though you know logically that it cannot harm you, much less scuttle off the page and attack you. This is because a powerful programme of fear of spiders is running in your subconscious. Again, consider the effects of placebos – dummy pills or inert medication with no therapeutic worth – that relieve symptoms or 'cure' medical conditions due to the subconscious influencing our belief that the sugar pill or fake potion has curative value. Again, look at the existence of every man-made thing that surrounds you – from the fertiliser on your lawn to a satellite in space; from the mercury in your tooth to the road surface outside your door; from the style of your hair to the Mona Lisa's smile. In the beginning the world that we know was a barren nothingness. Then the world became populated by the things that now surround us, the things we cannot imagine being without. How? Each and every one of man's creations was first a dream in the unconscious before its materialisation into matter. Our consciousness creates every aspect of our existence.

Stop for a moment to consider the phenomenal power of all of this. By dreaming a new and different future, it is possible to create a path out of the present and into another reality! Change and solutions may not occur overnight, but if you stay open to the idea (what have you got to lose apart from more fear, more hopelessness?) a stuck situation will eventually shift into something more beneficial. Whenever I have a problem, I make the *intention* before going to bed that my dreams will provide the answer. It's a powerful tool I've used often – even in writing many sections of this book you are reading. I go to sleep on a blank page, so to speak. The next morning, in a clear example of consciousness-manifestation, I find myself filling the page with an outpouring that has come directly from my unconscious. Have you ever been given the advice to 'sleep on it'? You are effectively being directed to plug into the power of your unconscious. Upon waking you will find that you have greater clarity, feel more relaxed, or less uptight about the issue that was concerning you. You may even remember an image or message contained in your dream that provides either the entire solution or the first steps towards resolving your problem. Not only can we learn from the messages embedded in our dreams (the symbols they contain and our emotional reaction to them are subtle and sometimes not-so-subtle clues), but the very act of lending significance to our dreams is a powerful force for change.

For many years I had a recurring dream. It was at a time when I was lost and unsure about my path in life. In this dream I would be choking on a dirty rag stuffed deep inside my throat. I'd wake up gagging, confused, my heart pounding. In a half-sleep, I would find myself forcing my fist into my mouth, convinced the rag was there. There was also a vague terror that I had forgotten something important, something linked to my survival. This dream reflected my general state of anxiety and fear of the future. It also contained a message. The throat is our channel of communication and self-expression: I was being shown that this channel was blocked, and I was to find a way of unblocking it. I finally overcame my fear of change and slowly began to find a new direction in life, one in which I was able to express my true self. Having served its purpose, the disturbing dream magically melted away.

Life is a dream that has already materialised. Our fears and beliefs about our own inadequacy directly influence the personal space that we currently inhabit. Here's the message: if your reality does not serve you, dream another dream. If recession is your excuse for remaining in fear, choose to focus on examples around you of people achieving and doing well despite personal obstacles, despite a depressed economy. On a global scale, thoughts, words and beliefs continue to create our planet. Consider a world in which violence and hatred is in the thoughts and minds of the majority. Conflict is more, rather than less, likely to occur – is it not? On the other hand, if thoughts of peace, harmony and community dominate, the likelihood of a totally different kind of reality will surely be the result. When we were younger we believed in our dreams and brought them into our waking life. Think of a child happily at play with their invisible friend or lost in some other imaginary world. Notice the absorption in that child's eyes; it tells you s/he is far from pretending. That child is, in every sense of the word, alive in a multicoloured, multi-textured present moment. If only that state could last. Regrettably, that child will soon be educated to grow up, to focus on being 'responsible'. S/he will be taught to believe that hopes, passions and dreams are an indulgence, a distraction to 'real life'. This will likely lead to an empty state of non-feeling, a losing touch with who we really are, and what we really want to do with our lives. Is it any wonder that we end up frustrated, in a place of anxiety, of fear, of settling with merely getting by? Furthermore, life confirms our predicament by continually testing any dreams we may have left, chipping away at our self-belief, our self-esteem. In the process, we soon leave behind the colour and magic of creation; we forget that we are *born* creators. Whether our longing is to have a fulfilling relationship, a healthy body or enough money in the bank – we stop living our dreams and give ourselves over to a consciousness-numbing culture of production and consumption, to the greyness of purely existing. So, how can we return to making our dreams a reality? We have to learn, in the face of life's many hurdles, to not lose faith in our unconscious. Tony Buzan (author of *Mind Mapping*) uses the example of a toddler learning to walk. Does that child give up trying because he has stumbled and crashed on to his behind one too many times? No. Not only does the toddler motivate himself to get up and try again, but as good parents we lovingly encourage that child to do so. It's time we relearned that same lesson and applied it to ourselves.

Our dreams are our gateway into possibilities we are unable to imagine with our often-fearful conscious mind. Through prayer, belief, intent, dreams, we practise magic all the time – unconsciously. If our unconscious really is the servant of our intentions, then we must make the deliberate intention that life *will* change – in a way that we desire... or far better than we can presently allow ourselves to believe.

In the following chapters of the story of my life, I will prove to you that when stuff happens, when the sh*t flies, if we trust in the power of dreams, our unconscious, magic is always the outcome.

Chapter 2

Transition

Death is not the greatest loss in life. The greatest loss is what dies inside us while we live.

Norman Cousins

My mother survived eight years in the UK. On 18th May 1970, at the age of 50 years, she passed away. Having experienced rheumatic fever as a child, the complications arising from irreversible damage to her heart valves seemed to accelerate once she arrived in England. I remember the terrifying sight of her the day she returned home from a visit to Eastman Dental Hospital: swollen jawed, bloody mouthed, and minus every single tooth in her head, extracted as a precaution against infective endocarditis (tooth decay bacteria) compromising her already weakened valves. My abiding memory of my mother is of a kind, warm-hearted soul whose benign disposition was frequently tested by crippling exhaustion, incessant aches, chronic pains, frequent hospitalisation, endless medical procedures, and the burdensome responsibility of having to raise four young children in a foreign country. Add to this the stifling role of the early 1960s housewife.

For a full-time working mother of the lower classes, whose husband worked the night shift and slept during the day, life was even less of a picnic. There were no food processors, washing machines or the convenience of online shopping to take the edge off the gloominess, the drudgery of my mother's life. Her chores seemed to consist of an endless round of hardships: bending over mountainous volumes of soiled clothes soaking in the bathtub before either hand-washing or lugging them in unmanageable dripping loads to the laundromat up the road; laboriously processing whole coconuts for our traditional Sunday rice and peas with a metal grater that would often shred the tips of her fingers to the point of bleeding; shampooing the unruly hair of two yelping, protesting girls before clamping us between her legs for the back-breaking, back-to-school combing and plaiting ritual; and even her one creative outlet, running up garishly-coloured 'Caribbean' dresses on the Singer sewing machine, would end up as just another chore when her creations were met with revulsion by me and my sister. The weekly grocery shop was dreaded by us children. It would involve our taking turns to accompany my mother along the length of the 'Cally' (Caledonian Road), popping into the fishmongers for fresh fish and a huge slab of ice (our window ledge 'fridge') before continuing on to the butcher, the baker, the greengrocers... The worst part was being required to stop beside my mother on every other street corner to allow her to catch her breath, and hawk and spit out the bad taste that was constantly in her mouth. As a child I was less concerned about my mother's suffering than I was about my own squirming public embarrassment.

But being chronically ill didn't stop my mother from yearning to live. She loved catching a glimpse of young Elvis on TV, delighting in his quivering quiff and the wild swivel of his hips; Tom Jones was her heartbeat, though, and I'm sure she had many a fantasy about running away to be adored by him in the Welsh valleys; while on a rainy Sunday afternoon, working the creaky wooden ironing board, her high quaver would accompany Jim Reeves' crooning that had the ability to transport her to loftier places far from the gloom of an English winter. I remember her fur-trimmed woollen coat, her heavy black side-zip boots and her hot-pressed hair held down by patterned silky scarves that tied in a knot beneath the chin. I remember that she would never think to venture out without red lipstick, face powder, and a dab of *Soir de Paris* behind the ear. The curious jottings in her Pitman's notebook were testament to the intelligence and ambition that had led her to leave Jamaica with the high hopes of continuing her career as a shorthand secretary. But life had other plans for her. The first and last job she secured on arriving in the UK was in a Jewish family-run factory in Farringdon. She electroplated gold jewellery, handling and inhaling hydrogen cyanide and other toxic substances.

There were enough mundane interludes in my childhood for me to assume that mine was an average, uneventful existence; certainly there was no indication of anything extraordinary looming on the horizon. But it would take at least three decades for me to comprehend the emotional legacy of my mother's long illness and eventual death. Having died three days before I turned 13, her death not only blighted every one of my birthday celebrations to come, but also conditioned my attitude to my own health. Unconsciously, I had become accustomed to 'mirroring' and absorbing the suffering I had witnessed in my younger years. My 'weak' heart, my low blood pressure (I had frequent swooning episodes), my rheumatic joints, all became causes for concern in later life. I would also dread my daughter approaching the age of 13, convinced I wouldn't live to see that landmark. When that date passed uneventfully, I spent the following years believing that my life would be snatched from me before seeing my fiftieth. And when my half century also came and went, a lingering superstition prevented me from fully relaxing until I had successfully reached the age of 51.

The day of my mother's passing was a cold, bright May morning. My father had collected her a few days before from the Royal Free hospital, one of her many 'observational' confinements (my father had quite rightly refused the surgeon's suggestion of an experimental operation on my mother's heart). I wasn't to know that the doctors had finally admitted they could do nothing more, and that my father had made the decision to bring Mummy home to die. Before heading out for school, I looked in on her in the downstairs back room that had now become her convalescence bedroom, and found her sleeping peacefully. I then went to say goodbye to my father. He was in the garden, emerging from the outside toilet, having emptied my mother's overnight throw-up bucket. He asked me how I thought she was doing. I recalled the afternoon before, Sunday, when she had surprised us all by emerging from her usual sickly stupor, roused by the musical chime of the ice-cream van pulling up outside. With enough energy to prop up herself on the pillow, she called for her purse and handed us sixpence each to buy a vanilla cone. Reflecting on this, I confidently told my father that she was getting better. His smile seemed different to his usual, his eyes overshadowed by a darting strangeness. All day at school I was haunted by that smile. I became increasingly upset to the point where I was compelled to lock myself away in the girls' toilet to try to make sense of the restless internal movements that I had become seized by. Eventually, exhausted by my inner turmoil, and not knowing what else to do, I burst into frustrated tears. As I emerged, red-eyed, from the cubicle, I bumped into my Spanish teacher in the corridor outside. When she asked what was wrong, what was I to say? My whole being was churning, but I had no name to identify the cause. After school, however, as I trudged the long, empty stretch of Elthorne Road, each leaden step that brought me closer to home crystallised what the feeling was. Ahead, I saw my father doing something I'd never seen him do before. He was at the iron gate leaning forward, looking out for me. Seeing my solemn expression, he broke into a smile, almost his familiar smile, and asked what the matter was. Never having known death or dying (both my grandmothers were still alive at the time), I looked him determinedly in both eyes. "She's dead," I announced. My father could only pause with mild surprise, nod wearily, and become silent.

During the short time my mother lived in England, her humanity had touched the hearts of many who had come to know her so it was ironic that it was a heart condition that had blighted her life. Whilst my father worked the late shift, it was often my responsibility to be my mother's bed-mate, making sure she was OK during the night. The experience of her swollen feet, like heat-seeking ice blocks beneath the blankets, affected me like an electric shock that caused me to reflexively whip my legs away. Though the reason for her persistently cold extremities was poor circulation, I like to attribute it to that familiar maxim, cold feet, warm heart. It wasn't surprising that her funeral drew the huge numbers it did – guests filling our house and spilling into the front garden and on to the pavement outside. Friends, acquaintances, neighbours, work colleagues and distant family came to pay their last respects and to view my mother's corpse positioned in the narrow hall in an open casket. Among the gathering I was half expecting to see the homeless vagrant who trudged along the High Street, invisible to all but my mother who never failed to stop and empty her purse of copper coins into his grubby outstretched hand. The adults clucked and tut-tutted and patted our heads as we passed beneath them, but I was too busy dutifully fetching and carrying to take in that my brothers, my sister and I were the objects of their concern and pity. I was also embarrassed. My father, unable to afford the immediate funeral costs and too proud to borrow, had reluctantly left my mother in the mortuary till he was finally able to amass the funds. Because of the considerable lapse of time, her body had begun to decay, and the putrid smell was thick and overbearing. Some mourners, caught between politeness and nausea, were driven to hold handkerchiefs over their mouth and nose. The lasting memory I have of that day, however, is sitting on my father's knee. He was exhausted, devastated, while I was dry-eyed and reassuring, insisting that everything would be alright. I was being faithful to my mother's middle-of-the-night refrains. When the pain became unbearable, she would cry out to God to be allowed to die, whilst begging me, "Take care of your father for me." For many years (it seemed an eternity), I would be tight-lipped whilst secretly bubbling up inside whenever anyone either mentioned my mother or expressed sympathy for my motherless predicament. It took many more years for the raw, open wound to finally heal, giving way to an outward approach to life that suggested I'd tidied away the fact of her death. When people commented that I must have suffered terribly as a child, I shrugged away their concerns, as I honestly couldn't identify with the poor, unfortunate waif who still drew compassion from others. But all of that was about to change.

In 1997 my partner, Richard, and I were looking into the issue of adoption, having agreed several years before that we would like, and were in a position, to give a home to a child. But we were unprepared for the extent of the social workers' invasion into our private life; the onslaught of delving and personal questioning. It was apparent that the prime objective was to uncover unresolved issues from both our childhoods that might possibly impair our ability to become successful adoptive parents. I liked to think that I came across as forthright and untroubled, but the more astute of the two social workers latched on to the fact of my mother's death and suggested that I submit myself to bereavement counselling. I had to stop myself from laughing out loud. My mother had been dead and buried nearly thirty years! But I wasn't getting past them. The two social workers joined forces and became adamant. In the end I relented. I figured that, compared to Richard, lumbered with a whole raft of therapy-based 'action plans', I had got off lightly. Where was the harm in a bit of gentle hand-holding, I told myself. I lost no time making the phone call and booking the visit. A week later, a lady from the bereavement charity Cruse appeared on the doorstep. When Beryl introduced herself, I half expected her to hand me a jar of her best home-made chutney. She was such an unassuming, grey-haired stereotype of an old dear. I silently summed her up as being long widowed, either familiar in the local hospital as a tea-trolley volunteer, or a reliable regular presiding over bric-a-brac at the church jumble sales. I offered her a seat in the front room, apologised for what was going to be a complete waste of her valuable time, and suggested that we get it over with as quickly as possible so that she could be on her way to whichever church hall was in need of her services. She paid no heed to my uptight prattling, took my hands, held me with her watery eyes, and gently smiled. The saying goes that the people we meet along the way enter our lives either for a reason, a season or a lifetime. Beryl had come into my life for one specific reason – to strip away an aspect of myself I'd held dear: my façade of strength and invulnerability. Thirty years of granite grief and unconsciously hoarded self-pity dissolved and poured out of me in a molten torrent of tears that I had no hope of stopping. It was an amazing and cathartic experience that left me drained, a raw wreck of emptiness. Up until that moment, I had no idea how much sorrow I had bottled up, unable to express, even to my loved ones. But if I'd thought that was the end of it I was sorely mistaken.

About 18 months later, in 1999, I was at a seminar hosted by Brandon Bays, a Californian motivational author and speaker. I'd been drawn to Brandon Bays after reading her book, *The Journey*, in which she describes devising The Journey process whilst curing herself of a large uterine tumour. Attracting hundreds of people, her seminars use methods that are heavily based on visualisation, Neuro-Linguistic Programming (NLP) and forgiveness, designed to uncover longstanding emotional blocks and bring about profound healing. My own experiences of the Emotional Journey process had brought to the surface unconscious issues to do with my mother's death and, after becoming a Journey 'grad', I had used Journeywork numerous times (without charge) to help scores of people, many of them friends and family members, often with extraordinary results.

Using Journeywork, I helped my son overcome a sudden paralysing fear of dogs that developed after he'd been chased across a field by a huge Weimaraner. The trauma threatened to scar him for life. Years later, now a teenager, he continues to have no problem whatsoever with dogs. It's as though the incident never happened. The session took a mere thirty minutes.

As a volunteer trainer at several Journey seminars, I helped many strangers. These included victims of rape, violent assault and incest; people on the verge of suicide; those struggling with depression, obesity and ill health; those suffering panic attacks and phobias, and those who were simply lost and directionless in their lives and looking for inner guidance. On this particular occasion, I was attending the Journey seminar as one of the team of volunteer trainers. Our role was to provide general hospitality and assist new delegates through the various Emotional and Physical Journey exercises. In the seminar environment, there are many broken souls seeking emotional and physical release, and countless stories of pain and suffering, and I was about to play a role I found extremely rewarding.

I got to know 'Ian' (not his real name) when we employed him to do some electrical jobs around the house. He came across as professional and assured, if perhaps a little cocky. I liked him because of his quality workmanship and because he had a surprisingly open mind, prepared to discuss all manner of topics, including the spiritual. Despite suffering from diabetes for the past 15 years and being insulin-dependent, he enjoyed drinking and smoking, sometimes, I suspected, to excess. I often urged him to take better care of his health and to recon- sider his lifestyle, but he'd only laugh off my concerns. One day he came to work smelling strongly of beer, and I decided to consult my trusted book, *You Can Heal Your Life* by the US author Louise Hay. Under the section for Diseases and Probable Causes, I looked up Diabetes:

Longing for what might have been.
A great need to control.
Deep sorrow. No sweetness left.

When I showed Ian the segment, he boomed with his characteristic laughter, arguing that the description read nothing like him. To my mind he was protesting a little too strenuously. I was aware that, despite his general upbeat manner, he was dealing with a number of personal problems, and could sometimes be subdued. So, I was hardly surprised when one day, out of the blue, he asked me about "this Journey work" I'd previously talked about, and whether I could put him in touch with someone who might guide him through a session. I read this as an unprompted cry for help, and promised to find a local accrediting therapist looking for case-study volunteers. After a week, I hadn't found anyone suitable but assured Ian that I hadn't forgotten. The next day, he asked if I'd be prepared to do it myself. I was surprised, but sensing his urgency I asked if he was sure – he might prefer someone anonymous to his situation. He said he was sure.

The next day, I settled Ian down in the spare room and began the Emotional Journey process – using techniques to first take him into deep relaxation and eventually into *Source* (a hypnotic state of boundless nothingness). Here, he encountered an issue concerning his parents that, despite always speaking highly of them, had eaten away at him since childhood, the extent of which, until that moment, he hadn't fully appreciated. After two long and emotionally draining hours, Ian came to the brink of, while not condoning or approving of his parents' behaviour, recognising that their actions were borne out of failing to do better for not knowing better. His entire body juddered and strained resisting this opening into forgiveness. Suddenly, he erupted on a huge, rolling tide of pain and rage that eventually subsided into a letting go of the past... an acceptance of both his parents' limitations... a deep and genuine embrace of love and forgiveness. When he opened his eyes, over three hours later, gone was the boyish swagger and cocksureness, and in its place were the moist and relaxed eyes of a man born anew. It was an emotional, exhilarating and revelatory experience for both of us.

A week later, Ian phoned to tell me some surprising news. For the first time in 15 years, his blood sugar levels had dramatically reduced and he hadn't needed to take his insulin. Concerned, I asked him if he was under the supervision of his doctor. He assured me that all was OK and that in any case he'd always been cavalier about taking the insulin. Four weeks later, he turned up to finish a few outstanding jobs around the house. I noticed an unusual 'air' about him. Over the course of an hour, he was becoming more and more agitated, his conversation drawling and lacking coherence. Curious and concerned, but distracted by a writing deadline, I retired to the study to continue working. Minutes later, the door crashed open. Ian burst into a tearful and rambling confession of unforgivable acts he'd committed in the past. This vulnerability was totally out of character for him, and a thought occurred to me: could his emotional turmoil be due to the insulin he said he'd stopped taking? During a momentary calm, he assured me that he'd taken insulin that morning and that perhaps he just needed something to eat. Before I could question him further, he had half-stumbled, half-staggered down the stairs and slammed out of the front door.

I tried to continue with my work, but alarm bells were ringing loudly in both my ears. Eventually I ran to grab my coat, phone in hand, dialling Ian's number. His mobile was switched off, which only raised my concern and suspicion. I found my keys and was rushing towards the door when the landline rang. It was the police! The officer asked me to confirm whether I knew a man of a particular description by the name of Ian. My blood ran cold. They said they'd found him weaving unsteadily across the road, and that he had narrowly missed being hit by an approaching car. I imagined the shock local headlines the next day, *"Spiritual Mumbo-Jumbo Reduces Man to Near-Fatal Emotional Wreck"*. As I hurried to the nearby bus stop outside Sainsbury's super-market, I tried to reassure myself that there had to be another explanation. I found Ian sitting slumped on a bench between two community police officers. He looked up with yellow-tinged eyes and though he was slurring his words he'd managed to tell the officers that he was diabetic and they'd promptly called an ambulance. Moments later, the ambulance pulled up. Ian's blood sugar levels were examined and the problem quickly diagnosed. That morning, after weeks of being off the insulin (without either his doctor's knowledge or consent), Ian, for some inexplicable reason, had decided to dose up. Perhaps it was realising that he was coming to see me, and knowing that I would have questioned him. In any case, after a long gap of abstinence following the radical reduction in his blood sugar levels, he'd suddenly medicated himself – effectively administering an overdose of insulin. Hence the strange, emotional, erratic behaviour.

Soon after, Ian visited his doctor who switched him to a more precise system of insulin delivery based on measuring actual levels of sugar in the blood. Months later, he called me from overseas to tell me that he was now living abroad and that his life was on track. More than a decade later, after having had no further contact, I bumped into him fleetingly in London. He appeared cheerful, fresh-faced and healthy and he promised to visit me soon.

During the afternoon of the second day, having listened to, coaxed and assisted at least a dozen delegates through their various states of emotional distress, I became aware that I was experiencing a weird combination of tension and jelly-like nervousness in my limbs. My emotions were brimming, threatening to engulf me. I was emotionally saturated, physically agitated, incapable of absorbing any more anguish. One of the other trainers noticed the signs of my imminent meltdown and swiftly led me, now weeping, to one of the small side rooms to sit in front of a senior trainer. This lady, who I saw through tear-blurred vision, expertly led me through an Emotional Journey process – progressive shut-eyed relaxation: guidance back to a painful, unresolved, part of one's life. The image of my mother instantly appeared. My heart began hammering at a terrifying speed. I couldn't understand it. Having experienced several Journey processes that had brought up issues based solely around my mother, I thought I'd cleared all the repressed trauma there was to clear. As the process continued, my entire body began to shake. Uncontrollably. So much so, that the chair beneath me began rocking violently from side to side. Though this alarmed me, I was unwilling, unable, to break the spell and open my eyes. I heard my trainer's voice calmly reassuring me that what I was experiencing was the Kundalinis[6] and that I was to 'let go' and welcome its powerful energy. Kundalini? I had no idea what she was talking about. I'd never heard of the word before. It meant nothing to me.

Let go! Allow! My greatest fear has always been of losing control, of breaking my critical hold on life. The very thing I was now being called to do. I'd been here before, this was nothing new. The impossible inescapable grip of unknown terror. But this time I was simply too exhausted, too broken to resist, and soon found my grasp loosening. As suddenly as I had been overtaken by Kundalini, the heavy presence of my physical body seemed to shoot upwards and dissolve into an extraordinary calm. Even the relative heaviness of my head, lagging behind among the planets, began to evaporate, leaving in its place an expanding softness. A softness that quietly emerged as what I knew to be... Me. Gently peeling away, further ascending... I sensed this Me edging towards a bright, faraway place. Immense and profound peace was now everywhere, shimmering in a boundless space. An etheric quality resembling a thought drifted around me: "If this is death... why would I ever want to return, back there?" I was aware of the disembodied part of Me floating loose in the vastness, the stillness, a deeper echo of the non-existence of care or worry, the No-thing I used to experience as a child. A gate opened. The path ahead, my path, was wide and clear. This was the moment I came face-to-face with the dazzling, unblemished truth of my past: all those years of clinging, not to the fact of my mother's death, but to the devastating belief that her absence was proof of one thing. *My mother had made a clear choice. That choice amounted to a personal rejection of me. My mother had decided to 'leave' rather than to stay. In her mortal wisdom, she had withdrawn her care, her warmth, her love and 'abandoned' me.* It was the deep ache of this 'abandonment' that had given a backbone, a story, to my life. And it was this story I was now being compelled to witness and to say goodbye to. Forgiveness came easily. Through heartfelt acceptance I surrendered, releasing those dense unconscious emotions anchoring the story in place – the pain, blame, disappointment, anger, rage, rejection... finally laying my mother to rest. Still in the brilliance of that vast space, I slowly opened my eyes to the world. I saw and knew that my life would never be the same. I could now live free from the destructive shadows of my mother's death.

What I learned on that day, a turning point in my life, was that physical death is not the end – not for the person who has passed, and not for the person who has been left behind. I also learned that if we allow ourselves to overcome our own instinctive resistance, and flow with the pain and anguish of bereavement, however deep that may be, what follows is the magic of transformation – the opening up of a beautiful bud of growth and change. An analogy is the daffodil dying back, its energy returning to the bulb to re-emerge into fresh bloom the next season. Meanwhile, its death is the force that creates that fertile space in the soil for additional life to shoot up and to thrive. Similarly, when our loved ones pass, their vitality returns to the soul before reappearing the next season in the next human incarnation. For those of us left bereft by what seems like an unfathomable void, this is the golden opportunity to evolve in that empty space left behind; a chance, especially, to let go of attachments to the old 'story' that formed our past relationship with that person. In relinquishing that story, we not only deepen our understanding of ourselves, we accelerate our journey to our Higher purpose.

In that moment of clarity, confronting that old belief that had been hindering my progress, I recognised the magic that was calling to me. I was transported back to the time when my mother was still alive, to the tan-coloured suitcase (the very same suitcase that held my father's diaries) kept high on top of my parents' wardrobe. Inside that suitcase it smelled like 'new' and it contained my mother's best unworn lingerie and nightdresses. It was her 'just in case' suitcase. Just in case an unexpected tragedy befell her, the understanding was that that suitcase would be whisked to her hospital bedside to clothe misfortune in dignity and style. The tragedy was that, despite frequent hospitalisation, my mother died never having worn a single beautiful item in that suitcase. All the lace and satin and pastel chiffon that had promised so much had been 'too good' to wear and had silently died with her. Horrifyingly and unbeknownst to me, I too had acquired my own 'just in case' suitcase. Instead of lingerie, I had filled my case with all the joys and laughter of living my life to the full – it was a case heavy with the weight of my happiness deferred. Like my mother, I was walking through life, carrying this suitcase, lumbered with the belief that I was undeserving of its contents. Why? Because she had 'abandoned' me. Not just in death, but over the years when she had been too exhausted, too sick, too depressed to embrace me with eyes that shone with the reassuring light of her love. Until that fateful day, I never noticed the presence of my suitcase, much less that I was carrying it out of a false sense of personal rejection. Instead of accepting that happiness is my birthright, I had been allowing a bogus belief to affect my relationship with myself, with others, and with the world. After my revelation, my life certainly didn't change overnight, I still had a road to travel. Unlearning various behaviours that were born out of this belief would take time and discovery. But my first step was an important one, experiencing the liberation of my soul from a prison of sorrow. If I had not surrendered and welcomed the magic waiting in the shadows, that sorrow would surely have devoured me and become my epitaph.

When we shed all the weight and all the baggage of all the habituations and handicaps and expectations of a relationship that once defined us, the death of another can be the open door through which we enter to embrace our own freedom. But it needn't take a death to find liberation. Like the story of Ian, when we open up to fundamental truths about ourselves we allow our own transition from an old self to a deeper, higher, *Knowing* of who we really are. You can begin the process right now, by asking yourself two simple questions:

- Am I burdened by the weight of carrying my own suitcase, unaware that the fullness of my life is contained inside?
- Am I willing enough, brave enough, to go along with the crazy idea that magic awaits me once I open up my suitcase, right here, right now?

Chapter 3

Synchronicity

Though we can't always see it at the time, if we look upon events with some perspective, we see things always happen for our best interests. We are always being guided in a way better than we know ourselves.

Swami Satchidananda

If I believed for one moment that life was nothing more than a string of random or accidental events I might never have developed the all-pervading sense of hope and optimism that has sustained me during the low times, the bad times, and even the reasonably-OK-but-not-so-brilliant times. Life has shown me too often that I am not alone, that a force greater than my own limited beliefs constantly has my best interests at heart, and that this invisible force is helping me to join the dots. My job is to take notice, to *allow*. For, despite the many defeats I have suffered, there has invariably come a time when, looking back, I have gratefully understood why it had been necessary to take or avoid a certain path: why I never achieved the job I desired; why a particular friend had to disappoint me; why I couldn't attend the school of my choice; why the book or the script was destined not to succeed at that time; why a relationship had to flounder, or come to an end. Each mishap or misstep along the way, taking me into the depths of despair, has in hindsight always been a strengthening experience, in synchrony with my ultimate purpose on this earth. A magical silver thread would always, eventually, pull me out of that disheartening place, set me back on my path, and on to my next stop towards my journey's end. Perhaps you're in the thick of it right now, being sorely challenged by life, in which case you probably can't appreciate what I'm talking about. No matter. If all you can do is put blind faith in my words, then do so now. You are here for a reason, a unique purpose, a mission that no one else on this entire planet but you can accomplish. The world is a lesser place without your singular contribution. There are magical stepping stones calling out to your every stride. Wherever you decide to tread, a series of what you might call 'coincidences' or 'flukes' will gently (and sometimes not so gently!) nudge and guide you towards the people, the places, the situations that in your heart of hearts is who, where and what you need to be. It may not feel serendipitous at the time, but accept that a greater plan is falling into place and a magical doorway about to open.

It was the year 1968. I had earned my thumb-sucking privileges by passing my 11+ and being awarded a place at the prestigious Dame Alice Owen's School. In those days, if you were from the working classes and selected for a grammar school place it was akin to winning the lottery, coming, as it did, with the assurance of a future of social and financial elevation. My parents were overjoyed, my father in particular. His child had been in England barely six years, and for this to happen! Our family elation, however, was short-lived. 1968 was also the year that the Conservative MP, Enoch Powell, delivered his famous "Rivers of Blood" speech, and single-handedly changed the course my life was to take.

Here is the means of showing that the immigrant communities can organise to consolidate their members, to agitate and campaign against their fellow citizens, and to overawe and dominate the rest with the legal weapons which the ignorant and the ill-informed have provided. As I look ahead, I am filled with foreboding; like the Roman, I seem to see the River Tiber foaming with much blood.

After assessing the mounting racist climate, my parents reluctantly decided that rather than sending me to the highly sought-after grammar school, it would be less of a risk if I attended the same secondary modern as my sister. By their reckoning, I would be safer in a multi-ethnic environment than being the only black target in an all-white school. Not quite appreciating the opportunity that had been snatched from beneath me, but fully aware that I was missing out on some kind of privilege, I was sent to shelter beneath my older sibling's protective wings. From Day One, with my sensitive disposition and the reserved air I'd inherited from my father, it was apparent to me that I would never fit comfortably among a crowd of confident, brazen girls. Whilst my class paired off into Country Dance partners, dinner-table buddies, and walk-home best friends, I was always among the remaindered. It was a situation I couldn't even redeem during the playing of sports, as I both loathed games and was handicapped by severe spatial awareness difficulties when it came to catching or handling a ball.

Three years on, I had come to detest everything about my failing all-girls school in North London – in particular the pimply crew from the neighbouring boys school who would congregate outside each lunchtime and hang like zoo creatures off the iron gates, leering, hissing and calling out to the uninhibited and flirtatious, until a hysterical Miss would charge across the playground and see them off with her whistle. I begged to leave, complaining to my father that the teachers were deficient and the children unruly. In the end I was forced to pull my ace card: I was learning zilch, and would end up with no qualifications to show for my entire schooling. That did it. My father immediately launched into panic mode. Sadly, in his colonial ignorance, believing that every school in England was an Eton offshoot, he succeeded in getting me transferred to the nearby comprehensive (known as the 'sin bin') where fights were a regular occurrence, and the only thing 'cut above' about its reputation was that this was 1971 and knives hadn't yet arrived in the playground. It was a disastrous decision and, once made, irreversible, as neither I nor my father was equipped with sufficient knowledge of a viable alternative. The intention of pairing me with my sister had backfired and I was now in a worse school, on my own, with no one to fend for me. It seemed that the universe was tripping me up. From this vantage point there was no way for me to observe the magical fairy dust that was being sprinkled on my path. What helped me, however, was discovering an interesting fact about myself. Whilst the prospect of being without my sister was daunting, there was a part of me that found it equally, surprisingly, thrilling. Alone in the world, I could define myself on my own terms; become any person I chose to be – a power reminiscent of that which I possessed in my dreams. I realised that the isolation of swimming out of my depth to expansive, faraway shores causes me to come *alive*; whereas the experience of following the instinct of the herd deadens my soul. Ahead of me, this lack of separation anxiety was to put me in good stead for the lonely journey the universe had in store for me.

The sweltering summer of '76. Aged 19, I'm in the final term of completing my 'A' levels at Tottenham Tech, and at the tail-end of a 3-year relationship with a boy of my own age. I'm also heavily pregnant. My father is so terrified of his emotions he passes me on the stairs and carries on as if he is blind to the outrageous bump projecting from my skinny frame. I can only imagine that his usual stern disapproval has been numbed by a deep inner sadness. So much for his firm belief in my academic future. Thank God my mother is not alive to add her own weight of disappointment. At college, I continue to ride out the pitying glances from my lecturers and the superior smirks of my fellow students. I've already planned how I'm going to make up for scuppering my immediate chances of going to university: I'll delay enrolling until my unborn child starts school. Everyone is sceptical when I tell them this, but this isn't even wishful thinking. I can already see my future – and it is not among the other pram-pushing gymslip mothers I encounter on the streets.

During my entire pregnancy my father continued to ignore the obvious. I have come to realise that it was both his way of failing to deal with the situation and his method of not rejecting me. Under his parental roof, we became part of a surreal existence of distance and manners. About to become a parent myself, I soon began to feel the suffocation of his petty Victorian patriarchal rules; his fearful, restricted view of the world. Hopeless as it seemed, I dreamed many dreams of starting a new, independent life for myself. As if in answer to my prayers, as soon as my daughter was born two related events occurred in quick succession. First, the local Council, through its 1970s slum clearance and community regeneration programme, slapped a compulsory purchase order on my father's condemned three-storey house. We'd moved into this house ten years prior, after our family of six vacated the two cramped rooms in Offord Road we'd inhabited since our arrival in England. Through my father taking every available shift at the postal sorting office, in 1966 he managed to purchase his first UK property for an unimaginable £3,500. Part of the reason for the bargain price (even then) was that the house came with two sitting tenants (who promptly moved out when their new black landlord moved in), and it was in an area designated for future redevelopment. So in 1976, as the UK was experiencing a sea change in the decentralisation of government departments to address local issues of deprivation and poor housing, my father was awarded a modest compensation deal and we moved to a newer, much smaller, house. I saw this as the perfect opportunity to make a clean break from the boyfriend who had failed miserably to measure up as a would-be father; and who was an even greater disappointment once our daughter was born. The prospect of single parenthood was daunting enough, but the idea of a future tied to a broken and problematic relationship was even more terrifying. Whilst living in the new house with my father and younger brother (my two older siblings had both left home by now), numerous housing associations had begun springing up in the area, and my friend Reima suggested that I put my name down for a flat. I was initially resistant as I couldn't see why anyone would want to reward me with shiny new accommodation when I was already, if not ideally, reasonably placed with my father. My friend persisted till I finally, more to please her than myself, went through the formalities, after which I gave the idea no further thought. Then came the next magical happening. Before my daughter's second birthday I was handed the keys to my first independent home – an unexpected and miraculous development.

Sadly, my relationship with my father had become so strained at this point that I purposely organised the packing and removal of my few belongings to take place while he was at work. Sitting in the front passenger seat, cradling my daughter as the removal van pulled away from the house, I saw my father walking briskly up the road towards the house. Our eyes met briefly, but we said nothing, neither of us ready to forgive or forget the time when he had brought a girlfriend to live in the previous family home and caused an explosive domestic situation. That drama had since played itself out and the girlfriend was now out of the picture, but the damage to our relationship had already been done. Though over the following months we would gradually repair the fall-out and get back on speaking terms, it was a sad-sweet occasion when I opened the green front door of number 11 and stepped inside the Finsbury Park maisonette that was to become my oasis for fourteen eventful years. I had been gifted with an incredible space in which I was to develop my creativity, to explore and experiment with becoming an adult in a grown-up world. That same year I bought a cake conserver, an extravagantly large glass dome over a matching flute-edged glass dish.

It was a totally impractical item for my miniscule kitchen, but it represented my unconscious *intention*, a gesture towards the future. As happy as I was in my little two-bedroom home, for as long as I lived there I was forever looking outward to a time when I could afford to purchase my own property. As the years passed, though there were no obvious signs on the horizon, the presence of the cake dome seemed to draw me closer to that day. I had no savings, I was living on a meagre income but, unannounced, an image came to me. Mysteriously like *déjà vu*, emerging out of the ether, it was a large red-brick house.

Five years on, after a number of deadening jobs to make ends meet, my bright, beautiful 5-year-old daughter is starting her first year at school, and I am about to embark upon a 3-year BA degree course at Bedford College, London University, the first member of my immediate or extended family to have achieved such dizzying educational heights.

As I filled out my 1980 UCAS form, I was too excited to consider properly any of the downsides of pursuing a university education whilst single-handedly raising a young child. The isolation, the juggling, the stress, the alienation would be part of the dream of expanding my horizons and arriving at a distant shore. After years of punching below my weight, I would at last be meeting challenges to stretch my potential. When I arrived at Bedford College I was an almost-mature student, one of the oldest by five years. The majority of my intake mostly lived in halls, got involved in politics, frequented the student union bar, and hung around the college grounds, generally having a sociable time. I, on the other hand, running a home combined with all the responsibilities of young motherhood, would be found in one of two places: the library, or on the bus heading home to collect my daughter from after-school club. On the whole, though, university life greatly suited me. I was desperate to *grow*, and the luxury and privilege of studying fuelled a huge inner drive for knowledge. It was an eye-opener to discover the great philosophical, psychological and humanist thinkers such as Plato, Fromm, Weber, Durkheim, Marx and Freud. My preferred subject was Social Theory and my absolute favourite lecturer was Steve Schenk, with whom I ran a great double-act. I, the wide-eyed student, hungry for answers to impossible metaphysical questions; he, the font of all universal knowledge, as I saw him, volleying back with open relish equally impossible rejoinders. I can see him now: lounging in that worn high-back leather chair, gingerly steepling his fingers, the dandruff-flecked shoulders of his dark jacket occasionally jerking in amusement, or very still as he summoned delicious comebacks from behind closed eyes. In the magical setting of Steve's tutor room, with the view of the lawns out of the tall Victorian window, I was encouraged to put aside my logical rational left brain and slip into a creative dream-space that required nothing more than stepping out of the way of myself. I didn't know it then, but the universe was yet again preparing me for the future, this time revealing the theoretical connection to those deeper realms where I would eventually access my ability to heal. With Steve's help, I graduated at the age of twenty-seven from London University with a respectable 2:1 in Sociology. My great regret is that when I looked back and thought to thank him, it was too late. He had already passed.

I decided that I wouldn't rush into finding a job until I had discovered exactly what it was I wanted to do with the rest of my life. While my contemporaries were already staking their claim in the jobs market, I sat at home, dreamed many dreams of what I could become, and waited for inspiration. Before long, I found myself in a cul-de-sac of despondence. The graduate careers in the jobs pages were unappealing, entirely not how I saw myself: deadly dull, way too serious, boringly grown-up. After years of having had to accept futile jobs (my first was aged fifteen –

summer vacation work in an industrial laundry, sorting the stained long johns of Pentonville prisoners into huge steaming vats; then shop assistant work; supermarket shelf-stacking; domestic cleaning; contract cleaning; office temping; and a few relatively respectable but drab years as an Inland Revenue Tax Officer, then a *Yellow Pages* office clerk) in order to support first myself, and then my daughter, I knew exactly what I *didn't* want to do.

During my first uni summer break I returned to the island of my birth for the first time. I wasn't to know, but this was going to be the set-up for magic to sparkle in my life. My Jamaican host, Sylvia, had found me a temporary secretarial job in downtown Kingston that helped fund taking my daughter to neighbouring Miami and on to Disney World in Orlando. Working in the same department was an ex-pat Englishman who held what in my eyes was a grand and impossibly glamorous jet-setting post as a junior consultant for the World Bank. He was intrigued by this 'Jamaican' secretary with a London accent, and we became friends. Months later, whilst visiting his parents in the UK, he dropped in on me in Finsbury Park. This coincided with the time I was searching for a meaning to my life, and floundering. The television happened to be on in the background, and he pointed at a reporter on the screen. An old school friend, he commented, mildly surprised. I, on the other hand, was quietly gobsmacked. The only intimate knowledge I had then of television was that if I turned the knob (no remote control in those days!) I would be transported to a nether world of mystical giants that included my daytime heroine, Oprah Winfrey. And there I was, in the company of a real person with a real connection to one of those TV 'untouchables'.

If nothing in this life happens by chance or by accident, then the timing of my friend's visit was impeccable. He was absolutely meant to be in my home at that precise moment while that particular programme was being aired in order to utter those exact words, because the effect was instantaneous, tremendous. It was as if a huge chunk of masonry fell from the ceiling and crunched into a dust cloud before me. In moments of the dust clearing I became unlocked from a trance of 'stuckness' and acquired a startling shift in perspective: I *knew* my vocation. I certainly didn't know the *how* of getting there, but I knew the *what*. As far-fetched or ridiculous as it might have sounded to my family and friends at the time, I knew that my career would be in television. Writing for television.

That flash of inspiration unleashed in me a tsunami of creativity. I became a writing vortex, filling up notepads and lined exercise books, scribbling on cereal boxes and the backs of brown envelopes. I began remembering certain events in my past, seeing the clues that had been silently beckoning to my future. I recalled how in primary school I was usually top at spelling, mostly out of a morbid fear of Mrs Christmas' evil jab in the spine for every misspelled word; the folded-paper illustrated stories I attempted to sell for tuck money to my 11-year-old class-mates; the reading and writing competitions organised by my local library that I'd consistently enter and win; Mr Beef, my English teacher, condemning our entire hopeless moronic shambles of a class, declaring that not one of us would amount to a single damn thing, except... Carmen Harris (you can imagine how many extra friends I acquired that day); and the time I submitted my first Year 7 essay to my Commerce teacher, Mr Morgan, the embarrassing memory of which clung to me for at least a few decades. I was perplexed by his amusement at my best efforts; in fact, he was openly in stitches. Addressing the homework essay title – "The Large-Scale Buying and Selling of Goods" – my opening paragraph had read: *"Donna's well-manicured fingers turned the pages of the glossy mail order catalogue..."* How was I to know that in big school, unless you were specifically in an English Literature class, 'essay' did not mean 'work of fiction'?

Six months following my TV epiphany, I had come to the end of a frenzied exercise in purple, overblown vanity that resulted in an impressive typewritten stack of A4 pages. My first romantic novella! I proudly sent off my manuscript to the publishers Allison and Busby, fully expecting a lucrative contract by return post. I didn't get my heart's desire, but what I did get went a long way towards building my confidence and confirming that a career as a writer wasn't an entirely impossible dream. Instead of the usual outright rejection slip, I received a very encouraging handwritten letter from the lady herself, Ms Margaret Busby (now OBE). I interpreted this communication as an indication that my work was shite, but quality shite; that I shouldn't necessarily knock on her door again, but I could possibly delay seeking the day job for a little while longer. I was so chuffed, I paraded the first few chapters in front of my friend Valerie, who then showed it to her partner, Alan, who showed it to Charlie, a theatre director friend of his. I had no idea this networking conga would eventually pay dividends.

Meanwhile, one day I excitedly purchased a new monthly black magazine, a groundbreaking publication in the early 80s. I was looking forward to reading about sectors of the UK black community doing well for themselves, hoping to experience a bit of reflected pride. To my dismay, each page was littered with enough spelling and grammatical errors to have resurrected Mrs Christmas from the grave for one last jab. It was unforgivable. Unable to stop myself, I rang the editor to complain. Without being at all defensive, Winsome Cornish (now MBE) listened patiently to my indignation, at the end of which she asked plainly whether I thought I could do a better job. I said I certainly could. That's how I landed myself the post of *Chic's* subeditor and occasional contributing writer, making intermittent trips to the magazine offices in the then emerging landscape of Canary Wharf. It wasn't what you'd call a proper job, more very poorly paid casual work, but among the other black journalist shooting stars (one of whom would become a respected author, and another a well-known TV presenter), working on the magazine became my first official assignment as a writer.

Days later, the theatre director, Charlie, turned up at my place in Finsbury Park. Over a mug of tea he explained that he had read the first chapter of my novella that had been shown to him by Alan, via Valerie, and that he was impressed with my knack for writing dialogue. Would I be interested in writing for the next series of a TV comedy he had been involved in devising? I think my solemnity genuinely shocked him. Or perhaps being Jewish, he admired my chutzpah? I responded that I was familiar with the programme in question, but that I couldn't write for it unless I was able to change some of the characters who, in my opinion, were over the top and just a bit silly. Rather than pricking the air out of my pompous balloon head, the director's generous parting shot as he left planted a tiny seed in my eager, fertile imagination. Had I thought about writing for the theatre, he asked? Theatre? I knew next to nothing about the world of stage and greasepaint. My first visit to the theatre had been in 1974 on a one-off family outing with my father to see the colourful South African musical, *Ipi Tombi*. My experiences since that time had been far and few between. Despite my appalling ignorance, I dared to ask, *Why not?* After all, I was used to writing or making up stories my whole life, and a theatre play was just a story set on an elevated wooden platform. Right?

Immediately after the director's throwaway suggestion, I tried my hand at a theatrical tragicomedy centred around two generations of a Jamaican family. The result, I thought, was amusing and not a bad first stab at something for which I had had no previous experience. With no money to finance its production, I befriended a group of 'theatre people' and invited them back to my place with the lure of a home-cooked Jamaican feast (cooking is a skill I have and something I enjoy doing). Little did the invitees – young creatives on the lookout for opportunities – realise that each one of them had been carefully selected to accord with my ulterior motive. The line-up consisted of several actors (many have since gone on to work successfully in TV and films), a West End theatre lighting technician (who remains a good friend to this day), a community theatre director (also a present-day friend, now a lecturer, who worked prolifically for many years in theatre, TV, and as a Radio 4 producer/director) and myself (aspiring writer). After the meal I made a 'spontaneous' suggestion that we might all like to have a bit of fun, reading individual parts for a play I just happened to have written. My unsuspecting guests (though they might have twigged when I rapidly produced twelve freshly photocopied and bound scripts) promptly fell into the spirit of the evening. By the end of a happy occasion filled with excited chatter, much laughter and bellies full of chicken stew, there was unanimous agreement that the play deserved to be staged and that we should create a vehicle to do just that. Hi-Time Theatre Company was born, and my writing career was off to a proper start. In no time, it seemed, my plays were being read and staged at Battersea Arts Centre, Riverside Studios, the Albany Empire and Islington Town Hall, and receiving some bland-to-favourable reviews in publications such as *Time Out*, as well as an extract reprinted in an anthology[7] compiled by Second Wave, an arts organisation whose patron at the time was Glenda Jackson.

Around this period I was accustomed to reading bedtime stories to my daughter who adored books. She especially enjoyed it when I improvised my own humorous tales. Had she not been so responsive, I might not have joined the Adult Literary Institute and enrolled for their short weekday morning course, Writing for Children. Encouraged by the tutor, Elizabeth Hawkins (a real published author! – that fact alone was an amazing motivator for me), I typed up one of my stories and sent it off to the first publisher that came to mind. Heinemann liked *Naomi's Secret*,[8] and it wasn't long before the first proof, followed by the hardback copy, landed on my doormat, and not much later that another of my books, *The Big Red Trouble*,[9] was rolled out by the same publishers. A few years on, two more of my children's stories, *The Moving Mystery*[10] and *Charlie's New School*[11] were also published, this time by Orchard Books. Onwards and up, always on the alert for fresh openings, I came across an advertisement calling for writers to submit entries to a comedy-writing competition. I almost talked myself out of entering, not for one moment imagining that anything would come of a personal submission. Eventually, I knocked up a silly little sketch that featured a warring married couple, a sugary doughnut and a bleeding finger pricked by a darning needle. It made me chuckle enough to send it off to Noel Gay TV, the production company headed up by Paul Jackson (then producer of Channel 4's *Red Dwarf*, subsequently head of BBC Entertainment). Several weeks later I received a letter announcing that I was one of six winners and that my 2-minute script had earned me an amazing £1,000! My first significant returns from a budding writing career. I was finally on the road to the rest of my life!

I look back thirty years ago and remember my utter devastation when I failed to secure an Office Manager post advertised by my housing association. It was my first serious job application, and I had total conviction that, among the applicants, I was the obvious and ideal candidate. When I was rejected I saw it as the worst possible outcome. Having very little money at the time, the promise of a career offering the security of regular income and a local, child-friendly environment would have been the solution to all my problems. What I didn't fully realise was that, unconsciously, it had always been my *intention* to become a writer, and my latent creative spirit would not have survived the confinement of a stultifying desk job requiring 9–5 commitment and occasional evening duties.

What the magic of the universe delivered instead was erratic income, very little security and the requirement to travel to a variety of offices across London. This may have appeared to be a very poor gift indeed, but it turned out to be ideal conditions for an aspiring writer. Having to resort to temp typing, slipping in and out of different work environments, actually fed my hunger for freedom and variety. It also meant I was able to remain detached and uncommitted, maintaining that all-important creative space in my life (and head). I eventually became accustomed to an irregular, itinerant working routine that would ultimately chime with the lifestyle of a freelance writer. Now, looking back with the benefit of hindsight, I recognise this turn of events as being one of many 'coincidences', the result of universal magic responding to my unconscious *intention* and accordingly steering the course of my life.

After a series of incredible leg-ups, the universe was busy lining up yet another leap forward into my future. Thus far, I had been enjoying the ride and playing my part by writing with determination and commitment, often well into the early hours of the next morning. But I was also feeling isolated, occasionally pining for adult company, needing to hear other than my own voice. I began to scour the local papers for a part-time job that would bring in some extra money and tear me away from the obsession of my typewriter, if only to sit at someone else's. I found myself answering a small ad that led me to a rundown house in Archway. The instant the door creaked open and I clapped eyes on the shuffling, unshaven figure emerging from the darkness, my gut instinct shouted: *About-turn! Run!* But more concerned about looking ridiculous (I was young, foolish), I chanced my life and tentatively stepped into the gloom. For the next two hours inside that dingy bachelor pad I perched nervously on the edge of a soiled chair in front of an Amstrad computer. For my 'protection' I refused all suspicious offers of refreshment and kept one eye on the door whilst the Polish stranger directed me to type up weird indecipherable codes that I was convinced had some sinister purpose. During the entire bizarre experience, my grubby-trousered, would-be-mass-murderer skulked inches behind me, rasping sourly down my neck. When my time was up, I flew out of there like the proverbial bat out of hell, making assurances that I would indeed return the next day, knowing full well that wild horses on speed would not drag me back there. Even now I get the heebie-jeebies recalling my narrow escape from the clutches of Fred West's Krakow cousin. Then again, it may well have just been my burgeoning writer's imagination. I continued my search, and the next local ad I answered in the *Ham & High* proved to be a call from the universe.

Copy Typist Wanted. Three Mornings a Week.

I turned up on an altogether different doorstep, this time in elegant Maida Vale. As the heavy black door swung open, I instantly recognised the figure standing in front of me. Of all the people whose ads I could have answered, that silver thread of synchronicity had brought me to the home of an ex-lecturer (turned independent business consultant) of my old university. Though his department had been Psychology and mine Sociology, our scholarly connection, I'm sure, helped secure me the job. And so began my 8-year sojourn at John Nicholson Associates (later to become Nicholson McBride Limited – NML), one of the most enjoyable and educative periods of my life. The moment John sussed that I was capable of independently constructing a sentence, three mornings a week soon morphed into three full days, and my title swiftly changed from Copy Typist to Resources Manager of a fast-growing 'crack outfit' consultancy whose byline is still 'Psychology in Business' (interestingly, Psychology was my first choice when applying to university, but my mathematics credentials seriously let me down). I couldn't have landed a more perfectly placed job at a more opportune time in my life. Under John's tutelage I learned the advanced craft of writing – the succinct, pithy, informative sentence, and my guiding maxim – *Less is more.* It was here, too, while witnessing my boss rattling off book reviews for *The Sunday Times* and numerous articles and publications, that I discovered that the real art of writing lies not in writing but in *re*-writing; and that the perfect *bon mot* doesn't necessarily fall effortlessly from one's head, regardless even of whether that head happens to be Oxbridge-educated. Soon I was penning training modules for business managers, rolling out the company's monthly newsletter, devising briefs for role-playing actors and scripts for corporate videos and audio cassettes. The emphasis on excellence, creativity and openness, the focus on people and extracting the best from them, absolutely fed my soul. And even my own extra-curricular writing was a source of appreciation and encouragement by the boss and my colleagues. About this time I was looking for a TV agent and scanned the *Writers' and Artists' Yearbook.* I came across a top agent, and despite the fact that her books were closed to new writers I decided that I would try anyway. I sent off an impressive-sounding letter about myself and my glowing ambitions for my own future. Soon I was sitting in an Islington office before Gilly Schuster and Cecily Ware, whereupon they both took a liking to me, and I have been a client of that agency ever since. And then it happened: My Big Career Break. Without any prior experience, never having read a 'How-To' manual, I was commissioned to write two series of my own original TV sitcom, *Us Girls!* This is how the universe contrived this massive slice of magical good fortune...

The reader, Heather Peace, who had recommended my winning Noel Gay short script had moved on to work for BBC Light Entertainment as a script editor. Being new to the department with a rather clean development slate, she naturally contacted the writers in her Filofax, myself included. It was a late Friday afternoon. She called and asked whether I happened to have any written-up ideas for a sitcom. I immediately said yes, very firmly. Thank God the Internet was not yet a global phenomenon. I promised to send in my 'idea' by first post, mentally scrapping all plans for the weekend as I would be spending it empty-head-scratching and eventually labouring over a half-hour domestic about three generations of black females coexisting in the same house. A couple of weeks later I was summoned to meet the Head of Light Entertainment, Robin Nash. In his plush office on the seventh floor of the BBC building in White City, he congratulated me on my script and remarked that during the department's weekly script meeting, *Us Girls* had stood 'head and shoulders' above the slush pile that balanced precariously on a large glass coffee table in the centre of the office. Barely weeks later, after an exciting process of auditioning, rehearsals and tech-runs, the pilot was being filmed live in front of a studio audience in Birmingham. My ideas, my thoughts, my words carefully being brought to life by professional actors. It was wild! Exhilarating! Unreal! The pilot was a roaring success and led to the commissioning of twelve further episodes over two series, resulting in an eventual broadcast on prime time BBC1. The opening episodes pulled in a respectable audience of over 8 million. An amazing coup for a first-time writer completely new to television. Other TV and also radio work started beckoning, including my engagement as team writer on a national soap that would last for ten memorable years. For most of this buzzy, creative, period, I was still working part-time at the consultancy, and John and my work colleagues couldn't have been more supportive or happier for my success. There was, however, another synchronistic twist involving NML about to emerge. An altogether different variety of magic seedling was beginning to sprout, and it had nothing to do with writing. At least, not in its early sapling stages.

One morning at NML I was summoned to John's office and given the stern 'request' to select and attend an external corporate course in order to support my ongoing professional development. My immediate response was to try to wriggle out of it, having successfully resisted all previous attempts at gentle persuasion up to that point. Though I was involved in writing such material, I couldn't see the point of sitting through half day workshops entitled 'Connecting People and Processes' or 'Mobilising Communication', when I had no ambition, neither was I cut out, to move up into the ranks of the high-earning consultant. Quite frankly, the thought of standing up and delivering training to a group of professional suited males terrified me. Public speaking in general was the stuff of nightmares for me. But my boss was adamant, and so was the universe. A day later, the latter promptly delivered, through the incoming post, an unsolicited flyer: *The LifeWorks Seminar, a Paul McKenna / Michael Breen Self-Hypnosis workshop.* The blurb stood out from all the other flyers promoting dry-sounding managerial programmes, pulsating with colour and vibrancy, and shouting: *Pick ME!* It was an obvious soft option and, to be honest, the lowbrow appeal for me was the thought of being entertained by a well-known TV hypnotist. To my surprise and initial disappointment, the two-day course was attended not by regular punters but mostly male attaché-carrying business delegates. I was to learn that there would be no mesmerised audience member with a red onion clamped between their teeth, believing it to be a juicy Royal Gala apple... ho-ho-ho! This was an audience with Paul McKenna's corporate alter ego.

My disappointment soon turned to revelation as I was gently inducted into the world of 'enlightening' workshops. Listening in awe to Paul's descriptions of the principles of Altered States and Goal-Setting, I discovered a real sense of coming 'home'. Were these not the same principles (constantly dreaming of; reaching into; the future) that had been guiding my own journey through life? Though I may not have realised it at the time, a series of synchronistic events, including my employment at NML, had been handing me both the tools and a systematic approach for moulding and designing a life of continued personal development. It marked the beginning of my pursuit of alternative processes that would eventually lead to discovering my Gift.

When you begin seeing coincidences as life opportunities, every coincidence becomes meaningful. Every coincidence becomes an opportunity for creativity. Every coincidence becomes an opportunity for you to become the person the universe intended you to be.
Deepak Chopra

This is exactly how I was beginning to see my life during this intense period. Each time I chose to open up to the creative flow, the universe responded with the magic of opportunity (*'fate'*) and the miracle of synchronicity (*'coincidence'*). It seemed only natural to be responding to a responsive world, but I do realise that for a lot of people this is quite a privileged perspective to have. When things are going our way, we may catch the occasional glimpse of universal magic, but we don't all consistently receive the world in this fashion. Indeed, many of us seem to hold the belief that the story of our life is a chaotic tale of being born, by some kind of genetic fluke, to random parents, in arbitrary circumstances, and thereafter stumbling haphazardly from one chance scene to another, until... The End. Wow. Having such an outlook, it makes perfect sense why so many of us feel so isolated, depressed, unsupported, powerless and at the mercy of invisible forces that are 'out there' and out to 'get' us. I believe that our journey is far more meaningful, more hopeful, more magical than such a fatalistic viewpoint. If this were the true scenario of our lives, we might as well have been born as fruit flies! I believe that we are both the main character and the playwright of our own life story. Consciously or unconsciously, we not only get to choose the part we play, we also select the story that needs telling, and co-author that story with other major and minor role-players (friends, family, authority figures, strangers, acquaintances). We are that powerful, if only we knew it. Another compelling principle we may not be aware of is that for every action we take in life, there is a corresponding reaction. Our thoughts alone amount to action. That day in my living room, the thought (*action*) that I could become a TV writer became such a firm belief, even despite all the initial setbacks and rejections, it sustained my creative flow (*reaction*), and led to a synchronising of opportunities that resulted in my work becoming visible to the right people at the right time (*magic*).

Every waking moment we are sending mental instructions into the universe. Through the power of our minds, we begin a chain reaction that will ultimately effect changes in our emotional state, our physical health, and our life's journey. Though the precise *how* and *when* of what will come about may not be immediately evident (I had no idea at the time how and when I could/would become a TV writer!), if we are consistent in our thoughts and disciplined enough in our efforts, we will arrive at the destiny of our dreams... or somewhere better. The universe, as the infinite creator, the ultimate story-builder, holds the key to the workings of synchronicity and the presence of magic – the *how* and the *when*. Being a creative writer, I too am a story-builder; perhaps this fact explains my clarity around the topic. As a writer, whatever the tale, my overriding aim is to devise an exciting/gratifying story that places my hero/ine in a difficult or virtually impossible situation, apparently with no way out. My end challenge is to come up with a credible resolution, one that neither my hero/ine nor the viewing/reading audience could predict. It would be quite easy to concoct a 'cheat' – i.e. random – ending, but this wouldn't employ skill, and neither would it be satisfying for me or my audience. Truly brilliant films are like watching the universe in action. Challenging. Exciting. Unpredictable. Magical. It's the thrill of a magical rollercoaster ride eliciting a range of high and low emotions that culminates in a fulfilling ending, but an ending that is always justified (i.e. made credible) by the character's own actions and motivations.

If we open up to the idea that in life's grand scheme there is no such thing as a random outcome, we might begin to take personal responsibility for our own story, and to feel more secure about the world in which we live. Sure, there are those forces, in nature for example, that we cannot always predict or control, but what we *can* control is how we *perceive* the outcomes that personally affect us. I could very well have admitted defeat at the first rejection of my writing, seeing this as evidence of the universe being pitted against me. Instead, I chose to perceive those rejections as a sign that I was perhaps knocking on the wrong door. So I tried knocking on another, and another. And sure enough, behind one of those doors, the magic was waiting. The choice is ours. We can believe that we are mere flotsam on life's turbulent surface, having no say in how or where we get washed up; or we can believe that through our own *intentions* and the act of *allowing* magic we can determine, in every situation, how life's challenges will bear upon our existence.

Here's a true story of comic 'coincidence':

I was living in a housing association maisonette, a single parent and a first-year student at London University. One day, I returned home with my daughter and realised that not only had I lost my keys, but I hadn't had the prior sense to lodge a spare set with a friend or family member. I shared my plight with some young Christian neighbours living across the road, and their visiting Christian friends. There we were, a small group of us, gazing up at my third floor window and discussing my predicament. A passer-by's brusque comment was that the only solution was to call out the fire brigade to hammer down the door. This would have been at a significant cost, never mind the bill to repair the resulting damage. Living on an annual student grant of £1,900 stretched thinly to cover rent, food, clothing, bills, travel and living expenses, this was a frightening prospect. Yet, the situation was impossible and it seemed that calling the Fire Brigade would be my only option. One of the neighbours confidently reassured me, "Don't worry. The Lord will provide." It was very strange. Though I have never been remotely religious, I found those words deeply comforting, to the extent that I took the bizarre incident that followed almost completely in my stride.

One of the Christians' friends murmured thoughtfully, "What we need is a ladder." Almost instantly another of them cried, "Look!" We swung our gaze across the road towards a shadowy figure that had just emerged from around the corner. He was in a great hurry and under one arm he carried a ten-foot long *extending* ladder! After a stunned moment, I bolted after the thin streak of a man, stopped him in his tracks and explained the situation. He looked across at our group and replied that he was happy to *sell* me the ladder. It was 'hot', you see. He'd only just 'nicked it' from a nearby building site. When I pleaded with him that I just wanted to borrow it, he let out a put-upon sigh, sized up the height of my window and began positioning the stolen ladder against the side of the house. Quick as greased lightning, he had skinned up the rungs and slithered through my half-open window. On the streets below, we were jumping in jubilation – me, because I'd saved myself a small fortune, and the Christians because their Lord had indeed provided. A moment later, the colour drained from my face. It dawned on me that I'd just given permission to a self-confessed criminal – *a burglar* – to let himself into my home! I had few possessions, but the little I did have was *all* I had. I felt sick. The thought of this stranger rifling through mine and my daughter's belongings... Suddenly, the front door opened and our man appeared. He'd been in and out in less than a minute. My anxiety melted into relief and gratitude. This was the most amazing crook I'd ever met! I tried pressing him with the few pounds that was all I had. He brushed away my offer, grabbed his ladder, hotfooted it around the corner and vanished as mysteriously as he had appeared.

Decades later, I still wonder whose *intention* the universe was serving that day – mine or my Christian friends'? Perhaps two birds were being sacrificed with the one proverbial stone, as one of the Christians eventually became the reverend of a major UK gospel choir, and this story would have been the perfect modern-day parable to illustrate the divine power of God (or synchronicity) in action!

There was a very good reason for Enoch Powell foiling my chances of a grammar school education. If I had become a plummy Dame Alice Owen girl, I might never have fallen from grace and developed the driving force of a single parent that would shape me into becoming the kind of writer that I am today. Nonetheless, it is my personal opinion that during those fast-track early years, though I worked long and hard, seizing glorious opportunities and flying by the seat of my pants, my body of work, though respectable, was far from outstanding. At each stage of the game, I would enter the scene as a novice player. Whilst still familiarising myself with the territory, I noticed that others would have already imbibed the rules and moved on to the next stage of acquiring mastery. They were the ones who received long-term contracts and multiple commissions, for instance. Meanwhile, I would be contract-less, surviving from one commission to the next (a part of me, admittedly, dreading the 'yoke' of more commitment). It was as if that silver thread was gently pulling on me from behind, urging: "No further down this road, save your efforts, there's another turning coming up." All the same, I do recognise that my achievements were commendable and I still pinch myself when I consider my output of articles, books, radio and TV scripts in many areas, including children's, soaps, dramas and sitcoms.

So, who or what am I to give my thanks to? Coincidence? Luck? Fate? Fluke? Talent? There were far too many breathtaking twists, quirky scenarios, incredible happenstances, to put my progress purely down to random coincidences. Talent had to be part of the equation, but it certainly wasn't the entire story. The universe is ordered according to our every thought, and I believe that at the same time as my career was soaring, my thoughts – consistently forward-looking, positive, energised – were in alignment with the life I was both consciously and unconsciously seeking. My conviction, borne out of repeated experience, had been that no matter how long it took, the universe would always, in the end, deliver. I implicitly trusted that it would. Yet, a decade later, in my early 40s, after having had two more children, coupled with the responsibilities of a long-term relationship and a large home, I seemed to have lost my original faith and energy. Somehow, I had allowed Life to get in the way. Or had I simply reached a turning in the road?

Yes, the large red-brick house did eventually materialise. I knew from the moment I stepped inside that Edwardian three-storey that it was to be mine. It had, and still possesses, the most amazing energy of light, peace and benevolence that most visitors automatically comment upon. Again, synchronicity's helping hand led the way.

Lying awake one night, upset and frustrated, I was mulling over the multiple mortgage application rejections that my partner and I had received. We had tried every bank and building society, but due to our dual freelance status and lack of a financial track record, we had finally run out of options.

The phone rang. It was my then script editor apologising for calling at such a late hour to discuss my latest redraft of a drama we were working on. She immediately picked up on the weariness in my voice. I blurted out the depressing tale of my partner and I having found the home of our dreams, only to be days away from having it snatched from us. I couldn't believe what I heard next. "Lisselle," she said, calmly calling me by my pseudonym at the time, "I can help you." It turned out that her husband was the CEO of an international bank specialising in non-certified mortgages! The timing, the 'coincidence' could not have been more perfect.

A few weeks later, mortgage approved, the wheels of the universe began turning in full, till we were finally handed the keys to our beautiful home. In this house, my cake dome eventually found its rightful place in a larger kitchen.

Chapter 4

Failure

The only real failure in life is not to be true to the best one knows.
Buddha

"OK, this next character. So, what do we all think?"

"Well... (deep sigh)... he's not actually going anywhere, is he?"

"I couldn't honestly come up with anything."

"Quite frankly, I think we've done all we can with him."

"Absolutely. Done him to death."

"Do we all agree with that?"

(Agreeing murmurs.)

"Hmm. I think you've got a point, but before we go down that road, let's explore a bit, dig a little deeper. Ask one final question."

"What's that [boss]?"

"Who hasn't he shagged yet?"

A perplexing mumbling went around the table, a bit like the beginning of Twenty Questions. Everyone seemed to be sharing the same thought: this bucking Italian Stallion had already bedded most, if not all, of the eligible females in the entire fictional neighbourhood, who else was there for him to fornicate with? This was one of our quarterly script meetings, during which heads would be scratched, brains racked, and pencil nibs blunted and doodled on official BBC notepads. Not to mention the cups of coffee and bottles of Perrier that would be consumed in sufficient enough quantities to lubricate the two-hour long session aimed at jazzing up (or, in this case, sexing up) each character's storylines. I had a tendency to drift off, my thoughts wandering out through the window, following the clouds in the clear sky. To be honest, it wasn't just these meetings. Meetings in general bring out the flakeys in me. I don't seem to have the mental stamina for prolonged seated concentration. At least at home there was always the opportunity to abandon hard thinking in favour of useful diversionary activities like descaling the kettle, baking a banana loaf, or re-grouting a few bathroom tiles before returning, freshly charged, to the task in hand.

"How about Lorna?" (not her actual fictional name).

My thoughts fluttered back into the little meeting room crammed with an unfeasibly large conference table, a refreshments trolley and an excess of unoccupied padded chairs. *Lorna!?* Of all the characters they could possibly choose to hitch together, Lorna and the Italian Stallion would be the absolute last for one very persuasive reason – they had absolutely *nothing* in common. Not a spark, not a glint of anything that could remotely pass for attraction between two people. Not even mutual hatred. It would be like speed-dating George Clooney and Camilla Parker-Bowles (no disrespect to you, my heart-throb, Clooney). The two might share roughly the same age (give or take a decade or two), but park them on a sofa beneath romantically dimmed studio lights and what could they possibly sweet-nothing about? Oh, well... someone else's problem. I began returning my gaze to those rather interesting candyfloss clouds, when I sensed a stillness in the room.

"Lisselle?"

It took a good few seconds to register that my name was being called. I jerked my attention away from the window, back into the room. All eyes were upon me. What I'd failed to pick up on during my daydreaming was that the episode under discussion was none other than mine, and now my opinion was awaited. I quickly gathered myself. There really were only two options: go along with the desperate ratings-seeking suggestion or argue my case. I hastily rehearsed a response in my mind that would bridge both respect for my own artistic integrity and regard for the rather generous hand that was feeding me:

"OK, fine, if that's the plan, I guess it could work over a period of

time – if we gave the audience a few weeks, at the very least, to overcome any resistance to such a bloody unlikely idea, but a DAY! Are you kidding me?"

Yes, a day. That's the miracle I was being asked to perform, when in the preceding episodes written by other members of the team, not one writer had included a hint, not a smidgen of chemistry between the would-be lovers in question. No matter. Lisselle would easily knock up a steamy 30-minuter cliffing on the couple locked in a nauseatingly feverish soap snog. The idea was ludicrous. But did my opinion count? Not really. When you're feeding a voracious, long-running, award-winning, prime time monster, voices are sometimes heard but, unfortunately, not that of the writer. This was certainly a far cry from the days when I began as a rookie on the series; when I likened the collaborative experience to being part of a cosy cottage industry.

Those halcyon days. Yesteryears when I actually looked forward to the hour-long trip to the studio office, heading out to meet a bunch of droll, chain-smoking characters a hundred times more complex and fascinating than the fictional ones presented onscreen. We varied from the posh, middle-aged, former housewife whose assured style of writing dated back to the inception of the series; to the lank-haired trendster plucked from a recent fringe theatre success, for whom this was his first pants-wetting episode. Back then, the execs were mostly women from a literary background. They wore trusting, intelligent faces and, so long as we didn't detract massively from the overall signature of the series, they pretty much left us writers to lovingly craft, over a generous period of time, our own unique product. My father, when he was alive, used to say that within five minutes of watching an episode he could tell whether or not it was mine, such was the scope for the writer's personal stamp. This artistic freedom gave us a certain conceit that our suggestions and our every whim really mattered to the powers-that-be orchestrating from above. In this very fortunate position of being rewarded handsomely for engaging in enjoyable work that allowed individual expression, we could be forgiven for thinking that we were a select group. Alas, I wasn't to know that this was a rather extended honeymoon period and that the beast would eventually morph into something totally unrecognisable. The twice-weekly episodes had already crept up to four with more being threatened, and with each successive exec producer bringing in their own set of stringent rules whilst bestowing increasing story control on non-writer producers, the pips were rapidly being squeezed out of the creative process. The writing was on the wall, so to speak. As I grudgingly accepted my assignment, meekly bowing to the 'suggestions' of my betters eyeing me from the head of an ironically round table, I began to understand the true meaning of the word 'hack'. Worse, I could see my future stretching before me – desperately unhappy, chained to an overheated fax machine spewing out endless redraft notes, round-the-clock surveillance by an hysterically oppressed script editor, incessant phone 'meetings' and email bombardments, all underpinned with the tacit expectation that the writer would be available morning, noon and night. Once, after having sent off a 'final' draft following an intense and exhausting few months, I booked a well-deserved week's holiday in the sun. When I casually informed the junior script editor of my intentions her immediate response was loaded: should there be further 'tweaks' required, my entire script would be handed to another, hungrier, writer. I cancelled the holiday; there were no further revisions to the script; and a few days later it was on to the next gruelling commission. Of course, there was always the possibility that this bleak, fear-based climate wouldn't last. The execs might miraculously arrive at their senses and recognise that they were destroying the very X-factor, the writer's authentic voice, that had been the bedrock of a series so loved by the nation for so long.

But I'd had enough. I'd been stifled for too long by the

requirements of the monster, and despondency was beginning to show in my writing. After ten long years, my soul hungered for liberation and true expression. It was time to venture out into the big, scary world, to walk the plank minus the comforting safety net of a steady income to break my fall. From a core contributor on a national show, I was about to become a freelancer out in the cold, tasked with convincing programme makers that I was a worthy, independent talent. Only problem was, this was the dawn of the 2000s and the world had changed. The industry was riven by fears about dwindling audiences. Its vision, due to a market fragmented by new technology, was shrinking rather than expanding. There were fewer and fewer opportunities for a cloud-chasing writer like me.

Despite the climate of foreboding, alongside my agent finding me the occasional stint writing on other programmes, I'd already started the ball of my optimistic future rolling. I was about to become a published novelist! My fresh sights had begun with the first tentative draft of an unsolicited screenplay that I'd shown to a producer friend of mine. Barbara was so impressed with the style of my stage directions she suggested that the story might lend itself to becoming a novel. I pounced on the idea. I had been here before, remember? I felt reassured, recalling the director who, years before, had visited my Finsbury Park home to praise my work, soon after which my success as a writer dramatically took off. Before long, my novel was writing itself, and I had great hopes of becoming an overnight literary discovery. Little was I to know that, despite past experience of writing in almost every medium – journalism, theatre, corporate, radio, soaps, children's TV, drama, sitcom, children's books – what lay ahead would be a hellish five-year struggle of defeat, and the steepest learning curve I'd ever embarked upon in my entire life. But at that stage I was determined. In-between the latest redrafting of my novel, I not only increased my speculative writing output, I outlined an ambitious personal success plan, jauntily predicting that at the end of three years I would be enjoying:

- No mortgage
- £200k savings
- Successful production/publication of:
  - 2 drama series
  - 1 feature film
  - 1 sitcom series
  - 1 children's book
- Novel published – a home and international triumph
- First steps towards setting up my motivational charity* – *Space-for-Grace*

Five years later, this was my actual progress:

- House remortgaged.
- Not quite bankrupt, but I've become an ARPPy – Asset Rich, Penny Poor.
- Original 6-part TV Drama series treatment commissioned. Producer raves about it, but fails to find a network interested in the idea. Fed up with the state of the industry, he naffs off to the East where the sun is orange and the future is bright, leaving my hopes in tatters.
- Treatment and one episode of a 6-part TV Comedy commissioned by a production company, but fails to find a broadcasting deal.
- Engaged by another producer to write a Film Script Adaptation based on a book he's successfully optioned. Author and her agent approve treatment, but until funds materialise there is no guarantee of anything.
- Treatment of Original Romantic Comedy Screenplay written and despatched to US production company, but so far no feedback. The only rave reviews have come from family and friends.

- Weekly column idea (and 8 samplers) intended for and rejected by *Guardian Magazine*; and no wonder – about every other newspaper in the land is now increasingly in favour of the 'celeb columnist'.
- 30,000 word children's novel written. About to embark on agent/publisher rounds. It's a great story and I'm full of hope, but I've been here before.
- Having set up an altruistic website, *MyBodyBuddies.com* (my small stab at putting something back into the community), I overlook the tedious fact that one essentially needs to drive traffic to the site. Lacking the necessary SEO technical competence and having neither the time nor motivation required to develop such an aptitude, I abandon the site. (Years later, *Embarrassing Bodies* website, based on the popular Channel 4 TV series, is a runaway success. The website is a sophisticated version of MyBodyBuddies.com.)

(*Never mind a charity for those in need, a little grace to cope with my own rapid disillusionment wouldn't have gone amiss!)

Clearly, something wasn't working. My recurring dream in which I would wake up choking and in a state of panic indicated as much. Bolting out of my sleep, I'd find my fist in my mouth, struggling to pull out the dirty rag 'blocking' my throat... only to realise that I was emerging from a nightmare. During the day, I was raiding the self-help shelves of numerous bookshops, reading my way through solution-sounding titles such as: *The Money Bible, The Cosmic Ordering Service, The Power of Now*. I was attending talks and workshops I could ill afford. Anything to keep the whiff of failure at bay, shore up my sagging spirits, and not lose sight of the belief that I was in control of my own destiny. The universe would respond to my needs. *Ask, and it is Given*, Esther and Jerry Hicks reassured me in the title of their then latest book. But the only thing I was being given, it seemed, was enough thick rope with which to hang myself. Soon, it became depressing and embarrassing responding to enquiries from friends. What was I up to these days? What interesting and well-paid project was I working on? My agent wasn't calling, and neither was the universe. I'd begin each morning with a heaviness like wet clay weighted in the pit of my stomach. If it wasn't for junk emails and Internet surfing providing the illusion that I was connected to the outside world, and a virtual sense that I belonged somewhere, I may well have given up and joined the checkout girls at my local Sainsbury's. Praise be for my children's adoring acceptance that Mummy was a writer, and Richard's unstinting support and belief in my work. Though at times it was barely detectable, I still, tenuously, held the conviction that as a writer I had something to say. I thought back to earlier times when life had seemed so easy, achievements so effortless, when the fruits of my labours appeared to ripen on every passing tree, falling abundantly and miraculously at my feet. Where had the magic gone? Were there lessons I needed to learn from the past in order to bring it back?

I started examining the patterns laid down in my life. What latent beliefs might be holding back my progress? I searched deep inside myself and came up with my strongest habitual emotions – fear of exposure; a deep sense of vulnerability. Perhaps it was no accident that I was attracted to working in television, despite always having shunned the limelight, the bright glare of publicity. If we are here to learn by confronting and overcoming our greatest fears, television was the perfect environment for me to expose this particular weakness of mine. One of the first actions I took the moment I convinced myself that I had earned the title of 'writer' was typical knee-jerk avoidance of my fears. I changed my name. At the very outset I projected that success would involve working and collaborating with many different people – legions of readers, script editors, researchers, directors, producers, actors, etc. It would neither be possible nor desirable to establish firm friends wherever I went, particularly in an industry known for chewing up and spitting out talent and fostering competition, politicking and backbiting. I saw myself as preparing to enter the lion's den, for which I would need armour, protection. A pseudonym would ensure that my real name was detached from a culture of insincerity and superficiality. But no matter how I dressed it up, this need for distance and invisibility was more profound and went further than I dared myself to imagine. It masked a deep-rooted insecurity, perhaps going back to my first school trip to the wilds of rural Surrey.

For most of our class, this was a first experience of being away from home and family. Sayers Croft, a residential educational centre, was where we would be staying for one week, sharing one of a cluster of single-sex wooden dormitories. The first day of the trip had turned out to be reasonably uneventful. But by Tuesday morning everything had changed. After being woken by our teachers, we jumped out of bed, routinely searching in lockers for our wash bags before trooping off to the communal showers in the neighbouring block. That's when the big brown cardboard box arrived. Our class teacher paraded it down the long corridor followed by a flurry of girls in pyjamas dying to know who it was for, what was inside. Miss Cartwright's exuberant march stopped at my bunk where she plonked the box down in front of me. I immediately froze. I have no idea why I so feared the attention, but I had especially not told anyone. Now I was forced to open the box in front of everyone with the contents revealing that I had just turned eleven. Among some other 'treat' items, my father had included a birthday card. On the front there was an embossed disc of transparent grooves so that when you placed it on a stereo it would play a scratchy *Happy Birthday*. After the oblig-

atory opening and emptying of the box, I became mystify-
ingly ostracised by my class. At least, that's how it seemed to
me. For a relatively relaxed few hours I had tentatively
belonged to the group, and now I watched them gather into a
huddle, whispering and darting glances back in my direction
whilst they plotted some minor act of humiliation or violence
against me. I had seen too many random outbreaks of arguing
and fighting to not know what this group was capable of. I
would have to keep my wits about me until the 'heat' of my
birthday had passed into just another day. For my own
protection, during field lessons I made a point of sticking
close to the teachers; and whenever I happened to be alone
and saw any of the girls approaching I would duck and hide.
I spent the longest day behaving like a fugitive, isolated and
in fear of a sudden 'attack'. When night finally came, my
trepidation grew steadily as I hurried into my PJs and
climbed on to the top bunk. During these final moments there
was still the possibility that the girls could make a final strike.
I dived beneath the blanket, only daring to breathe when Miss
Cartwright switched off the dorm lights. Absolutely no one
was allowed out of their beds after lights-out. I'd made it! I
was finally safe from any targeted troublemaking. My sincere
hope was that morning would bring some other distraction
and I would no longer be a marked person; I'd be allowed to
be part of the group again.

My eyes were blinded by a sudden bright flare. The lights
had come on! My entire dorm of classmates were sitting up in
bed. Five teachers stood in the doorway. All exploded into a
loud rendition of: "Happy Birthday, Dear Carmen!" My heart
rolled with fear and a mix of other fierce emotions. I might as
well have been peppered with mortar shells, such was my
mortification. Having already been wounded from having
apparently been excluded the entire day by my classmates, to
now discover the betrayal of my teachers who had been in on

the act of plotting this daylong ordeal the whole time! At the end of the singing a wrapped gift (a book and colouring pencils) was placed on my bed, and my heart reared up with fresh torment. The ensuing silence signalled that both class-mates and teachers were waiting for me to say something, do something, **be** something. I could barely acknowledge the present, let alone muster the wit and grace to entertain an audience. The teachers rescued me with a brisk lights-out and the scene fizzled into a disappointing nothingness. But the memory remained as a physical echo well into my adulthood.

It made sense that Lisselle Kayla became a wall behind which to hide. If fame indeed came knocking as a result of my writing, it would bypass knocking at the door of the real me, Carmen Harris. One day the knock came. I was asked to appear on TV – the popular Channel 4 youth programme *The Word* – to be inter-viewed by Terry Christian about my sitcom, *Us Girls*. My agent was delighted, but I couldn't imagine anything more horrific than having to perform in an energetically phoney way (the artifice of the programme demanded this) whilst being the focus of so many people's attention. I instantly turned the offer down. Public speaking is the number one fear for most people, even greater than the fear of death. If we examine this fear in ourselves, it usually stems from an unresolved childhood event. For me, the ghostly echo of the dorm immediately flooded back in the shape of a vague unknown terror. A few weeks later, however, I did accept another invitation, this time to guest on Radio 4's *Woman's Hour* with Jenni Murray. No, I hadn't miraculously overcome my fear of exposure. There were two reasons for going against my own better judgement. One: my then boss, John Nicholson, was so excited for me, as it was he who had indirectly arranged the engagement through an associate of his, a producer who worked on the show. As I had no plausible excuse to pass up promoting myself and my sitcom, it would have appeared ungrateful or cowardly to do so. Two: I reckoned that being on the radio was a safer option to television, as I'd be invisible to public scrutiny. The morning the BBC car arrived to pick me up, I came very close to cancelling. For days leading up to the interview I'd been regretting my decision and desperately seeking a way out of the obligation. What happened next was a perfect example of how our thoughts absolutely control our physiology and, ultimately, the world we live in. I obsessed and fantasised about sabotaging the interview, till the universe eventually delivered my get-out. A strain of influenza was going around; it was vicious enough to be reported on the national news. Many of my friends and relatives escaped the bug, but I conveniently caught – or, rather, manifested – it big time. Feverish and wracked all over, no amount of painkillers would lessen the chronic discomfort deep in my bones and muscle tissue, nor the aching eyes, the sore throat and the incessant thumping inside my head. The first few days were so bad the only relief I could find was to lie naked on the hard, cold floorboards. It would have been a totally acceptable excuse to cancel but, of course, I knew I couldn't let everyone down at the last minute. I crawled into the sleek black courtesy car in a hot daze, far too out of it to appreciate the privilege and luxury of being treated like a minor celebrity. Too soon I found myself in the middle of the interview, unprepared and ill-equipped to respond to even the most basic of questions. I was brain-numbed by the virus, struggling through a thick fog of pain and incomprehension. At one point I corpsed at the most trivial of enquiries (what's your name, possibly?) for Jenni, the consummate professional, to smoothly come to my aid. I left the studios in abject misery, embarrassed by my performance and feeling a total failure. A psychologist friend who listened to the programme said she hadn't noticed anything untoward. Perhaps she was being kind. Whatever, the overall experience was further confirmation that I was not cut out to be any kind of public figure. The idea of reinventing myself as a successful but 'invisible' novelist was becoming all the more seductive. I was staking everything on my debut novel *Soon Come Home* (two women – one white middle class, one black working class, meet in a mental hospital and embark on a spiritual journey that takes them to the island of Jamaica where they discover their true identity) becoming my defining accomplishment and rescuing my career from terminal decline. I simply had to succeed!

At some stage during the writing, I made the fundamental decision that it would be too easy to churn out just any novel. I'd already had four children's books published, and whilst recognising this as an achievement, they had been to no great acclaim. I wanted my novel to be the beginning of something new and significant in my life. For a start, it would be my first adult work to be represented by my actual name and, for another, through various self-development tools and techniques (more of these later), I had worked on my fears of exposure and was now ready to accept wide recognition for the success that was on its way. My aim was to reach the heights of some of the best writers out there, a tough challenge, but one that I felt was within my capabilities. After nine dedicated, hard-working months, I hugged my completed 58,000-word manuscript with stunned pride. I'd done it. I'd written my first proper novel. The next day, on the number 10 bus heading towards Oxford Circus for a celebratory shopping spree, my mobile rang. It was a friend, someone I'd previously met at a BBC function who happens to be a best-selling, international writer. Synchronicity in action, yet again. She already knew about my work-in-progress novel, and I was breathless with excitement telling her that I had finally finished it. Her response wasn't what I expected. Instead of congratulating me for my wonderful accomplishment, making the transition from TV script-writer to novel-writer, she quoted the depressing number of hopeful novels written in a single year against the percentage that would reach actual publication. I was stung by her negativity, her lack of encouragement, but rather than allowing myself to be knocked back, those hurt feelings had the opposite effect of spurring me on. I would prove to her and to everyone that I *would* get published! The next step would be to find a literary agent.

I visited two friends of mine, husband and wife, both successful novelists, and left them with a copy of my work. After reading it, they were so impressed they recommended me to the agent who represented them both. A couple of weeks later, this top agent had finished reading my novel and asked to meet me. My friends said this was a very good sign indeed. Their agent (let's call her Sue), who represented a very high profile writer of the time, was very particular, they told me, and certainly wouldn't waste her time on a face-to-face if she wasn't seriously interested. We met in the café of a little hotel near Bayswater. It was a pleasant getting-to-know-one-another rendezvous and we were both at ease and obviously liked one another. Sue told me how much she admired my writing, so I was more than surprised when she casually added that my novel possibly wouldn't be my first published book. I allowed a few moments for both the shock and the feeling of deflation to pass, before I set about convincing her that I was prepared to do whatever it took to become not just a published novelist, but a best-seller. Perhaps this was a little test of hers, as three months later, after I'd just finished incorporating her re-write notes, the phone rang. The voice at the end of the receiver was Sue's. She asked if I'd be able to write a little biog and a few lines of blurb about the novel... as she was intending to take it to the Frankfurt Book Fair! I whooped, fell to my knees, and kissed the carpet! My friend's (the male of the couple) first novel had been taken to Frankfurt by this agent. En route, it had been snapped up in a frenzied bidding auction *mid-flight!* Success! Success at last! I whizzed off the few pages to accompany the redraft, stuffed the lot in a big brown envelope, sent it off Recorded Delivery, and told everyone about my amazing good fortune. I then waited for feedback on the reworked novel and waited... and waited...

The day before Sue was due to head out to Frankfurt, I received another call. I trembled at her foreboding tone. She didn't mince her words. The redraft hadn't met her expectations and she wouldn't be taking it to Frankfurt. Indeed, she wouldn't, after all, be acting as my agent. I sank to my knees and as soon as my would-be-agent rang off, I blubbed like a baby. My critical inner voice made its appearance, that nagging, negative presence that lurks in all our subconscious: *Who do you think you are? Did you really imagine you could do this? Did you really think it would be that simple? International best-seller, indeed!* I crawled into a hole and couldn't bear to look at my manuscript for another six months, during which time I barely scratched a living from my other TV work. Though I shared a loving home with Richard and our two children (my first-born was away studying), this was a lonely, frightening interlude in my life, marked with all kinds of social, emotional and financial anxieties. It seemed that I had gone back in time. Though I'd swopped the housing association flat for our large red-brick Victorian terrace it seemed that we were no better off financially. On the face of it, I was living a very comfortable life, but the real fact was that in those recessionary times, I had joined the legions of Year 2000 Asset Rich, Penny Poor house owners. If writing wasn't my destiny, what was I to do with my future? I had some vague notion that I would like to be helping others, but no real constructive ideas. And where would the money come from to fund such altruism? I had limited savings (the bulk of it had already gone into restoring our derelict multiple bedsit property into a decent family home). Writing was the only activity I knew how to simultaneously enjoy and make money from. After stewing in the situation, I chided myself and came out of hiding.

When I was finally brave enough to re-examine my work, I saw how glaringly substandard it actually was. Though I exaggerate to make a point, and though I recognise that my novel was incomparably ahead of my novella all those years before, my writing still exhibited shades of the same overwritten exuberance. My critical voice surfaced once more to warn me against any misguided notions I might be harbouring about attempting another draft. I scoffingly reminded that cautionary voice that tens of people (admittedly, mainly friends) had admired my writing; that an established agent representing several No. 1 authors had *told* me, in person, that I was a talented writer; indeed, had very nearly accepted me on to her books. There *had* to be something in all of that. So, despite my subconscious grumblings, I set about immersing myself in yet another round of redrafting, learning from previous mistakes, and embracing that maxim from my NML days: *Writing is re-writing!* When the next draft was ready, I sent out a mailshot of three chapters and a covering letter to 25 top literary agents, pointedly ignoring a friend's suggestion that I might consider self-publishing. In my mind, self-publishing was an open admission of failure that went contrary to my big ambitions. It took about four months for the first of those agents to get back to me:

There is a great deal in this novel which is wonderful. The author writes with terrific immediacy… The best parts are the relationships between Jane and Martha, improbable and unpromising as it seems, and between Jane and Greg… the racial elements of the story are handled to perfection, being faced square on and treated like any other circumstance of the story… the first person narrative for Jane, and third for Greg and Martha work perfectly well; her visual sense and sense of place are vivid; her dialogue is good; her sensitivity is finely tuned; I'm really impressed with the microscopic and unsparing detail she gives us, and by how genuinely well she writes.

I held my breath during our subsequent telephone exchange and quietly rejoiced when she requested my entire novel. This time I would exercise caution and delay any temptation to announce or celebrate with friends and family. It was just as well. After submitting the full manuscript, several weeks later, the agent's initial interest ended in a lengthy letter with a rejection tagged at the end of it:

> *We are sorry we cannot take this story on the way that it is, but remember that this is a hugely subjective industry and this is one personal opinion... We would gladly consider anything else you are working on.*

Again, rather than crumple beneath the told-you-so's of my ever-present, ever-critical inner voice, I allowed myself a few months' cooling-off before I returned anew to the manuscript. Rereading it, I could see, once more, that this agent was also right. My novel wasn't ready. I still had a lot to learn. I explained to my unimpressed inner voice that these defeats were all part of the universe's larger plan, showing me that though I was not yet there – I would eventually crack this. I pointed out that despite all the rejections and disappointments there had always been enough encouraging voices to urge me on. The scales had also fallen from my eyes. When I'd begun writing my novel, I really had no idea of the extent of the challenges ahead (if I had, it's probable I might never have started). My naivety may have served me when I was writing my television sitcom, but this was an entirely different ball game. There was none of the psychological backup of an entire TV production team; each morning it was just me, my imagination, and the next blank sheet of paper. I'd been flogging myself to death in a 50-metre race, when all the while I was in the 100-metres. The question was, did I have the stamina to go the full mile? It was time to considerably up my game.

I harked back to my single days when having the time and space to read was a taken-for-granted joy and began to read voraciously – a luxury I'd not been permitted since having my two younger children. I selected my reading list carefully – no steamy potboilers, no throwaway chick-lit, only authors whose work had achieved literary status and whose success I would strive to emulate. Often, in order to get through an entire novel, I would resort to using the only time and strategy I had available to me – dawn reading and 'bog reading'. My children would stand outside, banging on the bathroom door, either demanding my attention or anxious that Mummy might have passed out on the toilet seat. I also enrolled for two terms at the City Lit as well as joining various writers' groups and local book clubs. I even attended the 2004 Orange Prize for Fiction ceremony and fanta-sised that instead of the black novelist, Andrea Levy,[12] stepping up to collect first prize for her debut novel *Small Island*, it was me, Carmen Harris, being feted for *Soon Come Home*. I learned an enormous amount during that time. By redraft No 6 my original 58,000 words had increased to 66,000, and the novel had gained greater levels of complexity and assuredness. It was time for the universe to reward my spirits with another little boost of magic. It came with a friend of mine being interviewed for a magazine about a business venture she was setting up. Synchronistically, the freelancing journalist conducting the interview just *happened* to be supplementing her poorly paid full-time job... as a literary reader in one of the largest UK publishing houses. My friend kindly mentioned my book. Danielle the reader/journalist responded saying that it sounded interesting and that I should send her a couple of chapters. I duly despatched the first three chapters and received a reply within days. Not only did Danielle love my work and want to see more, she had shown my manuscript to one of her editors who glowingly referred to my chapters thus:

> ... *a very good premise... and she writes with exceptional clarity of tone.*

But I was in a tricky situation. Though I had a TV agent, I needed a literary agent. At the same time, there was the very real possibility that this publisher might read my entire novel and reject it. If this happened, being turned down by a major publisher, I would be handicapping my search for literary representation. My novel, effectively, ran the risk of becoming soiled goods, dead in the water. I told Danielle about my reservations and that my priority was to first engage an agent. She understood and maintained her interest by sending regular emails to check on my progress. My connection with this reader turned out to be greatly to my advantage. Quite a few of the agents, once they realised that a big publisher had expressed an interest, rushed to the fore with immediate offers of representation, often without even requesting sight of my work. I ignored those. I wanted someone who was interested in *me* the novelist, and my long-term writing aims, not just in making a fast and easy buck. In the end I went for an agent who had obviously taken the trouble to read my work and had suggested intelligent and thoughtful improvements. Equally, I impressed her with my willingness to take on board many of her suggestions.

> I'm on the bus with the children, returning home after a trip to the local swimming pool. My mobile rings. I search for it in my bag among wet towels and leaky bottles of shampoo and conditioner. It's my would-be agent, sounding quite breathy. She's back from a holiday abroad, having taken my manuscript with her. She's read it and is now about to give her verdict. I hold my breath. Her pronouncement is: *"It's powerful. It's disturbing. It's life affirming. I'd like to represent it."* I am numb on the outside, trembling on the inside with fear and excitement.

After some more judicious editing (less is more! less is more!), I handed the finally completed novel over to my newly-appointed agent and she promptly sent it off to the publishing house reader on my behalf. After finally getting her hands on it, Danielle responded that same weekend. My novel did not disappoint. She'd devoured the entire manuscript in one sitting, and would definitely be recommending it to her publisher. She warned, however, that the company was not likely to publish unless the work received consensus from all four editors in the department. Several tortuous weeks of waiting later, she finally got back. The verdict was devastating. Only the literary editor loved the book as much as Danielle, but neither was able to convince the other three editors. We were back to square one. I thought broodingly of all those novels I'd recently read. I couldn't see that my book was any worse than some of those dubiously hailed as literary successes. In fact, in a few instances I'd rated my own work higher. What more did I have to *do* to get published? Did my book deserve to be rejected like this? Was I deluding myself? Was my writing *that* bad? *Yes! Yes! Yes!* cried my critical voice. And the universe now also seemed to be agreeing, because my agent confidently sent out my manuscript to twelve other major publishers... and received resounding rejections from every single one. She advised me not to become disheartened and to read the rejection letters because they contained many flattering comments about my writing. Taking little comfort from her words, I crawled into bed, hounded by a critical voice that was increasingly taking on my late father's cautioning tone: *There, there. Now you know you're not up to this, you can stop trying. Stop raising your head above the parapet. You'll only end up in a far worse place. Better to stay safe. Stick with what you know and you won't get hurt.* Eventually, fed up with hearing this negative voice doing me down, I contemplated my agent's advice, emerged from underneath the duvet, and dug out the rejection letters:

"I can see why you are excited about this one. There is lots to like about it, not least Harris' ability to get inside the heads of her

characters. And I admire the way she explores domestic truths in her story."

"The story is a gripping and relevant one, and I can certainly see that Carmen's years of writing for TV and radio have developed her skills for narrative and plot."

"This is an extremely interesting novel. I was fascinated to see the combination of a scriptwriting voice within the framework of a novel and thought she did it very well. Jane is completely believable and very real to the reader."

"I thought it was a stunning novel, very dark, powerful and incredibly moving. I think Carmen writes with great skill and helps the reader visualise and externalise the process through her filmic snapshots – it's brilliantly done and enables the reader to empathise more easily with a character whose very mental instability makes her difficult to comprehend."

"I hope you find a good home for this promising novel."

Yet still they had rejected my work! For all sorts of reasons ranging from *"unable to visualise the market clearly enough"* (i.e. which marketing box to post the novel in – which, actually, I took to be a compliment); to failing to convince the entire editorial team; to not sympathising enough with one or other of the main characters; to the writing being *"slightly more on the commercial side of things for my tastes"*; to the annoyingly vague *"not what I'm looking to acquire at the moment"*. But what caught my attention was that several of the publishers, though complimentary on the whole about my writing, had cryptically suggested that there was something flawed in the structure of the story. What could that be? I had no idea. I was so close to the narrative, it was now impossible to see it from a fresh perspective. My head hurt just thinking about it.

That night something prodded me awake. I opened my eyes and the problem miraculously presented itself to me. I knew it exactly! What's more, in my heart of hearts, I'd always known it. There was a very good reason I'd been running away from the truth: facing it would require a significant overhauling of my work. But the cloud had lifted and, despite the bruising I'd already received, I rolled up my sleeves and set to work. It was painful, but the words gradually came, my pace picked up and the story improved. I re-edited ruthlessly to cut out all traces of overwriting. Importantly, I also concluded why my book had been continually tested and thwarted in such a challenging way. It was because of the *intention* I had set for myself. I had been determined not to be a mere writer (I'd already achieved that), I wanted to be the Best that I could be, producing an important, meaningful book that embedded all of my beliefs about the inner and outer, visible and invisible worlds we inhabit. This mattered to me more than the risk of my work defying classification and marketability. In order to satisfy my *intention,* the universe had, of course, been obeying my command and rejecting each draft that wasn't up to my own high bar. Yet, its rejections had never been completely out of hand. Friends, readers, agents and publishers, all appeared at the right time to inject sufficient doses of advice and encouragement and to show me that, though I wasn't there yet, the effort of continuing was worthwhile. Even my international writer friend, with her gloomy prophesying that I was writing "against the odds", was part of this onward push. I'm getting there. I know I'm getting there... I kept telling myself.

My agent delivered the final killer blow. After being so supportive, so optimistic through all the many rejections she, sadly, had lost faith in pushing my work. Though not in me, she hastened to add, or even the novel itself which, she reassured me, she still regarded highly. She ended the call by requesting first look at my next book. By now, an incredible five years had passed since I had begun my best-seller odyssey. During that intense, blinkered time, everything around me seemed to have crumbled to dust. Alone in my bedroom, I totted up the loss – my TV writing career, my income, my status as a writer, my dreams of becoming a successful novelist, my belief in myself. There was clearly no more hope; certainly no more energy left to fight. There was nothing else I could do. I caved in to the immense disappointment, the sheer exhausting weight of optimism and bounce-back that I'd been holding up and on to for so long. I had done everything within my power to become the person I longed to be. I had followed all the rules, I had worked hard, I had kept the faith, and yet... the universe had totally and utterly forsaken me.

Tears of frustration and self-pity turned to bitter cries of anger and rage, an explosion of fury and darkness. What was the point in trusting that anything or anyone was looking out for me? What was the use in believing in God, or the Universe, or Grace, or Spirit, when playing by the rules could get you nowhere, amount to nothing at all? Why couldn't I have stayed, like many of my peers, and continued to work on the soap? Why did I have to want more than I already had? Who did I think I was, believing that it could be so easy? That anything I had to say could make a difference, to the world or even to myself? Why did I have to always be so dissatisfied? *Now*, look at me! I had lost everything! I had not only disappointed myself, I had let down everyone around me! I was nothing but a failure! A loser! I looked upwards to the heavens above the ceiling and screamed in the silence of my room: *"What the fuck do you want me to do with my life?"*

This was my dark night of the soul. We all have at least one in our lifetime. It was the moment I stopped, and the world seemed to stop, too. I stopped running, seeking, chasing after the illusion of the perfect image of who I was 'supposed' to be. It was my moment of utter surrender; the moment I ceased resisting the momentum of my life, giving up the need to control and reject all that failed to meet my limited ideas of success. It was the moment the universe heard and responded to the absolute Truth in my cry for help. It was the moment, in knowing there were no other choices open to me, that I accepted the situation, in the purest sense, for what it was. In so doing I opened the door on the magic that was waiting there all along. The magic that, if I *allowed* it, would usher in *real* change; a revelation of my life purpose, my ultimate path of least resistance.

I was having tea in the garden with S, a good friend of mine. She started complaining about being overweight, about her failure to curb what she saw as a compulsive eating habit. When I argued that she was far from overweight, she referred to the past when she had been so good at focusing on what it was she wanted in life, particularly during the years when she was studying. I watched S wolfing down a chorizo omelette followed by strawberries and cream and suggested that we leave the garden and do a little healing process. We settled in the front room where I asked S to focus on the feelings that came up around her weight issues, and to tell me what they were. She immediately used the words "lazy"; "lacking discipline". Being acquainted with S's background I knew that the area that most needed healing in her life was her relationship with her father. I asked her to hear her father using those same words as an attack against her: *"You're lazy! You have no discipline!"* Instantly, S clutched at her chest, feeling a palpable discomfort in the heart area. I asked her to now refocus on how she would like to see herself in the future – slim, relaxed, content, etc. After S described this image, I then instructed her to put all her thoughts aside. Whilst I worked on the energy field around her heart and solar plexus, I told her to "Just notice what you notice." Using the chakras in the palms of both my hands I scanned her aura (the egg-shaped area around the physical body) for 'interference'. I felt an uncomfortable sensation of heat, static, density, and made movements to clear the area till it felt light and slightly vibrating. This is what S later enthusiastically wrote on her Facebook status:

Carmen, only one week since the amazing healing you gave me and the results have already appeared!!!!! You won't believe how much weight I've lost in one week!!! Love u. Xxxxx... Carmen gave me healing last Saturday for my neurotic hunger and to lose weight as I felt unhappy with myself. I felt very 'strange' after-wards. It's incredible, only one week and I've lost two kilos and I'm not hungry any more as before. She is amazing! She really is a gift of God!! Carmen Harris is one of the best energy healers on earth! Wow!!!

My analysis: As children, unable to counter or defend ourselves from the beliefs of authority figures, we absorb and accept these beliefs as our own. The father's criticism of S became her own self-criticism and self-talk. Each time the accusation: "You are lazy! You have no discipline!" entered S's thoughts, consciously or unconsciously, it vibrated as a painful echo (*cellular memory*) in every cell in her body, manifesting physically as congestion or 'interference' in the heart area. As human beings, we are motivated by two basic instincts: to avoid pain; to seek pleasure. To avoid this feeling of pain in her heart, S had learned to seek the pleasure in food. The compulsive eating served to stuff down the critical voice; and the speed at which S ate was to squash down another bad feeling – the guilt of eating! Nothing is more powerful than those messages from our subconscious. We can tell ourselves all we like that we desire to lose weight, but if the agenda of our subconscious is: *eat to numb the pain* – we stand no chance. It's no wonder diets don't work! S felt 'strange' after the healing – a result of that particular message in her physical being now neutralised. Though it was still a 'mind memory', it was no longer a *cellular memory*, a trigger for bad feelings. Once we heal those subconscious messages that do not serve us, in the freedom that ensues we begin to take control of our life.

[Several months on, S and I met up again and began chatting about this and that. S mentioned how weirdly improved her relationship with her father had become, how she felt much more relaxed in his company than she'd ever been in her entire life. I asked whether anything in particular had brought this about, but she said there was nothing she could point to. In fact, the occasion she was talking about was the first she'd seen or spoken to her father in the longest while. I reminded S of our little session in the garden. She was astounded. There couldn't be any other explanation, she said.]

Miracles love to occur when we arrive at a state of allowing 'what is', often marked by the feeling that we have reached the end of everything. Somehow, when it seems that we have nothing more to lose, when we relieve ourselves of those preconceptions of what is 'right' and 'not right', of how and what our outcomes 'should be', we return to the innocence and wonder of our childlike selves, and life takes a different turn. In this space of *allowing*, something undefined can be born – something our limited minds could never have conceived. As children we are forever trusting of the next moment of each new day, even when we are powerless to know what that moment will bring. As adults, we fear the void. Yet it is here where we find growth, through relearning childhood openness and trust. In the void it is possible to confront the software of our subconscious that contains all the programmes of all the fearful beliefs and negative restrictions that have been installed over time via parents, authority figures, direct life experiences, and even our own peers. Among my own programmes I had learned caution from my father; betrayal from my teachers; unworthiness from my peers. For many years, through the voice of my subconscious, I had been running these codes without even realising.

Contrary to its often negative outcomes, however, the intention of our subconscious – by reminding us of earlier trauma and pain – is to keep us safe. These obsolete programmes once played a part in protecting us when our available strategies were limited by immaturity, lack of experience, or the inability to communicate, but today those programmes are the reason why we remain in the cramped little boxes of our past. In this tight space, we fear taking risks, we don't dare live, we hold back from fully embracing the colour, the magic and potential of our existence. So, why don't we simply challenge that dampening, hampering inner voice? Because our subconscious uses the powerful force of judgement: judgement of ourselves, judgment of others, fear of being judged. *Who am I to be this big, this powerful, this visible? Why would they choose me when they obviously prefer someone else? What if I am not liked, not accepted, not loved, not good enough?* We hear the voice of our parents, for instance, and we stop ourselves from doing, being, becoming. When we ignore the voice and break out, only to experience failure, this merely confirms that we were never meant to succeed; that we should never have left the safety of the little box. Failure plunges us into meaninglessness, confusion, identity crisis, self-blame. But rather than concluding that success is out of reach, what if we take the time to notice the presence of magic silently nudging us towards our life purpose? Instead of beating ourselves up over making the 'wrong' decisions, what if we empowered ourselves by viewing disappointments as either valuable lessons ('I was pushing against the wrong door, now I know'); or great experiences that are building foundations for achievements to come? After all, those of us who fail are always in excellent company. Look at our many famous and accomplished role models (Thomas Edison; Steve Jobs; Walt Disney; Oprah Winfrey, to name but a few) who 'failed their way to success'. However you define success, you are always capable of achieving. Believe. Work hard. Let go. And the next moment could be that moment of magic you have been waiting for all your life.

Chapter 5

Awakening

You will bring yourself the suffering you need to bring yourself so that you may awaken.
T. Scott McLeod

Though I wasn't to know it, over many years, decades, a certain kind of magic had been quietly weaving silver threads to form the backcloth of my journey towards this juncture in my life. Those miraculous happenings, however, were either too spaced out for me to pay attention to; too easily dismissed as 'flukes' or patches of 'good luck'; or cleverly disguised as what I would have then interpreted as 'bad luck'. During my teens, for example, after my mother's death, I seemed to spend a lot of time in the airless waiting room of my GP's surgery nestled in the middle of a new-build council estate. My symptoms were wide-ranging, from colds and flus, to aches and pains, to a peculiar non-specific disorder that could strike at any time. During such occasions it would be as though my chain had been yanked and every ounce of vital fluids had gurgled down some dark, myste-rious plughole. When it was particularly bad, a wave of nausea and dizziness would accompany the exhaustion and I'd find myself sinking in slow motion to my knees. Once, when my nameless condition (today it would probably be diagnosed as ME or Chronic Fatigue Syndrome) persisted longer than usual, I was referred to the Whittington Hospital where I became part of a longitudinal study of patients with similar unaccountably low neutrophil (white blood cell) levels, but nothing conclusive came out of this. For want of a more accurate diagnosis, my GP suggested anaemia and low blood pressure. My mother had suffered from clinically low blood pressure, and my visits to the surgery were at their most pronounced during the five-year period between my mother's death and the birth of my daughter. It is only with hindsight that it has become apparent to me that my physical symptoms were a cry from within, a reflection of deep emotional and spiritual needs not being met. I now regard certain intervals up to and including my forties, when I was periodically lost in the wilderness, as a time when I was taking the first halting steps on a journey towards finding my true self and discovering the path of *Light*. Some typical events spring to mind, each representing a catalyst that would eventually culminate in the dark night of my soul when, alone in my bedroom, I would cry out in forsakenness and despair.

Breast Lump

At the age of 21 I was browsing in a second-hand bookshop. Among the rows of tatty titles, one in particular caught my eye. I was something of a hypochondriac at the time, obsessed with disease and ill health. Despite every bone in my body urging me not to, I reached for the paperback, a true and harrowing account of a man nursing his wife through breast cancer from which, sadly, she would not survive. I became locked into a morbid curiosity, deeply empathising with the dying wife, and consumed the book uninterrupted over a few hours. The story was painful, unrelenting, despairing, and left me feeling emptied, haunted. Several days later, an incredible thing happened. A lump materialised in my right breast; I came across it while having a bath. It was significant in size and sited in a prominent part of my chest. I was amazed. This hard knot of tissue, the size of a pea, appeared to have emerged from out of nowhere. Literally overnight. My GP examined me and pronounced that the lump would definitely need "seeing to". The victim part of me felt ridiculously relieved, vindicated. All the silent hand-waving and attention-seeking visits to the GP had finally borne fruit and I could now be taken seriously as an unwell person. I was admitted to the Whittington Hospital for surgery where there was every possibility that I would wake up, in the doctor's euphemism, with a 'nasty' diagnosis. In the end, the tumour turned out to be benign. I'd had a lucky escape. At the same time I'd experienced something of an awakening. I knew without a doubt that in a single week my empathy alone had manifested an overgrowth of tissue in the same part of my body that corresponded to the dying wife in the book. The overgrowth may well have lain dormant beneath the skin for many months prior, but what was staggering was that it chose that moment to reveal itself. I was both frightened and inspired by the implications of this. This singular event pointed out to me the deep and inexhaustible well of power that resides in all of us. Our thoughts are the point of creation. Our thoughts create matter. Anything that we decide in our minds, we can manipulate into existence in the physical world.

Joint Pains

Both my Jamaican grandmothers suffered from a combination of rheumatism and arthritis. Those thin blue Air Mail letters in shaky Victorian handwriting spoke of little else – the knees, the ankles, the hips, the fingers, all 'troubling' them. As children we would be pressured by our parents to correspond regularly with Granny Sissy (Dad's mum) and Granny Jo Jo (Mum's mum) and to enquire each time about their aches and afflictions. Sometimes we would enclose alongside the ten-shilling Postal Order, in a registered parcel, Deep Heat and other strong-smelling medicinal balms.

During my forties when my own joints began to play up with pain and stiffness, I naturally assumed that I'd inherited the 'bad' genes on both sides of the family. My finger and knee joints were the worst affected, and I'd take cod liver oil during the winter months to ease the discomfort, which I accepted would worsen progressively with age. About ten years ago, the joint of my right thumb swelled up alarmingly, becoming too painful to bend. By this time I was far from the needy hypochondriac of my early years, shying away from the GP unless a visit was absolutely necessary. This was one such occasion when I needed a diagnosis. After a brief examination, the condition was confirmed as onset rheumatism. When I asked whether there was any treatment, my doctor shrugged and suggested ibuprofen and going for a rheumatoid factor test. I queried the usefulness of the latter – in what way would such a test *help* my condition? It would confirm the presence of rheumatism, I was told, and promptly issued with a white slip to present to the hospital. I went home and looked at the slip. The only use I could see for labelling a part of my body as 'rheumatic' was to be able to justify hypochondria: "Oh, my rheumatism is playing up... yes, it's been diagnosed. I suffer from it, just like my grand-mothers." I tore up the slip. There had to be a solution, a better way.

I decided to meditate on the matter, something I'd been practising at this stage of my life with varying degrees of success. I entered the quietness of my bedroom, sat comfortably, closed my eyes and focused on my breathing. During this calming-down phase, I made the *intention* to be 'open'; to drop all expec-tations and embrace, with all the innocence, the curiosity of a child, whatever might arise. Very soon, a disorderly queue of distractions began vying for my attention – my neighbours' soft voices carrying through the party wall... thoughts of the various household chores I was neglecting... idle inner chitter-chatter about all and sundry. But rather than resisting those thoughts and trying to push the insistent images out of my mind, I welcomed them. I'd learned the useful technique of imagining that my mind was an empty room with open windows at either ends through which all diversions were allowed to pass, in and out. 'What you resist, persists' – so the trick is to end the resis-tance against rogue thoughts and *allow*. Pretty soon I slipped into a still, wakeful unconsciousness. In this state, I 'spoke' to my thumb, asked it what the problem was... and waited. The answer floated back: *"Control."*

I understood immediately. For as long as I could remember I have plotted and schemed and visualised every aspect of my life, and when things haven't turned out perfectly, or the way I had planned or imagined because of events outside of my control, because of other people not playing ball, I would become worked up about it. Control was a personal issue I fully recognised, but had never properly confronted. But here was my unconscious telling me that this very attitude was contributing to a physical problem. Still in the quietness of *Source*, I visited all the joints in my body in turn, looking at them closely to better understand what was going on. The images that automatically sprang up did not resemble stiff anatomical parts. Instead, I saw tightly bunched flower buds, each representing my clenched, uptight unwillingness to unbend, to allow flow into my rigidly controlled outlook. An innate wisdom guided me to the next step. I saw myself holding a small dark bottle of potion. On to each closed bud I allowed a droplet of:

- self-love
- trust in others
- belief in others
- belief in myself.

In this state of relaxed wonder, I watched each bud slowly changing... unfolding... opening... into the most beautiful pink-hued, multi-petalled flower. When I ended the meditation, a little spaced-out, I flexed my thumb and it didn't feel so sore or so stiff. Was it my imagination? Wishful thinking? The only way to find out was to stop taking the cod liver oil and eliminate its lubri-cating effects at masking pain. I repeated the visualisation several more times and that entire winter, without taking any supplements, all my joints felt free and painless, and my thumb's inflammation soon got better. Since that day, whenever I start to feel twinges in any of my joints, I first of all become still and reflect on the deeper problem (until that moment, I might not even have an awareness that there is one). I notice my physical reaction at bringing up a particular thought or event, detecting where in my body I am unconsciously 'holding' the issue. I immediately relax, release those tensed parts of my body, and try to find a different way to look at and respond to the problem. Purely from my own observations, I have concluded that it is possible that many chronic conditions such as arthritis and rheumatism can arise over time as a result of low grade, repetitive, incremental forms of stress. In other words, driven by our thoughts and unserving beliefs, unconscious pressure, flexing, tensing, holding and clenching can cause long-term injury to the body's tissues.

Tooth Issues

Another example of my early recognition of the connection between the power of the mind and its magical remedying of physical symptoms happened during a family holiday to Brazil, soon after I'd had root canal surgery. We were staying in a holiday villa belonging to our friends' parents and I was in the little kitchen overlooking the porch, cooking breakfast while absentmindedly snacking on, of all ironies, Brazil nuts. I suddenly heard a sickening noise resound in my ears. It wasn't the sharp crunch of a nut; it was the uneven sound of something disintegrating. I spat out the shattered fragments of the temporary crown that my dentist had warned me wasn't up to the strength of a normal crown. After cursing myself, my immediate thoughts were: a) when would the excruciating pain start up; b) where, in this haven of holiday eateries and a million itsy-bitsy bikini shops, would I find a qualified dentist? Thankfully, the pain didn't materialise, and we were already booked to return to England the following day.

I'm at my dentist's surgery in North London. He's frowning and sighing at an X-ray of the damage. I hold my breath and dare to ask, is it alright? He tells me that I've shattered the crown (*this I already know*) and the remaining stump of my original tooth is broken down into the canal (*this I feared*). The only solution is to extract the whole tooth (*this frightens the hell out of me*). I'm holding it together to stop myself from having a crying meltdown. This is my idea of an utter nightmare.

Thanks to being brought up in an era prior to the NHS' programme of preventative dentistry I have far too many fillings. Back then, in the 50s and 60s, wearing dentures was considered normal, inevitable, and every adult I knew sucked on a pair that came out at night. I still remember the popular Steradent advert featuring a set of false teeth submerged in a bedside glass of pink *Plink! Plink! Fizz!* effervescence. Multiple fillings aside, however, I prided myself on at least possessing a full set of my own teeth, so the threat of an extraction was really a big deal! I begged the dentist to find an alternative solution. In response, he patched me up temporarily, handed me some pamphlets on bridges (ghastly) and tooth implants (gazillions of pounds each), and told me to come back in a week with my decision. As I left the surgery, a sheer cussed determination came over me. I decided that by whatever means, whatever it took, I would *not* be losing my tooth. I set to work employing every means I knew – from staring insanely at myself in the mirror and commanding my tooth stump to get better – to meditating day and night and picturing my tooth (what remained of it) still solidly rooted in my gum. By the end of the week I had acquired a sort of walking, woozy conviction that I had in fact healed the tooth. So much so, that I was braced to go elsewhere for a second opinion if my dentist dared contradict my belief. After the second X-ray (more of a formality, my predicament a foregone conclusion) I sank into the reclining chair, noticing the gruesome line-up of extraction tools before me. I could feel my already pounding heart gear up a notch. As my dentist snapped on a pair of latex gloves, I began my opening gambit.

"Do you believe in the power of meditation?"

I'd recently changed from my soft-spoken English dentist near to retirement to this young Asian, possibly fresh out of dental school. Though he was probably British born, I figured that he might be sympathetic to such other-worldly concepts. He smiled at me, which was hopeful, and said yes, he believed in such things. I told him that I'd meditated on my tooth all week and that I'd like him to look again at the second X-ray he'd just taken. He gave me a sidelong glance but, to his credit, he picked up the large fawn envelope, pulled out the X-ray, held it up to the light and peered at it for a very long time. After a while he began issuing thoughtful, indecipherable noises. He also looked perplexed. Finally, he spoke.

"Yes. I think we can save it."

I hadn't realised that I'd been holding my breath. The relief of hearing those words forced a lengthy exhale that sent my stomach muscles rippling like waves crashing to shore. Never before or since have I wanted to hug and kiss a member of the dental profession as I did then. I restrained myself and, after a fitting for a new crown, walked out of the surgery on cloud nine. To this day, my tooth stump is healthily intact. Again, the awesome power of the mind and its connection with the physical self was being revealed to me.

Eyesight

I began wearing glasses around the age of eight years old when my class teacher noticed that I was squinting at the blackboard. Unable to make out the blurry, chalked squiggles that floated confusingly in front of my eyes, I felt ashamed of my little secret.

Talking or whispering was strictly forbidden during lessons, so I was forced to lean towards the nearest pupil to copy their work, which they often delighted in covering up. Eventually, I was put out of my misery when Mrs Christmas moved me to sit at the front. But the squinting continued, so my father was advised to take me to the opticians. Since being fitted with my first pair of glasses way back then, each visit to the opticians has resulted in a changed prescription – always stronger than the last. In my forties my prescription had reached -4.25 in one eye and -3.75 in the other. This meant that, without glasses, friends would virtually have to walk up to me and step on my toes to guarantee recognition. Nowadays, I have mostly eschewed wearing glasses: I can decipher the smallest print in the dimmest light unaided; I am comfortable watching TV without glasses (though subtitles remain a challenge); I can make out the numbers of buses before they pull up right in front of me at the stop; I can read shop signs from across the road; and I can identify friends approaching from a few paces away. Not quite 20:20, but my vision has infinitely improved. Here's how...

During my forties my myopia was becoming noticeably pronounced, and a pair of spectacles was something I'd become accustomed to hiding behind. I remember the day I realised the actual extent of my short-sightedness. When my early morning alarm went off I would have to stretch to pull the clock to within inches of my eyeballs to see the time. Without glasses, the world was a shadowy underwater movie. This particular morning, I dropped the clock whilst reaching for it. My young daughter ran into the room to pick it up for me, and when I looked to thank her, I was horrified. She was standing by my bedside but, in the early morning light, I could barely see the features on her face. It dawned on me that I was literally losing sight of my children. I instantly saw the importance of making an appointment for a long-overdue eye test. This led to a further shock. I was told that I would now need to wear bifocals. The rookie twenty-something optician seemed perplexed by my distress. Her expression said loud and clear, "At your age, shouldn't you expect this?" I walked out of the Oxford Street branch of Vision Express both shaken and outraged. Despite my advanced years, I was still into wearing fashionable clothes, even short skirts; I had no difficulty keeping up with my young children's physical activities; and I was often mistaken for being up to 15 years younger than my actual age. Even if I was approaching middle age, I was certainly not ready to join the grey brigade of half-moon-swinging-on-a-neck-chain-spectacle-wearers. The solution had to be 'out there' somewhere. Hadn't I proved this to be the case so many times before? If I asked the question, the solution would surely come my way.

> **Journal Entry:** ... Now that I am extending my vision, I notice the many commonplace vistas that are new to me. I see rooftops meeting the line of the sky; I see the landscape of buildings far beyond my visual reach; I see the tops of shops and offices when before I would only have bothered to notice what they looked like at street level.

My eldest daughter and I attended a Vision Training workshop led by Leo Angart. A tall, lean, elderly German author, businessman and trainer, he travels the world educating spectacle-wearers and ophthalmologists to the true nature of eyesight, and how certain exercises can sharpen, improve and cure vision restrictions. He holds himself up as a perfect example – a spectacle-wearer for over 25 years, he acquired 20:20 vision two decades ago. Like me, he'd been prescribed bifocals and thought he was far too young to wear them. I was so excited and inspired by what I was hearing during the workshop that I removed my glasses from my face, dropped them into my bag and turned to my adult daughter.

"This is how I mean to go on," I told her.

From that day, I religiously practised Leo's series of vision exercises such as cupping, swinging, sun gazing, and near/far focusing. I also examined any childhood beliefs I may have acquired about what was 'unsafe' to see in the world. Myopics tend to have elongated eyeballs, the eye muscles distorting from habitually focusing on the details of life, the immediate world around them. Several memories came to mind. The earliest ones were of arriving in the UK, fearful and confused about my new environment, shrinking and retreating into the safety of my inner world. There was a definite belief that the outer world was not to be trusted, and that it held far fewer treasures for me. Over the years, I'd developed the habit of rarely lifting my head towards the horizon, looking beyond the lines on the page, the cracks in the pavement or the person in front of me. I definitely felt less comfortable looking up and out than I did down and within. To this day, I have an extremely poor sense of direction, I get lost very easily, and continue to be challenged by spatial awareness difficulties. It made perfect sense that in giving favour to the muscles operating one way rather than the other, the shape of my eyeball had distorted over time. Learning to live without my glasses would seriously challenge the vision I held of my place and position in the world.

> **Journal Entry:** ... After weeks of rain, sleet and then snow in March(!), the sun decided to come out. And how. Have I just become unaccustomed to its brilliance, or is something else happening to the world around me? No, there's definitely something different. My eyesight is returning. It's as if my eyes, accustomed to interpreting the world as a dull blur, have been washed clean. In the bright sunlight, words, colours and details lunge at me for attention and scrutiny. The world has moved infinitely closer.

After my workshop vow, and after struggling through the blurry discomfort of surviving without glasses 24/7, a dramatic incident happened a few days following the workshop. I was shopping in a department store when I was assailed by an overwhelming reaction to... everything. It was as if my optic nerves had begun to rebel at straining to pull the environment into focus, by having a nervous breakdown. I can only describe the sensation as a tsunami of overexposure to all my senses. The world around me became super-heightened – colours, sounds, shapes, smells, textures, temperature, taste. Life's normal filters had suddenly been ripped away and uncensored stimuli flooded my ears, eyes, nose, tongue and even fingertips. The harsh rustle of new clothes, the chemical taste and smell of contract carpeting, the icy touch of metal rails, the blinding glare of fluorescent lighting, the cloying warmth of the overheated store... I felt bare, vulnerable, nauseous and dizzy. I staggered around, my heart thumping like a fish on dry land, till I found a spot behind a rack of clothes, whereupon I collapsed into a trembling, gasping heap. Anyone watching might have thought they were witnessing a junkie going through withdrawal symptoms. It took a while to recover and to pick myself up and head home, a shaky journey, shopping abandoned. I later thought about what had happened, and much later read with interest Mihály's article (see Notes).[13] By removing my glasses, the screen behind which I had been accustomed to feeling protected from the world, I was in effect challenging a 'survival' mechanism that had served me for many years. My subconscious programming had reacted by issuing a red alert. This was my make-or-break point of improving my eyesight. If I stuck it out and overrode these danger signals, I would eventually convince my subconscious that I could indeed remain safe in the world without the shield of a pair of glass lens.

My persistence paid off. A few years later I took my son to have his eyes tested at my local ophthalmologist. He enquired about my own eyesight and I told him the story of how I'd improved my vision from -3.75 / -4.25 to -3.00 / -3.25. I could see from his blank expression that my words were outside the scope of his professional tolerance. He shrugged his shoulders and retorted, "Well, you're at an age when your long vision is improving anyway." I didn't have a good enough reply at the ready, but had I been quick-witted I would have asked him how was it, then, that my near-sight which had seen marked deterioration along with my far-sight had so dramatically improved? And why wasn't I now in need of the bifocals that had been prescribed by a fellow optician just a few years earlier? At the time of writing, I wear under-corrected lenses (-2.00 / -2.25) which I use infrequently, mostly for when it is important for me to see details in the distance (e.g. actors on the stage at the theatre) or to read important faraway particulars (e.g. airport flight information boards). There is obviously room for more improvement, and I would continue the process were it an ultimate personal goal of mine to achieve 20:20 vision. But I recognise that I have made great strides from the beginning of my quest when in order to read the computer screen without glasses I had to massively increase the font. Today, I am back to normal font; sight of my children has been restored; and I defy any person, young or old, to be able to read small print in dim light as effortlessly as I am able to. That is my own personal definition of success.

Other People's Conditions

About six years ago my elder daughter introduced me to the book *You Can Heal Yourself*. In this amazing book, the author Seka Nikolic (an exceptional energy healer whose popularity and amazing healing powers mean that her clinic appointments can only be made weeks in advance) describes how she first discovered her healing abilities, and introduces the reader to the idea that we all have healing potential. It is an easy-to-read and inspiring book, in which many people testify to Seka's incredible healing powers. About a year after reading it I decided to take my younger daughter to see Seka about a problem for which conventional medicine seemed to have no answers. Following that visit, I wrote my own testimonial for Seka to add to her considerable list of case studies.

About 18 months ago I visited Seka with my then 7-year-old daughter. At the age of about nine months she contracted severe chicken pox and as a result, as well as her eczema worsening, she developed a worrying scalp condition. Dry and itchy and bursting into weeping sores every few weeks, nothing seemed to cure it. She had many treatments, both conventional and homeopathic, and one shampoo prescribed by our GP literally stripped the skin from her scalp and left it red and raw. I had virtually resigned myself to her condition, hoping that in years to come she might outgrow it. A few months after reading Seka's book, however, my daughter started to complain regularly about pins and needles in both feet. It seemed to me that this and her scalp problem had something to do with her body's circulation. Exasperated, I decided to give Seka a try.

During the half-hour session, Seka was very warm and reassuring towards my daughter and soon located the "blockage", as she called it, to an area in the small of my daughter's back. As Seka worked over this blockage, she brought my attention to the back of her hand, to see how her skin had turned a strange bluish hue, only returning to normal colour when she moved her hand away from my daughter's lower back. Stranger still, as she worked in this area, the air crackled like electricity. Despite this slightly startling experience, however, it was a very relaxing and calming session and thirty minutes went in no time. I had imagined that I'd be asked to return for more visits, but Seka said that the problem wasn't too bad and that one session should do it.

On the way home, my daughter was both baffled and bemused by her 'treatment'. I told her not to think about it too much or expect anything, but to just stay open to the idea that things might get better. A week later, my daughter's head erupted into a worse than usual case of the sores. Though my partner was sceptical, somehow I knew that this was my daughter's body purging itself of the condition.

Two weeks later, there was no sign of the sores and my daughter only complained about the pins and needles once. Two months later, she had a couple of mild recurrences of the sores and a few more complaints about the pins and needles (bearing in mind she was previously complaining about this almost every other day). My daughter is now approaching nine, and since these minor occurrences, she has suffered from neither complaint – not once. This was a condition that baffled the doctors for over six years and took Seka only one relaxing half-hour session to cure. Oh, and the eczema also became a thing of the past.

Carmen Harris

Several months later, my son complained about a sprained ankle. I automatically thought of Seka, the title of her book, and the calm *knowing* that had descended upon me as I had watched her administering healing to my daughter. It was a soft inner awakening that had whispered, *"Yes, this woman is amazing but, really, we can ALL heal!"* I confidently told my son that I was going to heal his ankle by using my own healing powers. As he'd already been to see Seka[14] and had been impressed by the 'magical' electrical crackle she'd created around his head and body, and because children are ultimately trusting, he was entirely open to the idea. I spent twenty minutes with my hand hovering above his ankle, noticing that throughout he appeared very calm and relaxed. I'm not sure what I expected at the end, or indeed whether I had arrived at an obvious end, but it was acceptable to both of us when he announced that his ankle felt "a little better". Of course, after seeing her brother getting this 'special' treatment, his sister was next in line with her own ailment.

Around this time, my son who is an avid footballer was regularly experiencing excruciating growing pains in both his legs that would usually occur in the middle of the night. After taking half a junior Calpol he'd wake me up asking for a massage till the tablet took effect. I didn't particularly like the idea of my child on regular medication, however mild, but when you're woken from your sleep, exhausted and half drowsy, by a howling 13-year-old demanding an instant fix, you soon give in, especially as the half dose usually took effect after 15–20 minutes. One night, he crashed into my bedroom groaning that he'd just taken Calpol and wanted me to massage his leg till the tablet made it feel better. This particular night I was alert enough to engage with him. I asked him, out of ten, what's the level of pain? He said seven. Instead of a massage, I told him, I'm going to put my hand on you. Typically, when I'd start to massage his leg, he'd thrash about so much I would have to gently restrain him. But the instant I hovered my hand near the pain with the *intention* of healing, he became very calm and still. As I lingered just above his knee, I felt tingling in my palm, like pins and needles. After a minute I asked him whether the discomfort was still at the same level. He said it had gone down to a three. I turned over to go to sleep and told him that he'd be OK. In less than a minute he was sound asleep too. Normally I would have been massaging his leg for at least another fifteen minutes.

After these events, it became a regular thing for me to 'heal' my children of their minor complaints, each time with increasingly tangible results. Over time, Richard himself began transforming from a downright sceptic into at least allowing his curiosity to get the better of him. He had a headache one morning and when I suggested putting my hands on him, he didn't laugh or ridicule the idea. After a 20-minute session his headache was gone. More remarkably, he slipped on some ice on the pavement and hurt his knee. After a few days of seeing him limping up and downstairs and hearing him complaining about the pain I sat him down and began a session. Twenty minutes later, he *walked*, rather than limped, away. The next day the pain had gone. Totally. He then offered me the challenge of the tennis elbow he'd endured for nine months. After one session he told me in amazement that the pain had dramatically reduced.

During these 'healings' I would feel sensations in the palm of my hand. In the beginning, it was so indistinct I half dismissed it as my imagination, but another part of me kept remembering Seka's book. Proof was growing at such a rate I could no longer deny the fact that I had tapped into my own healing powers. The ultimate verification came unexpectedly one day when my sister informed me that her close friend's daughter had been hospitalised. When I decided to visit Samantha, little was I to know that the story that was about to unfold was in fact the universe weaving its magic, answering the heartbroken cry I'd made in the isolation of my bedroom.

Chapter 6

Beginnings

Beginnings are sudden, but also insidious. They creep up on you sideways, they keep to the shadows, they lurk unrecognized. Then, later, they spring.
Margaret Atwood

In early 2009 my cries to the universe had been prompted by a sense of everything falling apart, but I was about to realise that everything was, in fact, falling into place. The brown stuff was about to reveal the magic. My sister, Jasmine, has a close friend, Yvonne, their friendship stretching back to secondary school years. I'd vaguely heard that Yvonne's daughter, Samantha, had been poorly for a while. I didn't know the full details and assumed her illness was just one of life's ups and downs. One day, my sister rang to tell me that Sam had been hospitalised and was now seriously ill. I recalled a time years earlier when Jasmine had visited our large dilapidated house we'd just bought in a recessionary housing market. She was accompanied by Yvonne and Sam. Sam had been in her early teens, going through that sulky, moody phase that often characterises girls at that age. But underneath she was still the quiet, polite, and thoughtful kid that I remembered years before. Now she was a 34-year-old mother of three children, diagnosed with ovarian cancer. Despite my intense dislike of hospitals I felt an immediate pull to go and see her at UCH in Central London. As I crossed the road from Warren Street underground I had no idea that this was to be the beginning of a new and defining chapter in my life. In my heart I'd always known that I was searching for something, but I had no name for this vague longing. I may have had a strong sense of what it wasn't, but I had yet to encounter what it was. The stuff that life was throwing at me certainly didn't seem to hold many clues. In any case, like most people, I was too busy getting on with the everyday to notice any of the deeper patterns of my existence. It would only be in retrospect that I'd be able to look back over the years and see that a larger hand had always been guiding me on to a path that had never stopped calling to me.

When I arrived, Yvonne and Sam's younger sister were at the bedside. Sam's tumour, now in its terminal stages, was considered inoperable by the doctors. She'd been advised by the hospital that there was nothing more they could do. Sam, attached to a catheter, morphine drip and various tubes, was drifting in and out of consciousness. Her condition was fast deteriorating. The day before, I was told, Sam had been able to react to questions by feebly squeezing an offered hand, but now she was completely unresponsive. Without any clear intention and simply moved by deep compassion, I walked to the side of the bed and placed my outstretched hands a few inches above Sam's abdomen. I had seen Seka Nikolic take this position over my own children, so it was a combination of mimicking and what felt intuitively right in that moment. I certainly wasn't expecting what came next. In seconds, my hands became engorged with blood and prickly with heat. I was astounded when this sensation intensified till my palms felt as though they were virtually on fire. The sensation was a quantum difference to the vague tingling I was accustomed to feeling in my experimental healings. What was going on? My instinct told me that whatever was happening was beneficial to Sam, so I held my position, silently concentrating both hands on her abdomen, monitoring the sensations I was feeling, and noting the activity taking place around the bed. I observed the palliative care nurse arrive and stand on the other side, checking Sam's breathing. Behind a professional demeanour, I sensed her concern. Sam's eyes were closed, she was still unresponsive, and through her partly open mouth her breathing had become shallow and rasping. The nurse left and briskly returned with the doctor. After a brief examination, the doctor ushered Sam's mother and sister away from the bedside. I later learned that he was advising mother and sister to gather the remaining family to say their final goodbyes. Meanwhile, screened by the curtains, I'd begun talking softly but firmly to Sam. Where this *knowing* came from, I had no idea. I was simply in its flow. I told Sam that I knew she could hear me; that I knew she wanted to get better; that the sensation in my hands was energy; that I was giving her this energy; that I knew she could feel it; that all she needed to do was receive it. Although Sam didn't appear to be responding, a force beyond logic told me to keep repeating my mantra. After several rounds, the curtains parted and my sister, Jasmine, appeared.

Extraordinarily, as if responding to the swish of the curtains, and as if awakening from nothing more than a deep slumber, Sam's eyes fluttered open. Smiling with instant recognition and obvious delight, Sam called out my sister's name, threw her arms wide and welcomed Jasmine into an embrace. Witnessing this from several feet away, Sam's mother, sister, the doctor and nurse rushed back with looks of utter amazement. In a state of undisguised shock, Yvonne responded to Sam's unexpected request for a drink. Everyone watched in silence as, unaided, Sam held the plastic bottle, raised it to her lips, then, looking around, commented that it was strange having so many people staring at her. Sam's mobile, resting on the windowsill, began to ring. She turned towards it and asked for it to be held to her ear, whereupon she began to engage in a conversation with the friend on the other end. The caller would have had no idea of the role they were playing in what was turning out to be a truly miraculous event. I was so astonished my legs had been quietly buckling. Reminiscent of those early years when I suffered from my unknown condition, I sank to the floor, slightly dizzy. I remembered I had an apple in my bag – a few bites would raise my blood sugar level which had plummeted with the shock of it all. By the time I staggered to my feet, Sam noticed me standing among the others. It was the first time that evening we'd made eye contact, and the first time we'd met in many years. I wondered whether she'd heard my bedside babbling, but she gave no indication that she had. I said hello and told her that I would return to visit the next day, if that was OK with her. The manner in which she replied made me believe that her unconscious had, after all, connected with me at some profound level. She gave me the sweetest angelic smile and gently murmured, "Isn't she beautiful?"

On the journey home and all through that night, the movie of that incredible experience replayed dementedly, over and over, in my mind. What's more, each time I thought of Sam my hands responded with a tingling and burning significantly greater in intensity than mere body heat. Unable to sleep the entire night, I wandered downstairs at dawn and noticed that my mobile phone was flashing a message. My first reaction was dread. An early morning text could only mean one thing – bad news about Sam. It was a message from my sister: *"Stayed overnight at the hospital with Yvonne. Guess what! Sam just got up to go to the toilet!"* Trembling with excitement, I phoned my sister. She described how, pulling along her mobile morphine and catheter units, Sam had got out of bed and shuffled into the bathroom, all by herself! I was shocked. Up until this point, apart from Richard I hadn't told anyone about what had happened at Sam's bedside. I was still coming to terms with the drama myself. When I filled my sister in on the story, she replied, *"Now it all makes sense."*

The next day when I returned to the hospital it was immediately apparent that my sister had informed Yvonne what had actually happened the evening before. Visiting friends and relatives were hastily despatched to the waiting room as Yvonne explained it was so that Sam could spend some time alone with Carmen, in order for Carmen to "do her thing". When I saw Sam I was taken aback. Not only was she sitting up in a chair, and not only was her head fetchingly wrapped with a fuchsia chiffon scarf to disguise her chemo baldness, but in a complete transformation from the person I'd seen lying in bed the day before, she was wearing make-up! She seemed very pleased to see me and when I commented on her appearance I was amazed to hear that she had actually applied the make-up herself. I went to work right away, holding both my hands a few inches away from her abdomen, whereupon I immediately experienced that unusual rush of heat and tingling. Sam told me that exactly where I was placing my hands she could feel a pulling sensation. At the time I could only guess that this was a good indication, a sign of healing. When I later returned home I found a passage in Seka Nikolic's book, *You Can Heal Yourself*, in which she describes this healing energy:

> As negative energy releases, some patients may feel the resistance of the energy as a painful pulling sensation, so I do like to warn people that this can happen. It's normal and it's actually a positive sign that blocks are releasing.

Attracted to Sam's courage and her will to survive, I visited the hospital every day. I remember one occasion when her family were imploring her to lie or sit down. But Sam insisted on standing, her splayed legs supporting her swollen body whilst she doggedly gripped the end of the bed frame. She told me with fierce determination that she wasn't going to lie in "that bed" and "wait for death." The day she'd arrived, the woman in the bed opposite had died, and that wasn't going to be her. I loved her spirit and told her that with that kind of willpower she had everything to play for. Of course she experienced her low moments, literally sickened by the drugs and the depressing prognosis, but she was always cooperative, always eager to continue with our healing sessions. Every day we tried a different combination of hands-on healing,[15] visualisation and deep breathing. When I tentatively suggested it, Sam was open to the idea that diseases are far from random occurrences in the human body. Disease is usually the end-result of unresolved, long-standing emotional pain. I urged her to look deep inside herself to find out what it was in her past she was holding on to. Now was the time to let it go in order to heal and find peace. I truly believed, I told her, that anything was possible. In fact, in anticipation of Sam's recovery I'd already contacted Seka Nikolic by email. I'd described Sam's plight and asked Seka whether she could reserve a cancellation appointment for Sam's eventual discharge from hospital. Seka immediately and wonderfully responded with a yes.

Sam genuinely seemed to benefit from receiving the energy that emanated from the palm of my hands, her spirits noticeably boosted after each session. Her mother was also aware and urged me to continue with my visits. During one visualisation, Sam described a waterfall that seemed to stop in mid-air. I was sure that the symbol was significant to her healing. Once that waterfall touches the ground, I assured her, you will know that you have finally found a way of letting go. And "letting go" wasn't to be confused with "giving up", I added. Letting go meant allowing one's spirit to return to oneself, to reconnect and find peace. By Wednesday night, two days after my first visit, I received another text from my sister: "*Sam is going to be discharged in 2 days. Amazing!*" What, in fact, was amazing was not that Sam was now considered recovered enough to be discharged – it was plainly obvious she was still gravely ill – but that she had defied the doctors and nurses who had believed she would end her days there on the oncology ward of UCH. They simply hadn't accounted for the bravery and resolve of this one special patient.

I wasn't present on the day, but Yvonne described the huge smile on Sam's face when they pushed her in her wheelchair over the threshold into the hallway of her home. It was such a joyous occasion! I continued my visits, now to Yvonne's house, and each time found a warm environment filled with love and caring. There would always be a number of cheerful visitors, Sam's children and her sisters reassuringly close by, someone cooking delicious nutritious soups in the kitchen, someone holding Sam's hand, someone talking to her, someone plumping her cushions and making her position more comfortable, Sam's favourite tracks playing, laughter, and her devoted mother always to hand. It was a joy to be part of such a supportive and loving environment. Though weak, Sam seemed to be in her element, smiling and joking and truly at home, away from the sterile and unsettling environment of the hospital.

Twelve days after that first visit to the hospital, I arrived at the house as usual. Sam was bolstered into an upright position in an armchair, sedated by a cocktail of drugs administered by the visiting Macmillan nurses. I tiptoed around her to begin the healing and was a little puzzled when the usual reassuring sensations were absent in my hands, particularly where I hovered over her abdomen. I began to scan Sam's entire body, from head to toe, looking for 'hot' spots, and becoming increasingly concerned. Wherever I roamed, my hands remained cold, unresponsive. Had my 'magical' powers deserted me? Instinctively, I knew this couldn't be so. It took a while for the possible meaning to sink in. I wandered towards the kitchen, assembling the words that would explain to Yvonne my interpretation of the situation. Before seeking out Sam in the front room I'd been with her mother, talking enthusiastically about Sam's progress. I had even made the crazy suggestion that it might benefit Sam to be taken on wheelchair journeys out in the fresh air and sunshine. The Macmillan nurses had agreed that this was a good idea. As I entered the kitchen, I was anxious not to dampen any of this optimism for Sam's recovery. Yet, if Sam was no longer receiving energy because she had made the decision to let go, then her mother needed to know that the time to say goodbye may have arrived. I found Yvonne in discussion with the Macmillan nurses, concerned about a DNR (Do Not Resuscitate) form Sam had purportedly discussed with the hospital. Yvonne was distraught because this discussion had never taken place, and neither her consent nor Sam's had been sought; yet the box had been ticked on both their behalves. She asked my advice. I reminded her of Sam's determination to leave the hospital; how she'd amazingly succeeded in her aim, arriving home to this hub of warmth and love; seizing the opportunity to deal with the necessary paperwork to get her affairs in order. I told Yvonne that giving the Emergency Services permission to resuscitate would inevitably lead to the trauma of an ambulance dash, and Sam returning to the very place from which she had been so desperate to escape. My opinion was that, whatever happened, Sam should be allowed to remain at home. I'm sure her mother, deep down, knew all of this, but she had become so accustomed to fighting all battles on all fronts on Sam's behalf, anything less would have seemed like giving up. The conversation was my lead-in to what I was dreading. I described to Yvonne the lack of sensation in my hands when I'd attempted to do healing work on Sam. We both became silent. I felt bad as other than a gut feeling I had no real way of knowing whether I was right to raise this alarm. At around 2pm when I left the house I said a quiet goodbye to Sam as she sat, eyes closed in the chair, still heavily sedated.

In the early hours of the next morning, two months after her 35th birthday, Sam passed peacefully.

Yvonne's Testimonial:

I cannot express enough my gratitude for the tremendous support, peace and comfort you brought into my daughter's (Sam's) life, who was terminally ill with cancer. Both during her stay in hospital and her final moments at home with us, Sam and I felt an overwhelming sense of comfort knowing that you were there. Sam always looked forward to your visits; you made her feel very special. After each of your sessions with her, Sam always appeared relaxed, yet full of more energy, taking control of her situation, expressing her love for others and most importantly, she did not seem as fearful of her illness. I remember Sam saying to me, "Mum, Carmen is so lovely. It's so nice seeing her, she makes me feel so good about myself." This would be followed by a determination to remain positive whatever the outcome. She remained positive and relaxed right to the end. I am certain the visits you made helped Sam in her passing, as she was not fearful when she passed. Actually, her dying words were to "tell everyone how much I love them. I have such a lovely family and friends." She then gave a big smile. And she then died. Carmen, you know the saying, "People come into our lives for a reason", and it is so true. Your coming back into our life at such a significant time was a BLESSING, and I know how much Sam, the family as a whole, and I appreciated those visits. I am forever grateful... Thank You. Love you (and mean it) x (one from Sam) x

I wrote a record of Sam's story and sent it to Yvonne for her to verify it as being factual and correct. She sent the following email in response:

From Yvonne:
It was difficult, but touching and reading this has helped. A request Sam made before her passing is now making sense (or I am trying to make it make sense?). At Sam's final moments she asked for Carol and I to sit her up. Both holding her, we sat her up and she then asked for me to wash her face with water (weird request, I thought). There was a bottle of water nearby, so I poured some into my hands and washed her face. Unfortunately, some of the water went in her eyes. She cried out, "Mum, Mum, not in my eyes!" This seemed important to her, but she kept smiling. I tried to get as much water out of her eyes as possible. She then said what I said in my email [above] and then gave that big, big smile and died. What's the

meaning of the water?

My Response:

To begin with, I was just as perplexed as Yvonne. When the realisation dawned on me, it gave me goose bumps:

It makes perfect sense, Sam wanting to be splashed with water. Having visualised that waterfall, finally, she was able to allow her waterfall to reach the ground. In doing so, she wanted to experience it on her skin. When she felt this, she knew she had called her spirit back from the pain of the past. She could then let go, into Peace and Love. If we had any doubts before that Sam is fine, then this should put all our minds at rest.

Chapter 7

Forgiveness

Forgiveness restores our faith, rebuilds our trust, and opens our hearts to the presence and power of love.
Iyanla Vanzant

Amazing grace had opened a door directly on to my path, and my life would never be the same again. I was a writer. I had never expressed a desire to become a healer. That far-out idea hadn't once occurred to me. Yet, when I stepped into the role, it instantly felt *right*. A perfect blend of all the strengths and qualities I recognise in myself – my attention to detail, my perceptiveness, my empathy for others, my sensitivity (to light, noise, smells, temperature, people's thoughts and emotions), and my writer's instinct for the subtext in human stories. After Sam, I immediately began to offer healing to people outside the circle of my immediate family, to relatives, friends, strangers – anyone in need, free of charge. I was being driven to find out exactly what this gift meant and why it had been 'given' to me. Having already experienced Journeywork, I now immersed myself in other alternative techniques. After Reiki I Attunement, I became a certified EFT[16] practitioner, and much later a Theta healer; following that, a Reconnective practitioner, all in addition to studying, experiencing and experimenting with other modalities such as NLP,[17] Quantum Touch, Quantum Entrainment, Deeksha, Crystal Healing, Emotion Code, Healing Code, Binaural Beats, Lucid Dreaming, etc. My fascination for exploring the inner realms of reality drew me towards the maxim "Teach what you need to learn" – the most effective means to deepen one's understanding of anything.

My first *Be-The-Change* gathering, a small group of women

invited into my home to experience 'universal energy', was nerve-wracking. As I stood in front of the eight attendees, demonstrating through practical and interactive exercises the subtleties of the world beyond the veil, I could feel each thud of my heart against my ribcage. However, over time, as I began to appreciate my own worth and my relevance to the world, the impulse to disseminate the knowledge that we all have the power to transform our lives overshadowed my lifelong fear of exposure and visibility. Since that time I have interviewed the famous healer Dr Eric Pearl, given an interview about my healing journey, talked about my personal journey to various public audiences, and performed healing on the late US soul singer, Bobby Womack[18] – all to camera. Not exactly world-shattering achievements, but all would have been inconceivable in my NML and Jenni Murray days when performing in front of an audience, however small, however informal, was my worst nightmare!

When I launched my website in the hope of attracting fee-paying clients, setting up my stall among other established healing practitioners, it was as daunting as the very first time I publicly declared myself as a writer. As well as temporary lapses of confidence when I'd convince myself that I wouldn't be good enough, there was also the whole issue of accepting money for what many would regard as a God-given gift. I've heard this objection raised so many times, often accompanied by hidden outrage. Back then, I allowed myself to feel guilt-ridden; now I have my own response to this argument. Everyone on this planet is the pure essence of universal energy, the source of all healing. Without exception, we all have access to the gift. However, to activate our healing potential, it's necessary to acquire:

1) a strong *desire* to heal others
2) the unshakeable *belief* that this is possible
3) a willingness to *nurture* and *develop* the ability over time.

These same motivations apply equally whether you are a conventional doctor or a 'woo-woo' healer. Yet, how many of us would have the temerity to demand that a medical practitioner give up their personal time, their expertise and energy and treat us for free? Why not? Doctors have the gift of healing, don't they? Quite apart from the obvious right we all have to earn a living, in my mind there is no conflict at all in a healer requesting remuneration for their efforts in helping to relieve real pain and suffering. Why should anyone who feels called to dedicate their life to one field or another be set apart from the rest of humanity? There is as much need for healers in this world as there is for plumbers and politicians.

I began to steadily attract more clients (in between my creative writing, which I still continue), building up an impressive body of testimonials from people outside of my circle of family and friends. As if to dispel my earlier doubts, my very first paying client sent me an unexpected email an entire year after her single session:

I want to take this time to thank you for the healing! I have noticed a considerable difference to my well-being, my self-esteem, my whole life, since meeting you last year. I have been able to say I truly mean it when I say I am feeling good, and I have felt this change since the dawning of 2010, and others can see the difference in me! Thank you so much for your intervention! (Z.S.)

All of these adventures and the many changes in my life came directly out of my experience with Sam. But possibly my most powerful reward was a lesson I had first brought to her attention that she, in turn, taught me: forgiveness and letting go. Her family were witness to the peace that transcended Sam's suffering when she was finally able to surrender to the story that had dominated her life. She led by example, showing how when we find a way to step away from the anger and bitterness of what others have done to us, what we have done to ourselves, we are restored to personal power, freedom and harmony. It's a tough one to accept, but no one robs us of our happiness – we first have to give our consent, whether knowingly or unknowingly. We do this by agreeing to hold on to the pain of past hurts. The need to be right, to be wronged, to judge, to be vengeful, all of which keeps us mired in the past. Taking this lesson on board, I drew up a hit-list of all the people in my life who had transgressed me in some way or other and for whom that hurt still lodged in my heart and mind: the betrayal of a 'friend' who stole the envelope containing my first earnings when I worked evenings after school at Medici Cards; the teen rival who, driven by jealousy, crept into the cloakroom of Jones Brothers department store where I was doing a Christmas stint and slashed my prized new Top Shop coat; the pervert doctor who during school medicals sexually fondled the line-up of bewildered 5-year-old girls, myself included; and so on. Using the powerful technique of EFT, each day I selected a story from the past and tapped the energy of its emotions out of my physical body. There was one obvious candidate for this exercise – my daughter's father. Many years had passed, but my cells were still vibrating with rage, humiliation and sadness at being left holding the baby. How could I tell? Whenever a certain name came up in conversation I could feel a silent but palpable rearing up in the pit of my stomach, a sure sign of unfinished business.

> Try it for yourself. First think of something that makes you feel peaceful, calm or loving (perhaps the laughter of your child, stroking your pet, beautiful sunsets, walks in nature). Notice how light and undisturbed your body feels, maybe even slightly tingly.
>
> Now, bring up an image or thought of something that encourages any of the lower emotions like anger, worry or shame (e.g. the last time another driver cut you up in traffic,

that overdraft that keeps you awake at night, your personal weight issues). Now notice how your body feels and where you feel that feeling. Perhaps there's a heaviness, tightness or discomfort in your head, throat, shoulders, chest, stomach or elsewhere.

This is what our energy feels like when it changes from one frequency to another – high to low.

Amazingly, it was only relatively recently that the thought occurred to me: I need to free myself from the vibration, the destructive power of this old story of 'boyfriend rejection', the seductive need to portray myself as both victim and heroine. My newly-learned techniques helped me to not only overcome the resistance against letting my daughter's father 'off the hook', but also to recognise the gifts that had come out of the relationship: my beautiful, talented daughter; the courage and strength I gained from my years as a single parent; how being released from a doomed and troubled relationship offered up the freedom to explore the wider world and to discover the inner truth of myself. Though I certainly wouldn't excuse the behaviour of any man who does not take responsibility for his own child, and though I have no desire to rekindle our friendship when we have so little in common, I was able to see him in the light of a journeying soul, forgive him completely, and finally release my attachment to an unserving story.

I received a Facebook Friend Request from Sipho. We hadn't seen one another for many years and, after exchanging online pleasantries, I invited her round for dinner to catch up on old times. During our conversation, she broke the news about Vinette, a mutual friend, also from the past. She was in a nursing home in Pimlico, terminally ill with multiple myeloma. After recovering from my initial shock, I said I would go and see her, but Sipho became evasive, reluctant to give me any more details. Vinette was very proud, she finally admitted, maybe she'd said too much already. Vinette wanted few people to know what was happening to her or to see her in her present circumstances. I'd already mentioned to Sipho how my life had changed since we'd last met and that I had become a healer. "You're not doing Vinette any favours, denying me the opportunity to give whatever help I can," I told her. In the end, Sipho agreed to at least pass on my concerns and offer of help. Vinette responded via Sipho by saying that she would, in fact, like to see me.

I'd known Vinette from secondary school when she gave a good impression of being a wild child. Though she was several years younger and attended another local comprehensive, she hung around the neighbourhood with the 'glam', the 'daring', the 'loud' older girls from my own school. Energetic and raucous, most parents would eye her warily and regard her as trouble with a capital T. My own parents had no cause for concern as Vinette and I weren't friends as such, usually acknowledging one other from a distance. Then one summer's day in my mid-20s, recently graduated from university, I unexpectedly bumped into her. She seemed to have mellowed noticeably, even saying she admired the fact that, despite being a single parent, I was doing something with my life, unlike the other Finsbury Park girls she had since outgrown. She told me that she was now living centrally and that she had an understudy role in a new West End musical. I expressed my own admiration of her and she offered me complimentary tickets to see her show. At the Apollo Theatre in Victoria, my daughter and I were mesmerised by *Starlight Express* – that young, athletic cast buckled into amazing skating contraptions, effortlessly whizzing and rocketing and leaping and twirling around the moody set of a steaming railway station. It was as though the performers had been born wearing their flashing mobile footwear! At the time, I hadn't yet discovered my gift as a writer and the entire theatre experience of lights, music, spectacular colours and action ignited something magical inside of me – a pull on my unrealised potential.

Vinette played a sultry character, Belle the Sleeping Car, and her gutsy voice bellowed out some raunchy numbers that were well suited to her natural vivaciousness. I learned that she had been a roller skating fanatic for many years, regularly frequenting the Bayswater rink on a Saturday afternoon. It was here where she was scouted by a casting agent and, after auditioning and demonstrating that she had a powerful enough voice to match her skating prowess, she landed the part on the show. I was impressed by her hard work, her talent, and her fierce ambition to better herself, which seemed to be fired by a belief that, having ostracised her entire family, she was alone in the world. That very afternoon after going backstage during the show's interval I witnessed the entrepreneurial drive that had transformed Vinette from a Finsbury Park urchin to a stage diva. She was in the Green Room wearing a cotton apron over her glitzy costume, hurriedly unpacking a mountain of foil-wrapped Jamaican fried chicken, patties, fritters and dumplings that she'd prepared in the early hours of that morning. She asked for my assistance to help serve and sell to the crew and her fellow cast members, and her hard efforts pulled in a handsome stash of cash before she was back on stage for the second half. After *Starlight*, she went on to work in various musicals up and down the country, latterly earning a decent living as a Tina Turner tribute act and astutely ploughing her income into a small portfolio of properties, two of them located in prime sites in Central London. But while there was this reformed and admirable side of Vinette, there was also a hard edge of bitterness still apparent in her personality. Quick to take offence, she seemed determined to see every good intention in a negative light. Beneath the respectability and grease-painted sophistication, she was still a street fighter. After one too many disagreements with her, I decided that life was too short to pursue such a trying and unpredictable friendship. Inevitably, we went our separate ways and lost contact with one another.

I approached the third floor of the nursing home and found Vinette in a private room, her bed pushed up against the corner wall. I wasn't prepared for what I saw. Even if the flirty, tiger-sexiness that she was accustomed to exuding was just a professional act (she once told me, wearily, that boyfriends were usually disappointed that her stage persona was not one she brought home and into the bedroom), it was still a shock to see the shrivelled, curled-up body that required round-the-clock nursing assistance, including frequent turning to prevent bed sores. Her voice was weak and croaky when she spoke, but her eyes were glinty and suspicious, scanning my expression for any unwarranted signs of pity or sympathy. As our conversation progressed, though, she slowly began to relax and drop her guard. One of the things she shared with me was that, though she wasn't religious in any way, she had been attending a spiritualist church before she was taken ill and had found joy in gospel singing and being part of the choir. It was clear to me that joining this community had helped to soften aspects of Vinette's nature and saved her from becoming the worst of herself. But not entirely. She was still possessed by her demons, and despite her weakened state she found the energy to give scornful looks to those nurses whom she felt were persecuting her in some way, kissing her teeth at the mention of them.

I broached the subject of healing and asked Vinette if she was willing to experience a technique called EFT. Her immediate receptiveness showed that she hadn't given up the fight to live. After some hands-on healing that transported her out of her pain into a calm and relaxed state, I took her emaciated arm and began tapping on the various meridian points. My probing soon raised the ghosts of unresolved early childhood issues; the lack of nurturing that had led to her difficulties in both giving and receiving love in adult life. The central 'story' affecting her mental/emotional and, ultimately, her physical health was her fractured relationship with her mother who had given birth to her at a very early age, a child herself. Vinette was both candid and emotional about all aspects of her upbringing, the harshness of her mother and the many traumas she had endured as a young child, exposed and unprotected from the abuse of others. As we worked, more of the edginess melted away with her tears. As with Sam, I visited the hospital regularly to give healing and, day-by-day, noticed gradual improvements. From being incapable of doing anything for herself, Vinette slowly began to regain some of her independence.

One day after phoning the nursing home and being informed that Vinette had been temporarily transferred to a bone marrow transfusion unit, I arrived at the Hammersmith Hospital. After reaching the appropriate floor I stopped at the double doors of the ward and decided that I had better first visit the ladies'. Fifteen minutes later, having got lost in the confusing warren-like corridors and medical blocks isolated by dedicated lifts and stairways, I arrived back at the ward. As usual, while other patients were surrounded by friends and relatives at their bedsides, Vinette was alone. This was what dismayed me the most about my visits, how despite her large family and glamorous show business associations, I only knew of three others who visited her. I imagined the reason was that Vinette had destroyed many friendships because of her beliefs about her lack of support in the world, which caused her to unconsciously engineer situations that brought about that very reality in her life. My visit was a surprise, and when she saw me her eyes lit up and danced with genuine appreciation. "I just thought of you!" she cried. "When?" I asked. She estimated around 15 minutes ago. The same time I had stopped outside the ward door. We experienced this kind of psychic connection a number of times in different situations, leading me to believe that on our life journey we had been destined to meet up and to learn something from one another, despite our obvious differences.

Several days later, Vinette was transferred back to the nursing home. When I turned up the day of her return, again, she seemed very pleased to see me. From that motionless figure curled up in the bed resembling the charred remains of a Pompeii victim, Vinette had become much more bright and alert. She was sitting up in an armchair and after telling me that she was doing even better than I imagined, she went on to describe how the TV remote had been out of her reach on the bed in the corner, but rather than call out to the nurses she'd been able to crawl on all fours to get it for herself, then crawl back to the armchair. This was astounding! Never mind the crawling; just the fact that instead of turning to face the wall she was now starting to take an interest in the world. I was so pleased, I persuaded her to pose for several photos so that we could begin documenting her progress. I added that soon she wouldn't even need to call out for the assistance of the nurses, as she'd be well enough to get up and stroll the corridors. I'll never forget the sudden look of naked rage (or, was it terror?) that came into those eyes. "Don't you DARE tell me WHEN I'm well enough to do anything! I'll get better in my OWN TIME!" she yelled at me. Startled, I began explaining what I'd really meant, that I was pleased that she was improving so quickly, that... She was in no mood to listen. Amid her mounting, ranting hysteria of accusations, I stopped trying to defend myself. What was I apologising for? What had I done wrong? My comments had been totally benign. I'd even arrived with an M&S ready meal that I had been hand-feeding her at the time (she hated the food at the home), and she'd been sipping on beet/carrot/ginger juice that I'd prepared freshly and lovingly and brought from home. Her anger fired up my own anger. I stood my ground and so did she. Soon we were having a full-scale row. Out of the corner of my eye I became aware of the elderly patient in the room opposite stirring in his bed, and nurses in the doorway peeking in to see what was going on. I suddenly saw the ridiculous situation – me, arguing with a terminally ill patient – and came to my senses. "You know what – why don't I just go?" I said, breaking off and gathering up my coat and bag. As I turned my back, I heard Vinette mutter, "Yeah, and don't come back, like the rest of them." Now, that wound me up all over again. I went over to the armchair, levelled eyes with her, and said firmly, before storming out, "I'm going, and just to prove you wrong, I WILL come back!"

I was due to attend a meditation meetup at a yoga centre in North West London. Fuelled by upset and anger, I hurried inside the building, half an hour early. I found the organiser sitting cross-legged in the dim light of the otherwise empty room, surrounded by mats, cushions and scented candles. Barely introducing myself to the poor unsuspecting guy whom I'd never met before, I shattered the tranquil ambience by blurting out the whole upsetting story. He listened silently, waited till I'd ran out of oxygen, then calmly replied, "Good on you for not letting her get away with it, sick or no sick." I felt vindicated hearing a stranger take my side. Then something occurred to me. A detail that in the flare-up of emotions I hadn't stopped to notice or consider: *She has the bloody **energy** to argue with me!* That gem of a perspective stopped me in my tracks, breaking the spell of my own righteous indignation. Laughter bubbled up in my chest and rose in my throat. I found myself roaring out loud, "The diva! She must be *so* getting better!"

30/1/11

Hi Vinette,

When I said, I thought, encouragingly, that on my next visit you'd be walking the corridors, I expected a smile, a laugh, or even a rolling of your eyes and an "I wish". The last thing I expected was for you to erupt in anger. When I described you as a "Be Strong

Person", the type who others don't offer help to, because they mistakenly think you're OK, I was showing empathy with your situation, not criticising you.

I know that the healing has helped you enormously. I know because I can see obvious improvements each time I visit, and because it has also helped many other people who have received it from me. I also know that your own determination and strength to get better is the greatest factor in your healing. But neither my healing nor your determination is enough. Healing comes into its own when we heal the heart. When we recognise that the past is only the past and we choose to walk away from that past.

On our journey through life we encounter much pain and often the situations we find ourselves in we feel we don't deserve. But these are our life lessons – opportunities to grow away from the past; to decide not to repeat patterns that don't serve us; not to inflict upon others what has been inflicted upon us. If we have been denied justice, this is our chance to show mercy. If we have been denied love, this is our chance to show and to give love.

Each time I came to see you, I came expecting nothing. Far from being a 'bully', I only wish you to get better, if you wish that for yourself. It is your choice, and there is nothing I can do, nor would want to do, to alter another's choice. If you want me to stop coming because you see me as 'bullying' you, then I will respect that. But if you want me to continue seeing you to give healing (something that other people pay for, and which I give to you free of charge), then I am more than happy to continue. But this also is your choice. I'm leaving it up to you how you decide to continue your journey.

With love,

I kept away and heard nothing. Some days later, I contacted Sipho and asked if she could surreptitiously enquire whether Vinette had received my letter. Sipho told me, with some humour, that when she'd asked Vinette had "vaguely" recalled seeing "some letter" that had arrived in the post, "but hadn't read it". Relieved that the diva had at least received, and most probably read, my sentiments, I let the situation lie. My hope was that in some small way she might start examining the link between her thoughts and feelings and her current ill health and isolation. The ball was in her court. Several days later, my mobile rang. Upon hearing the feeble voice croaking on the other end, I automatically assumed it was an old person who had misdialled. Then I recognised the tone. I'd only ever heard Vinette's strong, forceful voice over the phone before, long ago in the past, but it was definitely her! Considering that only a few weeks earlier she had been unable to raise the weight of her own head from a hospital pillow, her ability to pick up a phone, dial a number and speak into the handset was an amazing accomplishment. The obvious effort she was making to reach out to me totally softened my heart. As we spoke, I didn't quite get the apology I deserved, but in her own way she expressed her contrition for flaring up and misinterpreting my genuine intentions. Whatever anger I'd felt was now a thing of the past, and I promised that I would see her soon. But events overtook my plans. Richard became ill with a dangerously inflamed gall bladder and was himself hospitalised, so my focus was diverted to my family. Though Vinette preyed on my mind, with two younger children to look after as well as visiting and tending to Richard, there just weren't enough hours in the day to travel to and from the other side of London. About a week later, I heard from Sipho that Vinette had passed peacefully.

The funeral had a modestly respectable turnout, though far from the numbers I had imagined, given Vinette's colourful showbiz past. Among the crowd, I saw her younger brother for the first time. Allowing a few weeks' grace, I later contacted him, explaining who I was, the work I'd been doing with Vinette, and how sorry I was that I hadn't been able to continue my hospital visits. During the conversation, I was frank in describing the fractious relationship I'd had with Vinette, my impatience with her stubbornness, her moods, her paranoia and negativity, to which he exclaimed, "You *knew* my sister! You really *knew* her!" He'd experienced the same frustrating relationship throughout his life with Vinette, he explained, but towards the end he had noticed that a major change had occurred in her. In fact, he had been able to cherish those final precious moments they'd shared. At last, he said, he had reunited with the big sister he had always wanted.

We are all influenced, to greater or lesser degree, by our emotions. Whether painful or pleasurable, benign or challenging, the range of our emotions come and go, 24/7, throughout our existence. There are, however, three important emotions that can unknowingly become 'signature' to our lives. *Anger, sadness and fear.* The process goes like this: in the past, we experienced an incident that overexposed us to one of these emotions. Because this emotion was never fully resolved (we weren't allowed to express it; we were forced to repress it, hide it, swallow it, etc), we limp through our life stories, responding to triggers that reignite the same underlying, unhealed emotion, over and over in different relationships, different situations. *Same sh*t, different pile.* Vinette and I were more alike than either of us would have cared to acknowledge. Two strong-willed women, we shared in common a signature emotion that was neither sadness nor fear. I recognised only too well Vinette's patterns of defensiveness, self-protection and deflection – typical automatic responses to a notion that one's personal power is being threatened and under attack. My own reaction to Vinette was that I couldn't abide those qualities in her. But the saying goes that "it takes one to know one" and I certainly knew her anger. She was a mirror to the anger that was also in me: expressed in my need to be right/indignant/offended so that another could be wrong; my need to control so that I would not be controlled. That day when

Vinette was brave enough to call me on the phone, I fully expected that she would be seeking my forgiveness. It never occurred to me that I may have played a part in our argument; that I might consider accepting her own forgiveness of me. Looking back, in my enthusiasm to 'save' Vinette from her suffering, I may very well have overstepped the mark, appearing bullying and controlling. If I'd stopped to empathise with the pattern of anger that stemmed from Vinette's childhood rage at a world that had treated her so badly, and being forced to suppress that rage for so long, I might have allowed her the right of her outburst. I might have thought to forgo my own right to be angry and immediately apologised for any transgression she may have interpreted in my actions. Instead, I matched her anger with my own.

We are the root cause of everything that happens to us in our lives. There is no one to blame, to hold responsible or accountable but ourselves. The buck stops with us. Yes, it sounds harsh, and I hear your response: what about the person who is born blind, poor, disfigured, or suffers from real injustices of war, hunger, loss, pain? The fact is, we can play that argument all day long and where will it get us? Precisely nowhere. We are where we are in life, but we are never powerless. The defining strength we all possess that can never be taken away from us is our outlook. We always have the choice to find liberation in appreciating the best our situation offers, however grim that situation may be.[19] We can be grateful for what we have, or we can lament that which we are being denied by allowing fear, sadness or anger to run our lives. The path to freedom for both Vinette and for myself was to ask a simple question of ourselves: *despite my story, my background, my experiences – am I willing to give up my right to be angry?* If I had demonstrated through my actions that I had indeed been willing, what a powerful example, what an amazing gift, in that moment, I could have offered to both of us.

Forgiveness does not have to invalidate our own pain nor should it condone the unacceptable behaviour of others. The act of forgiveness is first an act of empathy, a deeper understanding of the flaws in our transgressor, but also in ourselves. We all do better when we know *how* to do better. The other person, like us, can only ever do the best they can with the current resources available to them, including the gift of personal insight. In the moment of conflict, our transgressor is blind to the true cause of their own struggle and suffering – their addiction to the alluring story of how their past should have been. Likewise, we are unable to see, in our story, our own attachment to blame, resentment, hurt and, most importantly, the withholding of love – both from our transgressor, and from ourself. For, in order to forgive others, we must first be willing, no matter what, to return to our own heart. Until we reach that place of self-clemency we will continue to find the same fault and difficulties in others that we (deep down) find in ourselves. The choice, as always, is ours. We can either submit to the constant re-triggering of the same painful emotion by the same person or scenario, each time in a different guise; or we can yield to the powerful lessons found in the consequence of our anger, our sadness, our fear, and move on. Until such time, life will continue to present the same opportunities for learning. However, the day will come when we finally *get it*, when at last we understand. On that day we will have expanded to our next higher level, and that particular lesson will no longer have cause to show up in our mental, emotional and physical existence. That doesn't mean that we will have arrived and the illusion of this world will cease to present problems and challenges. We are human – life will forever test us. What it does mean is that in any given situation, when we view life through the new magical lens of our own essence, the opportunity will always be there to reframe our suffering to: *experiencing* an emotion, *becoming* that emotion, then effortlessly *releasing* that emotion.

R has rheumatoid arthritis and, in addition, is recovering from breast cancer. Her relationship with both her parents was turbulent, particularly with her mother: Breast cancer is usually an indication of nurturing issues, and autoimmune disease a sign of self-rejection. In this case R had been insufficiently nurtured by a mother who seemed to hold a grudge against her. Once she blamed R for her own inability to be a good mother, as R reminded her of 'things' in the past she would prefer to forget. During one of our healing sessions a strong image came to me of a sailing ship on water, the people on board looking out towards land. When I relayed this to R she said that she loved being in the water, and we left it at that. The image surfaced a few more times on different occasions. The last time it returned I again mentioned it, and R remembered that at age 3–4 she was violently ill with dysentery on board a boat, forcing the family to cut short their sailing holiday and return to land.

During the following session R recalled making a vow that day, having seen the power that her ill health had to change events – i.e. forcing her parents to cut short the holiday. The vow was that she would make her parents suffer. R realised she could control her parents as well as receive the attention she craved if she were constantly ill. We had hit upon an *Aha!* This recollection made sense; why no matter how R tried, her disease would not abate. Rheumatoid arthritis is a result of the body's immune system attacking itself. In wanting her uncaring and sometimes violent parents to pay for their behaviour and to suffer guilt, R was effectively waging a war against her own body, conveying the message that it was OK to be ill – i.e. to attack itself. During the session we healed the belief of this little 3–4 year old trying to survive in the only way she knew how. Forgiveness of both herself and her parents was a big part of this. Today, though R's fingers are still deformed, the pain has noticeably abated.

Chapter 8

Spirit

A sparkle of white light out of the corner of your eye signals that an angel is near. A feather that mysteriously appears from out of nowhere. And the beautiful angels you see in a darkened room, or standing beside a beloved friend or teacher, confirm that the angelic kingdom visits you.

Doreen Virtue

Do you believe in fairies? Or, for you, do they merely exist in children's fables and adult fantasies? I can't say for sure that my eyes have ever witnessed the popular depiction of a fairy, but I readily accept, through other people's documented testimonials, that these magical unborn entities really do exist. Spirits of the deceased, on the other hand, I have definitely had personal experience of – as I will soon reveal. As a result, I can assure you that our spirit companions are present beyond and above this physical plane that we call reality, helping to support us throughout our entire lifetime. Angels, guides and messengers, as well as originating from the spirit dimension, also walk among us in earthly form as earth angels, helping us to express the highest gifts of our soul. All spirit beings do this by offering protection, guidance, healing, revealing our truth, answering prayer and caring for us during our final moments. In the midst of our troubles we can call on our other-worldly friends to lighten our load and bring magic into our lives. Unfortunately, the majority of us are often too preoccupied with material worries and concerns to notice that we are always accompanied. Add to this the fact that our friends frequently appear in guises that we don't readily recognise, it's no wonder it takes a stretch of our imagination to believe in their loving presence.

The first I knew something was awry was when I walked barefoot into the kitchen early one morning and met the confusing sight of the otherwise clean black and white floor tiles scattered with chicken bones from last night's dinner. Next, my attention was drawn to the black bin liner. It had been ripped to shreds in some kind of frenzy. My skin began to crawl as the puzzle pieces slowly started to fall into place. "Rats! Rats in the house!" Richard came hurrying down the stairs at the sound of my horrified screams. I was hopping, yelping and gulping like someone who had just tripped over a dead body. In no time the guy from Rentokil was sitting on our sofa watching me sign on the dotted line for every bell-bow-and-whistle strategy to de-infest our home. The end result was a series of large green metal traps strategically placed in the basement and both back and front gardens; high frequency sensors in the kitchen and family room; sticky rodent sheets in the bottom of cupboards; and a year's subscription to Rentokil's on-demand services. But despite all the expensive measures, nothing seemed to stem the flow of invading rats. At my wits' end, I seriously considered adopting a neighbour's cat, until the thought of half-chewed rat remains filled me with even more terror and revulsion. And then came the smell. That gamey, putrefying stench of dead rodent. The nightmare was that we had no idea where it was coming from.

We searched high and low, until Richard finally narrowed down a crawl space between the kitchen floor and the basement ceiling below. Incredibly brave, he bashed a hole in the basement wall and ventured through. Several nail-biting minutes later, he emerged in full rat-protection overalls and asked whether I first wanted to hear the good or the bad news. I shuddered. The good news was that the rat was dead; the bad news was that it was still moving – *writhing* with maggots! My partner's laughter followed me as I fled screaming to the attic, from where I refused to come down until I had cast-iron assurances that it was safe to do so. The rats continued to pay regular visits and the situation remained unresolved for *months*. The very last straw was opening the kitchen drawer to find myself staring eyeball to eyeball with a huge shivering brown rodent! At that point I was all ready to pack up, lock up, and move out – forever. Why me?! Why now?! I howled, tearing my hair out. We had lived in our house for approaching twenty years and had never experienced anything like this before – not even mice (though the Rentokil guy reassuringly explained that the rats would have devoured any trace of mice). The professional rat-catchers returned, inspected the house and garden once again. This time, one of their operatives leaned over the fence and casually pointed out the source of the problem. Next door had recently replaced their French doors, leaving a six-inch gap between the foundation and the bottom of the door frame. The local rats were entering via the garden into the basement of that house and scampering over to ours. At the time our basement was a dark, barely head-height space in which we stored years of accumulated junk. The walls were roughly plastered and there were many holes and gaps where much of the brickwork was missing. A rat's paradise. The area measured the whole width and half the length of the house, but I insisted that we immediately empty and replaster every inch of the space in order to eradicate all points of entry and escape. Richard brought to my attention that neither of us were exactly flush with the tens of thousands of pounds that would be required to carry out my master plan. When I doggedly investigated the cost of a basement conversion, calling in numerous quotes, it did indeed turn out to be prohibitive. But I kept telling myself there had to be a way. There just had to be!

One morning I noticed workmen emerging from Matthew

and Carrie's basement. Our neighbours, several houses down, had moved in only recently and, though I'd only spoke to them a few times, I nevertheless went through the open door to see what was going on. They were doing exactly what I was aching to do with our basement, refurbishing it! I was introduced to George, their Hungarian builder, who was undertaking the work for a fraction of my lowest quote. If his men were able to work on both basements simultaneously, he told me, it would reduce the costs even further. All of a sudden, I could see blue sky! When I contacted my building society I discovered that they had only recently introduced a low-interest loan for green improvement initiatives such as wall and floor insulation and energy-efficient boilers – necessary requirements of any basement conversion. Between the rats, George, and that low-interest loan, the end result was pure magic – something I could never, in my wildest dreams, have foreseen nine months earlier. It was as though the universe had been forcing my hand to take my calling to its next level in a pure demonstration of the brown stuff hitting and magic appearing. For out of the experience we now have a wonderfully light and airy additional space in our home that can double up as a healing room for treating clients. These days, instead of recalling my unexpected visitors as filthy terrorists, I fondly regard those rats as furry, four-legged guardians bearing an unexpected gift – but only just.

Psychics, mediums and clairvoyants have the ability to access the spirit world, retrieving information via extrasensory channels that most of us believe to be less than normal. I very recently visited an extremely gifted clairvoyant, Loraine Rees. She stated matter-of-factly, "You work with spirits; you're very psychic," followed by, "Whose birthday was it when your mother died?" I was gobsmacked, I hadn't uttered a single word upon entering the little makeshift room in the back of a hairdressers' in Barnes.

How did she know that my mother was dead, never mind the rest? She informed me that my mother was standing beside me, as she always was, and that she was very sorry that she had to go when she did. During our 20-minute session Loraine's voice would change as she disappeared into the dimension of the spirits, rapidly firing information at me that could only have come from an other-worldly source. At the end, she scrunched her face, rubbed her nose and commented on a sinus problem that had been bugging her for several weeks. By then, she'd discovered that I was a healer so I offered to help. I spent a few minutes feeling for interference in her aura and used my palms to clear it, after which she said she could definitely feel the difference. When we communicated six months later, Loraine told me that after the healing the problem had taken two days to go completely, but that it had never returned!

During my twenties and thirties I was in awe of these gifted people. My first contact with such folk began as my way of having a bit of a laugh with friends, but I soon became irrepressibly drawn to the idea of a living person acting as a conduit to the 'other side' and having a *knowing* of me beyond my own knowledge of myself. I offered my hand to many fortune tellers pitched up in market tents and to psychic seaside spinsters renting rooms at the Spiritualist Association, and was often told that I myself possessed psychic abilities, that a deceased uncle was my 'protecting' angel, that my late mother was proud of my achievements... etc, etc. Of course, I came across many who were obvious chancers and charlatans, but that didn't quell my fascination.

This is an email exchange I had in October 2010 with the initial proofreader of this book. Back then she was a published novelist and a consultant in the field of Work/Life Balance; today she is a coach, mentor and publisher of self-help authors:

Lucy: *"You wrote this a few weeks ago: 'Just had an image of you as* *a publisher of self-help books!' Since then, conversations with my publisher have led to him offering me a sort of partnership/commissioning editor role, which I'm going to take up. And he does do mainly self-help books. I had no thoughts of it when you wrote – although perhaps it opened my thoughts up to possibilities when we started talking about how he worked. I'm just really interested as to what your 'image' consisted of, and whether this happens to you often. I know a couple of people who are consistently right in their 'feelings' about the future – and I wondered if you were one too."*

Me: "When I was working on your book [reading it to give feedback] I had a flash of an image and a distinct 'feeling' that accompanied it, the sum total of which conveyed the information – Lucy... publisher... self-help. Sorry I can't be more specific than this but, yes, it occurs now and then. I keep telling myself to properly tune into it as it's a great help in my healing work."

Of all the soothsayers I encountered in those early days, there was one person who truly impressed me. Thirty years on, Anne Owen's website describes her as *"One of the best psychics around... a caring and devoted mother of two."* In the mid-80s, though, websites were a thing of the future and her clients found her mainly through word-of-mouth, visiting her at home or receiving 'remote' readings via the landline. My friend Reima first brought Anne to my attention and, game for a laugh, I decided to accompany her to Kent to pay this psychic a visit. Sitting outside Anne's reading room that evening, Reima and I prodded one another, giggling over who should enter first. Ever the adventurer, I went ahead and sat before a large friendly woman wearing sandals and an Alice band that kept at bay an unruly bush of jet-black hair. During the preamble I maintained my usual initial scepticism, holding back personal clues about myself. I can't recall everything I was told on that day, but I do clearly remember Anne startling me by announcing that that I was "good with words", and that I had a daughter who "loves the limelight". I started to listen more keenly, as my shy 8-year-old did indeed love the limelight, and was attending the Anna Scher drama school at the time. The half-hour session was full of insights and seemed to fly past. Afterwards, Reima, a career bank teller, went in. She received a prediction from Anne that she would one day "work in show business". On the way home, several pounds lighter in our pockets, we compared our readings. Reima was less impressed than I, scoffing at Anne's 'one-note' prophecies of limelight, fame and show business. Roll forward a few decades:

Reima phones me from her office. I can barely understand what she's saying as she's shrieking down the line. In the middle of a tea break, Reima had apparently experienced a *Eureka!* moment. Having been made redundant by her bank some years previously, through a rather serendipitous route, she'd ended up on a very different career path. Mug of tea in hand, there she was, at the desk of Break A Leg Management, her own community theatre/TV/film agency. The Anne Owen penny had only just dropped!

What lodges in my own mind from that visit to Kent was Anne's final pronouncement during my reading: *"You and your daughter are going to be famous together."* Ever since, I have been waiting for my own Eureka! moment.

April 2011 – To alleviate a sudden back condition, I'm having a healing session, lying on Kasia (a fellow healer)'s massage couch. As she runs energy through me, I hear knocking. It sounds like central heating pipes, but instead of coming from below the floorboards, it appears to be coming directly from underneath the massage couch. I say nothing. After the session Kasia enquires whether I heard the knocking. I say yes, and ask whether it was her pipes. She says, no, that knocking was for you. Someone was communicating with you. This feels strangely comforting, not frightening at all.

One day in 2011 my eldest daughter visited and in conversation mentioned that she'd attended a workshop where she'd met a businessman who had an interest in mentoring start-up entrepreneurs. So many times my daughter has proved to be the catalyst in my life, pointing out particular books, people and ideas that have nudged me towards my next level of transformation. This turned out to be another such occasion. For some reason what I was hearing resonated, so I asked my daughter to tell me more. The man's name was Robert, and he was to become my earth angel at a time when I was pondering my direction in life. Yes, I now believed and accepted that I had a gift as a healer. Yes, I was attracting clients and collecting an impressive number of incredible testimonials. But was there more I should be doing with my gift? Could I be reaching more people? Teaching more people? Empowering more people? Most healers I personally knew were accustomed to playing small, apparently content with seeing several clients per week. For some pressing reason, I wanted to make more of a mark. Vague notions occasionally floated into my mind that embraced elements of education and community, but I had no real conception of how this might either look or materialise, never mind the steps needed to move forward (evidenced by my confused, idealistic email below). Yet, my restless spirit had been urging me on. So, when my daughter suggested contacting this man to sound out some of my half-baked ideas, I did just that.

4/4/11

Dear Robert,

Excuse me for approaching you like this. My daughter told me that she met you at a workshop last weekend and that I should contact you as you have interests in the area of business mentoring. I would really appreciate if you could spare the time to read this email.

I am a professional writer by trade (TV, children's books), but two years ago my life changed when I discovered that I have the ability to heal. You may or may not believe in the possibility of these things, but if you read my personal story (via my website's link below) you will see that these things are indeed in the realm of the possible.

Since that day, I have been putting my gift to good use and often to amazing effects (see my website testimonials) – dealing with physical ailments like sciatica, back pain, breast lumps, allergies and fractures, to emotional distress ranging from performance anxiety, phobias, deep depression, to grief. I charge a reasonable fee and many times I heal for free when poorly people cannot afford to pay. However, my main thrust in life is to teach people that I am not unique and that we are all capable of healing. To this end, I have recently started a women's meetup group to discuss and demonstrate healing empowerment. Through this group, I also give free monthly distance healing to anyone who is interested. See one of my testimonials below:

Testimonial: *The healing was the most incredible physical experience I have yet had. When I settled, energy centred immediately on the solar plexus, feeling fuzzy. Gradually the sensation of a vacuum started to manifest between my ribs under my sternum, so strong that I wriggled a little to see if the pulling sensation was being created by my clothes, but it was internal. I gave in to observing it, thinking that it would probably go away then, but if anything it strengthened. It was like when leaves and debris are cleared from a drain and the water rushes in, sucked in and down. The breath was moving next to it but this wasn't the breath, it was quite distinct. Heart, arms and hands started to feel tingling and* *full, then brow sensations of energy within the space. This was truly powerful healing. Maybe it was the stronger for having spent two days preparing with yoga, but this felt like grace. Thanks Carmen for your gift. Thank you.*

Anyhow, this is the crunch. In these disheartening times of global recession and personal fear, we have lost sight of what is really important – our connection to our spiritual empowerment (please note that I am not in any way religious, but deeply spiritual). As a human race, we have tried the path of greed and more greed, and this is where it has got us. There are many, many people like myself who are not religious, but seeking another way to live a just and hopeful existence. This sounds all very metaphysical, I know, but on a purely practical level:

Think how much physical and emotional suffering would be ended if we could be taught how to help ourselves out of these cycles of fear and hopelessness.

Think how many people could be embraced if there was a place they could attend that did not speak of God in the denominational sense, but which offered the same levels of comfort and optimism, despite all that is happening in the world.

Think how many people in the care and prison systems could be helped to overcome their personal demons in quick, simple and effective ways to end cycles of self-abuse and criminalisation.

Think how businesses would be transformed if managers could be taught to dissolve the personal fear that drives them into making bad decisions and mismanaging their staff.

Think how different the world would look if people suffering the effects of war, famine and disaster could be taught simple techniques that could neutralise their suffering so that such negative emotions were not passed on to the next generation.

Ultimately, I am looking at ways to put my gift to wider use (to spread the word that extraordinary things can transpire from ordinary people) but, I admit, I am not sure what I am asking of you personally. However, if anything automatically comes to mind, I would be indebted to your business acumen. If nothing is instantly forthcoming, but you at least remember that I am here, should you have any suggestions in the future, for that, too, I would be grateful. Thank you for listening.

All the best,

After replying to my email, Robert suggested that we meet for lunch the next time he was in London as he often visited the capital on business. He turned out to be a large, kindly and rather old-fashioned suited gentleman from Somerset. Over grilled sea bass, we exchanged stories and it seemed that our rendezvous was about to conclude as one of those polite occasions that pleasantly lead to nowhere. Everything changed, however, when in the middle of attempting to describe the notion of energy healing, I broke off and made a suggestion. "I live close by, why don't you come to my house and then I can demonstrate first-hand?" He was up for it, so I led this complete stranger to my home and out into the garden. As I sat him down on a chair in the spring sunshine, I realised I was nervous. Many people are able to sense the energy or radiation that emanates from the centre of my palms, but there are the odd few who feel no sensations at all (though this is no indication that they are not receiving the benefits of energy). What if I'd dragged this poor man away from his barely digested meal to flap my arms in front of him, for him to feel... precisely nothing? How embarrassing would that be? I put aside my doubts and, with both hands, began to scan the energy at the crown of his head.

The moment I felt the slight resistance of his *aura*, he immediately responded, "Oh! I can feel some tingling!"

"That's energy," I replied, mightily relieved.

I then fanned my hands either side of his head and as soon as I engaged once more with his aura he commented, "Now that feels very different, like waves!"

I was so pleased, he was obviously very sensitive to energy. When a person is able to *feel* the presence of universal energy, it takes less to convince them that there is an electromagnetic field that surrounds us all. I then held out my right palm about a foot away facing his chest. After a few seconds, he cried out with disbelief, "I can feel the heat!"

This time I also expressed surprise. There was a pronounced intensity like a laser beam, emanating from the centre of his chest, striking the middle of my palm. And it hurt!

"I can feel that, too!" I exclaimed. "It's suggesting to me that you either have an issue around your heart or that you've had one."

He looked at me. His eyes were full of wonder, then they softened. "My dear, I had a heart attack four years ago," he said, and immediately booked a session for the following week.

Chakras are invisible to the normal senses and exist in the dimensions outside of our physical self. They operate like invisible vortices, pulling in energy and releasing energy in a continuous flow that creates harmony and balance in the body. There are many chakras but the seven major chakras, each linked to different organs and different parts of the endocrine system, are the Root, Sacral, Solar Plexus, Heart, Throat, Third Eye and Crown. Disease first shows up in the areas surrounding these chakras before they manifest in the physical body. I am able to feel 'blockages' or 'interference' in the chakras with the palm of my hand. After the second healing session with Robert, having worked on issues related to his Heart chakra, he surprised me by announcing that he so believed in my work and my good intentions that he would like to help me. He pulled out his chequebook and declared that he would assist me in setting up a healing foundation. I felt an immediate twinge in my solar plexus as the vision of scores of thousands of pounds flashed before my eyes. The words automatically shot out of me: "No! I can't do that. I can't accept your money, but thank you." I felt terrible, slapping away his kindness with what appeared to be ingratitude. Later that day, I sent him an email to apologise, explaining that I couldn't take his money as it would conflict with our client-healer relationship, that it might come across as exploiting his vulnerable state. The next time I saw him, he calmly wrote out a cheque for the session and, knowing that I couldn't refuse, added an extra amount, explaining that he wanted me to put it aside for people in need of my treatment who couldn't afford it.

On 7th June 2011, Robert sent me this text:

> *You are the best person to use this money to turn into kindness and good health. Go forth with great confidence in the powers you have. Let us hope the exercise acts as a great multiplier. If you treat one person, the odds are you also help their family and friends through their HAPPINESS and well-being. Love to you all.*

I put that much more modest sum of money to good use, printing 'Special' cards that I distributed to friends, family and some clients to be issued to people they personally knew who might benefit from free healing. I have since learned, though, that (apart from babies and young children) offering treatment without some form of reciprocation is not necessarily the way forward. When a person recognises and makes the decision that they have the ability to get better, *intention* alone is a powerful force for kick-starting healing. Some clients, though, initially see the challenge as all mine – to prove that I can heal them, not for them to confront their own resistance to healing. However, it is up to the client to not only demonstrate that they are ready to make life changes by showing up in the first place, but also to recognise the value of any healing they receive. Whether payment is a few pound coins or a homemade cake, that simple exchange of energy between healer and client is a necessary part of the therapeutic process.

Robert became my favourite client, a fortnightly regular to my home, and a great friend of the family. Occasionally he would join us for dinner before returning to Somerset or his Central London hotel. His extreme generosity, his great need to give, was a trait that could very easily have been exploited by others. When he visited, he would often arrive bearing small gifts for my children, for me, or for the home, and I strove to give in return, once by treating him to a memorable evening at the theatre, for which he was very grateful. The iPad that I use today, he bought for me. At the time, I had no interest in the technology and, in my ignorance, regarded it as a children's plaything. But he convinced me that I would find it useful for my healing business, and suggested donating me his old one that he'd been using for some while. Put in those terms, I was willing to give it a try and waited for several weeks during which time he ran a story about first needing to delete his personal information from the device. Having softened me up to the idea, he turned up one day with a spanking new iPad! We were very much alike, both willing to give but reluctant to receive. Part of his big-heartedness was a show of gratitude for the healing, for which he would always exclaim: "Thank you, dear. I don't know what I'd do without you in my life." His general health seemed to be improving, so when he told me a few sessions later that he'd been diagnosed with prostate cancer, I was taken aback. His doctor wanted to operate right away, but he had stalled, saying that he wanted to investigate all the available options. He asked for my opinion and, as is my general policy, I replied that I was not medically trained and could not intervene in any discussion between a client and their physician. In the meantime, however, I said that I would redirect my healing towards his condition. Several sessions later, Robert announced that his PSA levels, without any medical treatment, had reduced so dramatically his doctor was now satisfied with observing his condition rather than taking the drastic step of an operation. I later added Robert's testimonial to my website:

Dearest Carmen, one day you will be feted for what you have achieved, maybe at the moment a little bit of an unsung hero, there can be few if none who have been in contact with you that have not benefited from you...

I met Carmen by chance, my life was at the lowest ebb, I was unaware of her skills. She immediately diagnosed my past heart problems. She has also identified and discovered deep-seated emotional problems in my childhood that have caused my prostate cancer. In fact, she treated me for this condition whereby my blood cell cancer count has been reduced by over 25%. Moreover, my emotional welfare and well-being has been restored in a way that my deeply buried fears have been removed. My new life is a revelation to me. I am now happy as stress is no longer resident in my life. My treatment continues and I can only look forward with optimism and with a happier heart. Thank you Carmen.

R.T. (Company Director, Somerset)

According to reports he received from his doctor, Robert's overall health continued to improve – his laboured breathing, his swollen ankles and the fluid around his heart. He'd even resumed playing squash and talked about buying a bicycle. One of the most unexpected results from the opening up and healing of his Heart chakra, though, was his surprise discovery that he was a lover of art. He told me that this appreciation appeared to have come from "out of nowhere", and that were he to be born again he would certainly choose a career as a dealer in the arts. So great was his newfound passion, he partnered with a Cork Street artist, supporting the artist's work and investing in his gallery. He spent tens of thousands of pounds on artwork, buying so many framed pieces that he ran out of wall space in his own home and began displaying his purchases in the homes of his friends. On more than one occasion he hinted at the blank space above the sofa in my back room, but each time I would politely move the conversation on.

One day he came for his regular session and seemed in a particularly mellow mood. In fact, I commented that he had the appearance of a Buddha, sitting peacefully on the sofa with both hands folded in his lap. I enquired about his latest altruistic business venture with a young lady he'd met recently. (During our sessions I discovered that he financed a number of small start-ups from which he had little expectation of receiving any financial returns.) He replied contentedly, "Carmen, I've realised that I no longer need to rescue women in order to feel good about myself." It was an amazing statement. Eighteen months before, when I'd first met him, he was overwhelmed with stress, self-loathing and guilt about many areas of his life, in particular with what he saw as his hopeless relationships with the opposite sex. This issue had been intricately connected to an unresolved story to do with his mother. Was he telling me that the myriad aspects of this story had finally been healed? I gave him a huge hug, and told him how proud I was of him; that he had turned a significant corner and was finally on his path. He took me to lunch and we spent a lovely chatty hour or so together. I had no inkling what was just around the corner when I bade him farewell till the next session. A week later, I received a distressed phone call from a friend of his. I could barely hear her words for the gulping and sobbing. As I listened, I felt as though I'd become part of a movie that was slowly unspooling and confusingly losing its frames: Robert had visited the Cork Street art gallery and was on the train returning home for a game of squash. A couple sitting opposite him in the first-class carriage had noticed him take a call on his mobile, before he leaned back and gently fell asleep.

When the train arrived in Taunton, the last stop, the couple tried to rouse him but couldn't. Robert had suffered a massive heart attack.

Spinning with grief and shock, I was distraught for many weeks. Intellectually, I know that no healer can take either credit or responsibility for what happens in another person's life. The healer's sole task is to act as a catalyst, enabling a depleted body to absorb enough universal energy to set in train its own healing. The rest is up to an Intelligence operating in the smallest particles of all of creation; a force infinitely greater than the brainpower of the smartest human being. But that didn't stop me from blaming myself for not foreseeing Robert's death, for not being able to 'prevent' it. The situation had echoes of Sam. Whilst another person's earthly purpose might have been to summon the huge resolve needed to overcome a terminal prognosis – as such miracles do occur – Sam's sole desire had been to survive long enough to take care of her children's affairs. That was her will. This she achieved. No one has the power to alter another's will or final destiny. It is an arrogance to think otherwise. No matter how much I desired it, it simply was not within my gift to 'override' the fact that Robert's time had come. Even so, it took me a very long time to appreciate that, having journeyed from a dark, exhausting and abusive past to a place of growth and enlightenment, Robert had simply reached his last stop for this lifetime. He had returned home, and not a moment too soon or too late. Exactly 24 hours after his death, something happened that seemed to register this point. I received a 'delayed' text (these things do occur, but at the time it had never happened to me before). Apropos of no previous discussion, Robert's message simply read: *"Thank you for everything."*

February 2012 – I'm in the middle of a healing session with L, a friend and elderly actress. I decide to call on my guides for help and assistance with her issue. I lift my arms and, though I can't see my guide, I sense a presence and simultaneously get the feeling that my arms are clothed in draping robes. At that moment, L's eyes fly open. "Who was that?" she fires at me. I ask her to tell me what she saw. She describes a bearded man with long hair who had been standing beside me. I ask, "What was he wearing?" L replies, "Loose clothing, white or off-white in colour." I ask about the sleeves. She confirms that they were long and draping. She tells me that she doesn't believe in spirits, and were it not for the fact that she knows me and that the face was a benign one, she might have run straight out of the door. She jumps off the massage couch and, strangely, makes an instant beeline for the mantelpiece. "Who is this?" she asks, pointing to a family photo she must have seen a dozen times before. I say, "That's me." She says, "No, who is the man?" I say, "Richard" (whom she knows). She squints without her glasses and exclaims, "Oh, my God! That was the man! Older, but the same face!" This makes no sense to me. As far as I'm aware, at that moment, Richard is not a spirit, he is alive and well.

Eighteen months later, Richard has a session with the psychic/teacher/healer, Sidra Jafri, and is told that the spectre of his long-dead uncle (who died before Richard was even born) has been attached to his energy field for a long time. She helps him to clear the energy of the deceased uncle. When I hear this, a thought occurs. I ask, what did this uncle looks like? His mother furnishes him with a picture – the uncle could be mistaken for Richard.

Robert was my earth angel. We were destined to meet to confront our mutual heart-based fears and to take each other to our next highest level. He may have achieved his end, but I still remembered the palpable discomfort I'd felt in my solar plexus when he'd offered me what my heart and my unconscious mind had been desiring, as expressed in my very first rambling email to him. His greatest joy would have been to see me become a huge success as a result of his personal assistance. Putting his money to good use would have been fair exchange, my return gift to him. I now recognise that my rejection of his money, no matter how much I dressed it up as an issue of ethics, was a rejection of myself: *It's bad to receive; I don't deserve it.* These were the unconscious beliefs about myself that revealed a deeply-buried fear of abundance. We inherit these kind of irrational fears from our parents (Ruby Wax puts it perfectly in her book, *Sane New World:* *"Mommy and Daddy... jam their USB sticks into our innocent hard-drives and download their neuroses into us*), and mine had centred around hearing my mother and father repeat familiar adages such as these:

> *Money doesn't grow on trees.*
> *There's no more where that came from.*
> *I don't have any money.*
> *You can have too much of a good thing.*
> *What do you think I'm made of – money?*

In Jamaica my father had been a radio technician, a tailor, and also ran a small trucking business. In England, he became a postman, a job that provided security for his family, and a position, though lowly, that he held with pride. Although for many years he instilled in me that I was bright enough to become a lawyer, when I disappointed him with single parenthood, he fell back into a less ambitious vision of my future – the one he himself had been forced to accept. When I broke the news that I was quitting Yellow Pages to study for a BA and he expressed his horror – *"What? You leaving you good-good job in de Post Office?"* – it was the same pinching-back message I'd heard all my life: only so much is available in the world for people such as us; if you squander your allotted rations, there will be nothing left in the pot. I eventually became a Sociology graduate, but I was already a long-time graduate of this unconscious parental programming. The telltale signs were evident. Whenever money came into my life, I efficiently saw to it that it went out again, re-establishing the low-income comfort zone that I was accustomed to. There was danger and treachery in having too much money; meanwhile, there was safety in knowing that if I possessed only so much, I could only lose so much. So deep was my conditioning. There was also the ugliness that money represented. All around me, during the 80s especially, signs of Thatcherite 'Greed is Good' showed up in every facet of life, so vividly expressed in the ego-ridden power-dressing of that era. I had friends and personally knew people who had made a lot of money and whose lives reflected a hideous, selfish frittering that didn't appear to make them any the happier as people. I recall the sister of a friend who insisted on offering me a lift in her spanking new convertible who spent the *entire* 20-minute journey on a single topic of conversation – the car's customised white kid leather interior.

Yet to be poor is to live in a constant state of paralysing anxiety: fear of brown envelopes hitting the doormat; of repair, replacement and maintenance bills; of embarrassment at the shop counter; of being called to buy the next pub round; of the office whip-round; of rising prices; of dwindling savings; of world events. And to have had wealth only to lose it raises an entirely different set of neuroses: fear of being exposed as inadequate, a failure, a has-been; fear of being cast out of a world that was once yours. I look back now on my earlier attitude to money and cannot believe how *indoctrinated* I was! Who was I serving by acting so *small*? With wealth, I can not only help myself, but my family, my friends, my fellow human beings, the world! I knew all of this mentally, yet the old reflex had kicked in the moment I was offered abundance on a plate. Robert, my earth angel, was the person to bring my awareness to my own scarcity consciousness, and for that I owe him an immense amount of gratitude. I missed him deeply, but a month later I received irrefutable proof that he is still communicating with me, from the other side, the spirit dimension.

Richard and I are in Brescia, Northern Italy, staying with my friend, Samar. That morning I wake up and remember a vivid dream I had overnight. I dreamed of Robert. *He's sitting on a bench, his legs slightly apart, his right hand clutching the top end of something that looks like a sceptre, a cane or stick. It's the pose of an old man. I can't see his face because it is obscured by some kind of scribbled formula –* $E=MC^2$ *– Einstein's equation. Energy is Everything!* I tell Richard about the dream and later I will be glad that I did, or I would have convinced myself that I'd imagined it.

Franco, Samar's nonno (grandfather), has been poorly for some time. Once spritely and independent, he has now become housebound. I offer to accompany Samar to his home in nearby Crema. When we arrive, he is being visited by Samar's mother and his other daughter and there is also a home help present. He's sitting on a chair with his legs apart, a walking stick behind him. I introduce myself and ask if he'd like to lie on the bed for me to do some healing. He nods his agreement, and the four women help him on to his feet as he's very unstable, and lead him to the bedroom where they lie him across the bed as I instruct. They leave us alone and I stand behind Nonno's head and begin to direct energy into his crown. He opens his eyes and looks up at me in a worried/questioning kind of way – he speaks no English and my basic Italian is not sufficient to communicate effectively. He shouts out for Samar and she comes running into the room. He tells her in Italian that he felt tingling in both his feet. I tell Samar to reassure him that it's just energy being activated in his body and all is OK. He seems satisfied with this and Samar leaves the room. I continue and a few minutes later he hollers for Samar again. When she returns, he indicates that he had a pain in his right side... but that it has suddenly gone. I make the same reassurances and Samar once again leaves. After another few minutes he's calling out again! Samar appears and he describes hearing a voice very close to his right ear, distinctly whispering his name: "Franco! Franco! Franco!" I tell Samar that this sometimes happens. Spirits arrive. Samar again reassures him and once more leaves the room.

Nonno closes his eyes and finally settles down into the healing. Several minutes later his black bushy eyebrows concertina as he screws up his eyes and begins to thrash his head from side to side. His eyes remain closed as he shouts out to his granddaughter for only the fourth time. When she arrives he cries, still with his eyes tightly bunched, that he sees a light, "The brightest, whitest light!"

I ask him, "Are you afraid?"

He replies, "Yes."

I tell him not to be, to accept the light as it is there to heal him. I instruct him to direct the light to where he needs it most in his body. When I finally finish, the helpers arrive to assist him off the bed. As soon as he's upright, Franco waves the women away and walks shakily, defiantly, unaided, back to the front room. Sitting on his chair, he recalls with wide-eyed amazement the light that he saw behind his eyes, how it was the most amazing light he has ever seen, and that he'll never forget it. When I say my goodbyes he rises to his feet, grips my head between two shaky hands, pulls me towards him and plants endless kisses on my lips.

I would later learn of Franco's tragic yet heart-warming World War 2 story of being rounded up off the streets as an 18-year-old, and being taken to a prisoner of war camp. During those harsh years he would dream every night of his mother's rabbit and polenta. He believed it was his determination to savour it once more that kept him alive. One day, at the end of the war, his mother, believing her son to be long dead, was hanging washing in the yard. Turning and seeing the living apparition of Franco, she screamed. Later, having recovered, she lovingly watched her son tuck into his favourite rabbit and polenta.

I am honoured to have helped this hero and loving grandfather to transition into peace. When he died, five months later, a rainbow stretched from the open window to lie across his chest, long enough for Samar to take a photo of the beautiful comforting image.

It was only later that I saw how my dream paralleled reality – Robert/Franco sitting on a bench/chair; the walking stick/cane/sceptre; the energy/equation/light between the eyes. My Robert was communicating with me! I absolutely knew this. The message could only be one of support and encouragement: *Keep doing what you're doing. I'm here.* In order to send such messages, spirits and guides are able to manipulate the electromagnetic field – an explanation of why some people report lights flickering or equipment sometimes switching on and off. Spirits and guides also offer their vibration which we translate into thought. For example, my deep *knowing* in the presence of Seka Nikolic that we can all heal was a vibrational whisper that I translated into an articulated thought. It's important not to overlook intuition, dreams and gut feelings that give us access to the finer dimensions of the spirits and guides who are always trying to get our attention. Look out for hidden messages when, for example, your awareness is unusually drawn to the lyrics of a particular song; the appearance of feathers, especially where you might not expect to see them; repetitive symbols or numbers; unusual or pleasant smells; 'hearing' your name being called when there's no one around; sudden changes in body temperature or the surrounding environment; the coincidental appearance of creatures like butterflies or ladybirds. When you notice these things, be *still.* Judge whether what your senses are picking up resonates with you. What do you *feel? Where* in your body do you feel? Does that sensation 'feel' like a yes or a no? Does it feel right? Does it feel good? You might be asking right now, "Yes, but how would I know whether I'm simply making it up?" The answer is, who cares? Trust your intuition, give yourself permission to play, to tune in to your feelings, to go with it. This is the magical art of our existence. The signs that we pick up are capable of transporting us from a stuck or painful situation to shifting our perspective towards possible growth and change – from the brown stuff to the magic. Remember, spirit is always communicating with us, not to influence our lives, but to convey messages that lovingly promote our efforts along our path. When I sense spirit or my guides I sometimes smell the scent of flowers, or I experience a sudden rush of energy, heat, cold, or a tingly shiver – interference in my electromagnetic field. Sometimes it is the spirit or guide of my client, and when the familiar sensation arises in me, often the client feels it too.

T came to see me about exhaustion and deep feelings of sadness. Soft-spoken and gentle-mannered, he described his ongoing relationship problems. Digging deeper into his history, I realised that a greater issue was his father's death that had occurred the year before. T's father had been the victim of a senseless crime that had ended in his death. T had been living with the guilt and the helplessness of knowing how much pain his father had suffered during his last moments on earth. I explained to T that it requires a lot of energy to block emotional pain, and that as this grief for his father had not been properly released, emotional suppression was the likely cause of his unexplained exhaustion.

I began by scanning T's aura, and an image of T immediately came to me. What was interesting about the image was that whilst T's face was shadowy, the shirt he was wearing stood out. It had an iridescent, sepulchral quality that floated in the forefront, almost as though it was in a different dimension. I mentioned the image to T, telling him that it might not indicate anything at the moment, but a possible meaning could come to him later. The session lasted 90 minutes and was intense and cathartic.

We were getting ready to say our goodbyes, when T murmured, "I know what that shirt is. When I think of my father, he is always wearing a dark suit with a white shirt." In that instant, I felt something amazing – a shimmery wave of energy pooling at my feet. It rose quickly, pulsating strongly around the outside of both my legs. Rushing upwards with a silent *whoosh!* it exploded through the top of my head. All of this in a matter of seconds. I felt a powerful release and tears sprung to my eyes. When I looked up, there were tears in T's eyes, too. We were feeling the same emotions. Without a doubt, what I had just experienced in that room was the spiritual presence of T's dead father.

With a confidence that bypassed my thinking mind, I said, "He wants you to know that he's here and that he's OK. You mustn't worry." T nodded knowingly and replied that it was such a relief to hear.

I was having difficulty deciding on the design for the cover of this book. I was looking for the perfect image that would convey simplicity, magic, humour, and appeal to both sexes. Quite a tall order. After weeks of independently researching *thousands* of online images and then working alongside the talented illustrator Garth Mule, I was getting boggle-eyed. One day I was with the family visiting the seaside town of Bournemouth. As we turned the corner on to the beach road, something loomed in front of us: a huge and colourful hot air balloon bobbing in the blue sky. We all saw it, commented upon it, and moved on. But something about the image stayed with me. Several days later, in a quiet moment, it suddenly occurred to me: why wasn't I instructing my subconscious to work on the design problem during my sleep? I then heard a 'dimensional' inner voice: *the answer has already been given to you*. In that moment the huge balloon image crowded my mental screen. Next, the front cover revealed itself, entirely! Immediately I knew it was right! This was such an astoundingly clear example: through paying attention to my subtle senses I had exposed the existence of my helpful Guides.

Are you able to take that leap of faith that I might just be right; or would you rather believe that you are alone, unloved and unsupported in this world? Let go. *Allow*. Receive.

Chapter 9

Healing

The wound is the place where the light enters you.
Rumi

The first book I ever wrote was *Naomi's Secret*, a children's story that features a healer who sits on the bed of a little girl she has never met before, yet mysteriously knows the reason for the girl's tummy ache. During those early starting-out years, even though working in the healing arts was the furthest ambition from my mind, it seemed that my fertile imagination was guiding me towards a destiny that would eventually feel like a homecoming. Looking back over my life, it appears that I've never been out of tune with the subtle energy vibrations that surround us all. Even today my children laugh at my predictability. The moment I enter the living room I immediately ask for the TV volume to be turned down. To my ears, everything sounds *loud*: the radio, computer games, the hum of the fridge, the tick of an alarm clock. As a writer, I guess my audio sensitivity, the ease with which I am able to tune into other people's conversations (the merest whisper of tittle-tattle from the most remarkable distances) could be regarded as quite a useful handicap. My sense of taste, too, is overdeveloped. When I discover a flavour I'm not crazy about, my dislike is passionate and there's no persuading me to try the thing when I can already taste it in the vividness of my imagination. My son, 'the fussy eater', also has this finely-tuned tongue, and seems to have inherited my keen sense of smell too. The moment anything unfamiliar lands on his plate, he immediately makes a face and unleashes his sniff-o-meter upon it. This was me as a child, and even now. I am always the first to sniff the doggy poo that has been brought into the car on the soles of an unsuspecting passenger's shoes; I can detect a fart at a hundred paces, so there's no point denying that one in my company. Annoyingly, those offending odours usually cling to the tiny hairs of my nostrils and stay with me till long after the event, whilst at the other end of the smells spectrum I try to avoid the perfume departments of large stores. It sounds dramatic, but the heady combination of heat, bright lights, and the cloying cocktail of scents used to bring me to the verge of passing out. As for my eyesight, in my early years I tended to shun the brashness of 'out there' in favour of the comfort and mystery of my inner landscapes. Today, my inability to comprehend distances, my unreliable sense of direction, and my lack of spatial awareness are all connected, I'm sure, to my early childhood outlook. As my fear of the outside world grew, my vision contracted accordingly and myopia became the end result of capturing every close sensation and burying myself in a mountain of books. No wonder I was so atrocious at sports. Why would anyone in my netball team chance to throw the ball to me, knowing it would only slip between the gap in my outstretched hands as I made a good attempt at catching the air instead?

Talking of shivering during outdoor games, there's also the matter of my sensitivity to the cold. Coming from the tropics, I'm equipped to tolerate immense heat, but the winters during my childhood were the most unbearable times for me. From a respectable distance away you could hear the chatter of my teeth and the knocking together of my bony knees. My playtime haunt was usually the girls' toilets, but it was also the favourite patrol of the monitors. So, you'd find me gliding like a ghost up to higher and higher levels of the school to escape being evicted out into the grey and frost of the playground. Secreted away, I'd huddle with a good book, absorbing the belching heat of those old-fashioned cast iron radiators till I heard the wonderful peals of the end-of-play bell; whilst in senior school the warm book-lined library became my adopted place of refuge. I never minded my isolation from the other children, particularly as personal space was another one of my things. When anyone entered my invisible cordon, my nervous system would register trespass with an overwhelming sense of that person's presence and a flood of self-consciousness. A quick scan of their eyes would tell me whether they were genuine, dangerous, friend or foe – and that ability to discern is mostly still the case today. As for the frequency I emit myself, for many years my children would yelp whenever I touched them, or they touched me, recoiling from the electric shocks they received. Growing up wasn't easy in my oversensitive, overcharged, inner space. Yet, I have found that people seem drawn to me. Strangers, especially, are often compelled to sidle into my company and confess lifelong secrets unknown to their own family and loved ones. The first time I noticed this was when a careworn 30-year-old mother of four young children shared her entire life story with me. I remember being baffled as to why an adult would want to confide her sadness, her innermost yearnings, with me, a shy, unworldly schoolgirl. Perhaps, despite my unworldliness, people were drawn to me because, even then, I was deeply aware of a secret about the universe apparently hidden from most. It is a secret contained in a single magical word defined as:

> *capable of becoming; latent excellence; ability that may or may not be developed; qualities that could lead to future success or usefulness: inherent capacity for growth or coming into being; hold the seeds of movement, change, hope and possibility.*

Nine letters spell the word *'Potential'*: When potential expresses itself in our lives it is like a giant arising from a deep slumber, yawning and stretching to full height. It signposts our own potency lying in wait for us; a stronger, brighter personal future that we are not yet able to imagine. We read the word most clearly in the wonder etched in children's faces: the look of discovery and delight when they are presented with a thing or a concept for the very first time. The word focuses not just on what we *are*, but on our *becoming*. As a child I was always a silent believer in life's possibilities. Then, as now, I continue to trust that wherever I am in life, there is *more*, that my being-ness is forever unfolding. When I encounter adults who have lost sight of everyday magic and awe, who are in a state of uncertainty but ready to take the next courageous step, I am always happy to lend support and guidance. It was inevitable when I discovered my gift of healing and remembered my connection to the invisible world of *potentiality* that I would want to share my knowledge. One Sunday each month I host a small gathering of women to do just this. We play with concepts of energy and learn energetic techniques that open us up to the unseen universe. The women who come are images of myself some years ago when yearning, searching and seeking took the form of emotional and physical pain. There was something out there, calling to me, but as I didn't yet know its name I was often frustrated for reasons I struggled to articulate. It now delights me to be able to save others from years of stumbling in the dark; to introduce women to fellow seekers of the *Light*; to enable a group to recognise the oneness of our combined experience; to reassure soul-searchers that our pain comes from the ache of limbs reaching for the highest branches of our own true potential.

Four years ago, no sooner had I settled down in the specially created mezzanine den in my top floor bedroom than I heard my young daughter shouting that my first guest had arrived. I cursed myself for losing track of time while running around the house plumping up cushions, lighting incense, displaying crystals, preparing break-time snacks, lining up inspirational music CDs and printing last-minute revisions to hand-outs. Now there was no opportunity for the meditation that I'd planned to calm my nerves before the influx of visitors to my first ever meetup. My stomach began tightening and my palms started to prickle with tiny beads of sweat. I called out that I was coming, and breathed heavily as I uncurled from my sitting position and headed for the top of the stairs. Each step would be taking me deeper into my fears. Though I'd tapped on my nervousness the night before, I felt a sudden rush of adrenaline coursing through me and my heart racing. I couldn't have been better prepared for danger had there been a Bengali tiger prancing on the Welcome mat below. Halfway down, an image flashed before me:

My brother's wedding reception. During a second's lull in the speech-making, I've leapt out of my chair to add my little-sister contribution – but my nerves let me down: my brain deserts me and my head is a complete void. I look down the long decorated table at the rows of eyes staring at me. In the silence of expectation, I'm in the headlights of cold terror. Words eventually, thankfully, tumble out of my mouth. However, I don't recognise them. They are a mixed-up babble of incoherence, during which I hear myself refer to my brother as "my sister"!

Another memory speeds in front of that one:

I'm in a hotel conference room. I'm standing beside the flipchart with the office secretary, Kerry. Kerry finds it difficult to hold eye contact, she stutters and blushes deep red for the least thing. I'm hiding my own feelings of anxiety and vulnerability. The two shy girls of the company are about to deliver a presentation at this internal meeting. Besides terror, I'm also fuming at the injustice of it all – being forced to perform to a team of assured consultants who do this sort of thing standing on their heads, for which they are paid handsomely by the hour. The embarrassing thing is, the office secretary's performance surpasses my own. My surprise of being outed as last in class wells into a sense of public shame and humiliation.

Other memories flooded into my consciousness. Turning down appearing on *The Word*. My disastrous interview with Jenni Murray on *Woman's Hour*. When did this fear of limelight and audiences (I appear to be the exact opposite of my actress daughter) first come to dominate my adult life? I wondered. It was too late to consider the thought. My first guest, someone I had never met before, was in the hall staring up at me. As the seven other guests arrived one after the other, I was assailed by a knee-quaking wave of irrational mental what-ifs. *What if they don't like me? What if they criticise me? What if they judge me? What if they ask a question I'm not qualified to answer? What if my demonstration of energy transmission falls flat? What if no one is impressed with the subtle sensations they feel in their body? What if everyone feels nothing? What if they think the afternoon is a waste of their time? What-if-what-if-what-if...*

I ploughed on through my nerves, delivering my presentation, all the while wading through the smelly brown stuff. There were, however, surprising moments when I sensed myself uplifted by an unknown force. During those magical moments, I was confident enough to emerge from behind my sheaf of notes, daring enough to consider that perhaps I wasn't so bad, that this was something, given enough practice, I might even excel at. The mist of fearful anticipation slowly cleared and I discerned the reality of the situation – the attentiveness of my audience, eagerly absorbing the information that I was sharing; and during the interactive exercises there was laughter and camaraderie, my instructions received with a mixture of absorption and wonder. I recalled a snippet of information that one of the NML consultants once shared with me: this seasoned presenter found a small audience of intimates far more challenging than a full auditorium of strangers. The memory was reassuring. Finally, I was slipping into my stride, able to convince myself that I was doing just great, all things considered. By the end of the session, when the last person had (reluctantly) waved goodbye, I collapsed, as wrung out as if I'd run a half-marathon, and fell into an unconscious sleep. When I emerged, the entire afternoon seemed like a dream that had passed. I was elated that I'd got through it, and congratulated myself for feeling the fear of my worst nightmare, and doing it anyway. That's when the most overriding memory decided to make its appearance:

My first year at A-level college. Sociology class. There's a discussion about the recent black youth uprisings in UK inner cities. I blithely express my view – after all, there is no right or wrong in a personal opinion. I make a statement about the criminality of young blacks disgracing themselves in public. Michael Henry, fearfully politically astute, an angry young man for whom I'm no match, cuts me to the quick with his counter argument. My small-world take on black people is shown up for what it is – devoid of historical context or political analysis. I am still standing, surrounded by my peers and out of my depth. I had no idea I was so green, so ignorant of important issues. I feel foolish, exposed, an outcast.

This detailed recall was a revelation. I was recognising the moment I had felt the sting of shame and made an unconscious decision to travel through life with my head bowed; to take my father's unspoken advice to not draw attention to myself; to accept that lifting one's head above the parapet would only risk exposure and failure. I tapped various pressure points on my face, body and hands as that old memory resurfaced as fresh emotions, materialising as a painful knot in my throat. After tapping out the feelings of shame, embarrassment and fear, I re-imagined the scene:

Instead of shrinking and lowering myself into my seat, I walk calmly to the head of the class. I assert my entitlement to voice my own opinions, whether people agree with them or not. I don't have to be right, or clever. I just have to be ME. I feel strong, confident. I'm looking everyone defiantly in the eyes, including Michael.

I tapped until I was free of the anxieties and fear that accompanied that deep, visceral and powerful memory. My throat relaxed and the lump completely dissolved. The experience illustrated the point perfectly: wherever there is pain is where you will find the opportunity to access the *Light* and personal freedom. Going into the wounds of the past is how we bring about profound healing.

When you last paid a visit to your doctor about a particular ailment, perhaps you asked the question, "Why me? Why now?" Your health professional may have shrugged their shoulders in response and put your condition down to 'one of those things'. In contrast, when you come to me – whether your issue is related to the mental, emotional, physical or spiritual – I demand an answer to those seemingly impossible questions. I want to know not just *how* you are experiencing your symptoms, but *why* the organism of your body created those symptoms in the first place. I want to know what real or perceived fears have caused your individual cells to respond in such a way as to kick-start a whole-body survival operation. I want to know at what point your subconscious decided to write that particular protection programme. I want to know what triggers in the environment are alerting your body to continue activating that programme. For there are no accidents when it comes to the fine workings of our own physiology. Writing off mysteries of disease or discomfort as fluke or bad luck is merely an acknowledgement of our current state of ignorance surrounding the facts of who and what we are. This desire to get to the root of your problem will lead me to ask the same opening question as your health practitioner: when did the pain/discomfort/issue first arise? At this point I will delve deeper with the following enquiries: can you remember any life events around or just before this time? What feelings or emotions were you experiencing during this event? When was the very first time in your life you experienced these same feelings or emotions? Tell me *that* story. For ill health and chronic pain begins with the story of how every part of us vibrates with energy, and how these vibrations are translated into information that the body receives moment-by-moment, as programme instructions.

Sometimes the person will not remember exact details of their story – especially when a trauma happened at a very early age. But, that's not too important. Even if the experience occurred during the client's pre-verbal years, I have techniques for lifting the information from where it is held, deep in the subconscious. We are accustomed to thinking that our brain is the most powerful repository for memory. It is not. Every experience we have ever had can be located in the body at a cellular level. This explains why when you taste something that you thought you were consuming for the first time, your senses flood with déjà vu. This is the reaction of your cells recalling the information. Here's another example. If you were too young to remember the parent who abandoned you, should you chance to meet up again you might experience a deep intuitive familiarity – the cells 're-membering'. Each cell in our body contains all of our inner and outer-worldly impressions. The unconscious, however, will only finally *release* the *cellular memory* when the associated issues are resolved, and the subconscious perceives it as safe to do so.

Have you noticed how when you enter a crowded room you are immediately aware of who in that room you either feel drawn to or repelled by? You are picking up on individual vibrations. We all vibrate – every infinitesimal part of us. We vibrate at different frequencies, at different times, and our vibration changes according to our thoughts, moods and emotions. Our frequencies contain information about what we are thinking, feeling or experiencing at any given moment. We can actually detect our own vibrations. For example, when we are happy and joyous, we are light and energetic and talk about 'feeling high' – this is when we are vibrating at a high frequency. When we are vibrating at lower frequencies, we feel lacking in energy, heavy, depressed, and talk about 'feeling low'. Have you also noticed how you react to spaces, places or things – whether someone's home, a local park or an antique brooch – with a similar discernment of either good or bad vibes? This is because everything in the universe also vibrates at its own frequencies – the chair you are sitting on, the floor beneath your feet, that teacup, pencil sharpener, a blade of grass, the moon, sun, stars. In terms of energy we are no different to everything that surrounds us. With the palm of my hand I can detect those almost imperceptible movements and oscillations that surround our body, what we call the *aura*. When there is a problem in the physical body I am able to pick up from the aura (electromagnetic field) a variety of subtle and not-so-subtle sensations, ranging from dragging, to stickiness, to intense heat, prickling, and actual pain in my palms. By contrast, when the aura is healthy and flowing, it is like running my hand through the ripples of cool, clear water. I am able to do this, and so can you. We are all God-given this ability. There is an entire spectrum of frequencies that surround us in the universe – some of these we detect as colour, sound, smell, taste or touch. It is a matter of training ourselves to be still enough, sensitive enough, to identify the invisible frequencies that lie outside the bandwidth of our normal, everyday, taken-for-granted range.

An ex-lawyer came to see me about insomnia and feeling frustrated, lost and confused. Though Molly loved being a mother and looking after her three preschool children, there was a part of her that felt lacking in purpose. When I scanned her body I noticed that there was quite a lot of interference around her Throat chakra – our communication channel. I sensed that Molly's purpose lay in the area of expressing herself publicly, and that something was preventing this. During a visualisation exercise, I asked Molly to imagine herself seated in the front row among a packed audience at the Royal Albert Hall. The presenter on stage calls out her name and invites her to give a short presentation on what it's like to be a stay-at-home mum. Immediately, Molly's body stiffened. When I asked what she was feeling, she said tense and panicky, as much as 8 out of 10.

This reaction was an exact emotional replay of an incident that happened to Molly when she was 11 years old. This is the cellular memory that surfaced during the subsequent healing process: *Molly is about to take part in a ballet performance. She forgets her moves and freezes in terror on stage in front of the audience.* The root of the crisis actually occurred a few moments before, behind the curtains, when little Molly was among the other happy, excited children about to enter the stage. As adult Molly recalled this part of the memory, she surprised herself by bursting into tears, saying she'd felt alone, panicky, vulnerable and desperately needing the reassuring presence of her parents who were among the audience. This deeply buried memory had everything to do with what was going on in Molly's life, 27 years later. At that moment, behind the curtains, Molly's subconscious had created a survival programme that, from that moment on, would scan the environment for any situations that echoed this traumatic event. Upon detection, it would pull the plug each time Molly approached the 'danger zone'. For example, in order to keep her safe, to quash any possibility of her re-experiencing the original panic, vulnerability and exposure, whenever Molly began considering possibilities for her own future, the activation of this automatic defence would trigger unconscious acts of self-sabotage (falling ill, having an accident, being late, getting distracted, becoming confused, etc). Though Molly consciously wanted to get ahead, she wasn't allowing herself to risk opening the door upon her dreams due to the power of those unresolved unconscious fears. Allied to this, those feelings of frustration were the result of Molly denying the life force of her own creativity. During the healing I asked Molly to run the old 'movie' several times until the connection between the memory and her body's automatic reaction had been broken. At the end of the session, despite lying beneath three blankets, and despite having arrived feeling hot and flustered, Molly commented on how very cold she had become – a sure sign that her vibration had changed from dense, low frequencies to a higher, more life-supporting vibration.

Within a couple of *days*, Molly's life started settling into place when the perfect job combining her professional qualifications, unique personal qualities and recent life experiences unexpectedly fell into her lap! Shortly following on from that, she found herself spearheading a neighbourhood organisation that involved speaking in public and to the media. A total about-turn!

Whether we realise it or not, when we think a particular thought, our cells vibrate according to that thought. Instinctively, we know that neutral thoughts promote peace, well-being, good vibrations. It makes sense that living in the neutral present brings us greater serenity than dreading the future or mulling over the past: fearing what we *think* will happen or what we *remember* happening. When we fully inhabit a single moment, there is no fear in that moment. Even our perception of pain can be altered to an interesting fleeting sensation in the moment. Whereas ruminating on regrets and would-have/should-have/could-have-beens; or running imaginary what-if scenarios or anticipating what might possibly happen tomorrow can cause us anguish, pain and suffering. What's more, a fearful thought results in a lower, denser vibration, contracting the physical body on many levels – from the microscopic (blood vessels, neurons, muscle fibre) to the macro (muscle groups, tendons, joints). Hence, the headache, the stiff neck, the stomach cramp, the heartburn, the lump in the throat, etc. Over time, these contractions lead to disease and painful conditions such as arthritis, backache, tendonitis, ulcers, tumours. Whether we do it consciously or unconsciously, when we think a thought that transports us into future anxiety or past fear, we are alerting our hindbrain. This reptilian part of the brain exists to scan the environment for danger, ready to take necessary action to ensure our survival. Interestingly, the hindbrain doesn't make a distinction between what is real or what is merely a thought or memory. So, the *sight* of an actual spider and the *thought* of a spider will cause the same anxiety and panic in an arachnophobe. Both sight and thought activate the fight/flight/freeze response, also known as the *stress response*. When we experience trauma we encode the memory of that trauma in our cells. Until that memory is resolved, multiple triggers in the environment (a certain colour, texture, sound, taste, person, feeling, event, etc) can activate this cellular memory at any time, causing the body to go into involuntary stress. Chemicals such as adrenaline, glucose and cortisol flood the body, affecting our breathing, our thinking capacity and our heart rate, whilst our muscles become primed to flee real or imagined danger.

When a person comes to me I talk to them about their history whilst scanning their aura. I can sense how their vibration changes when they call up a particular thought or memory. As the person hits upon a distressing or unresolved area of the past or future in pictures or images, I can feel the static or interference in their 'field'. What they are experiencing and what I am reading is the stress response being activated – as if, instead of a visual replay, the trauma were actually happening in that moment. In other words, years after the original trauma, the old stress programme is still active. Why? Because at the moment of trauma we weren't able, or allowed, to talk about it, cry about it, understand it, acknowledge it, be forgiven for it. And neither does the trauma have to be as huge as physical, emotional or sexual abuse; it can be as benign as that first stern look in our normally loving parents' eyes[20] that we interpreted in that moment as utter rejection, that caused a stab in the heart at a time when we were too young to rationalise and move on from the experience. I am able to clear this interference with my open hand (often in combination with tapping various pressure points) whilst simultaneously raising that person's vibration to a higher frequency. The result is that when that person thinks that thought or raises that image again, their cells have been retrained to respond at this new higher frequency and their nervous/hormonal system reacts in a completely different way – calmed rather than stressed. When that person then goes out into the world the usual triggers cease to activate their stress response. Now that their cells are no longer in constant fight/flight/freeze their body is able to return to its normal functions of growth, healing, repair and maintenance. It makes total sense, doesn't it? Without resolving the underlying cause of our symptoms – recurring thoughts that keep us locked into survival mode and low energetic frequencies – our body cannot achieve optimal health.

Tom, an actor, complained of muscle strain in both arms after overdoing it at the gym a few days before. He described the pain as intense (7 on a 0–10 scale). Conventionally the arms would require several days rest for the muscles to relax and repair the damage. It seemed like quite a straightforward issue, and I began by scanning both his arms with the palm of my right hand. Immediately I could feel the prickly heat of interference in this area of his aura. I focused my intention to connect with, and direct, the universal energy that surrounds us all. Soon the pain noticeably reduced in both arms. With a simple physical trauma, this was the result I expected, but then something curious happened. The pain flared up again, in just the left arm. A stress response had been activated, indicating an unresolved story connected with this part of his body. Using the digging and probing techniques of energy psychology, I discovered that Tom had suffered a trauma (broken bone) to this left arm when he was 8 years old. The resurfacing story involved a family member and was a painful memory, both physically and emotionally. I asked Tom repeatedly to retell the story as I simultaneously calmed the stress response. When the suppressed shock of the decades-old story had left his arm, so did the pain. Completely. Tom was astounded. He said that during the healing he could feel waves of energy coursing through his body and described the session as: "Amazing."

Because everything in the universe is energy, healing works on objects, too. This was my Facebook status quite recently:

I almost can't believe this! A few weeks ago my iPad would not charge, no matter what I or my son did to it. I decided to project healing energy into it, even though my daughter thought I was being daft. Bingo! My iPad came to life and has been working ever since. But, of course, that could have been a fluke, right? No such thing as 'healing energy', right? Listen to this... A couple of days ago the indicator on my cold laser started jumping all over the place. This meant that it was un-programmable – i.e. non-functioning. I switched it on and off for varying lengths of time, but still the same crazy jumping. I started to panic, realising I'd have to send it off to the US manufacturers, that it would take time and money to repair it and, worst of all, my unique programmes would be wiped. I caught myself spiralling downwards and sternly gave myself a talking to. I'm a healer! I can do this! So, again, I projected healing rays into the laser. Bingo! It stopped jumping and started working! My family had been super-impressed with the iPad but this time, their response to my excited yelping was, "Yeah, we know. You already did it with the iPad. Old news. Yawn. Yawn." That really got me. The way anyone could regard something so miraculous in this humdrum way. But, then again, I know that 'magic' and 'miracles' (the subject of my forthcoming book) are nothing more than unexplored territories in the outer reaches of our everyday reality. Anyhow, on with this incredible story...

Yesterday, I remembered that my friend's laser was languishing in my front room. Unable to charge, it was totally inoperable and I had offered to arrange for it to be shipped to the States for repair, but due to complications too boring to go into, several months later it was still with me, no solution for its repair in sight. I thought – Hmm. Why not? So, last night I did the usual energy transmission and... dead, dead, dead. Disappointed, I went to bed, wondering about the unpre- dictability of the universe. But just now, about an hour ago, I had the idea that perhaps the reason why the healing/repair hadn't worked might be due to my slight resistance/lack of motivation to putting in the 'effort' because, after all, the laser belongs to my friend and not me (sorry, Sarah!). So, before attempting the healing again, I worked on neutralising or removing this unconscious resistance – in much the same way that I work on my clients' physical and emotional issues. Well, ladies and gentlemen... Voila! ... I believe these photos speak for themselves! [I uploaded photos of the laser, fully charged and beaming ultra-violet rays.]

Several months later, my iPad is still working; my laser has gone back to jumping all over the place; Sarah's laser is still functioning, but not optimally. The mysteries of the universe continue to fascinate and elude my understanding!

Chapter 10

Flow

Be like water making its way through cracks. Do not be assertive, but adjust to the object, and you shall find a way round or through it. If nothing within you stays rigid, outward things will disclose themselves.
Bruce Lee

It was snowing heavily. I could have been warmly tucked up in bed on that early Sunday morning, but I was braving the weather, about to rejoin a group of four hundred people in a hotel near Holborn for Day 2 of a wealth creation programme. Among entrepreneurs, small business owners, coaches and sole practitioners, I was hoping to learn a winning formula to help boost my earning capabilities. Day 1 had been interesting enough, but within the first few hours of Day 2 doubts had begun forming in my mind about the boot-camp type atmosphere, the tough-talking, self-styled guru, and the fawning drill of his followers. Dotted in among the audience, after every other statement their multimillionaire prophet uttered they would eject from their seats and punctuate the point with a loud single handclap followed by a *"Fuck, yes!"* By the afternoon, despite being surrounded by a sea of wide-eyed participants glued to the every word of this charismatic motivator, I had reached the conclusion that I was staring at Emperor's clothing. Whilst our man paced the aisles my concentration began to wane. My thoughts drifted towards the guru's self-professed wealth. More specifically, the ways in which I'd use that wealth, were it mine, to transform the world in my unique way; how, instead of fashioning mini-me-millionaires, I'd make a radical difference to poor, suffering children; how I'd play my part in opening hearts and minds to the world that exists beyond the illusion of pain and struggle; how I'd dedicate time and energy towards making spirituality accessible, everyday, and *fun!*

The increased volume of our man's voice broke through my daydreaming. I was looking down at polished black shoes on the carpeted floor. He had paused to stand in front of me. I held my breath, convinced that my inattentiveness had been rumbled and I would now be made an example of. Short in stature, our facilitator's voice boomed to encompass the entire lecture room as his next words peppered me in the gut.

Are you telling me that if you had the cure for cancer you'd still be sitting here, in this room? If you had that much belief, that much knowledge, that much power, why wouldn't you be out there, running up and down the street, shouting about it?

I felt my stomach lurch and my heart race. When I looked around, heads were nodding thoughtfully, people waking up to a realisation that they lacked total conviction in their own brands, products and services – so, why the surprise that the world and its riches wasn't beating a path to their door? But no one seemed to be winded in quite the way that I was. As our business prophet clicked his shiny heels and paced along the row, I reached for my notepad and began scribbling. How had it never occurred to me before? From my scores of testimonials, I quickly listed those of my clients who were facing the world's greatest health fear – cancer:

- *Chenelle* – 2 sessions: Suspicious breast lump 'disappeared'.
- *Robert* – 4 sessions: Prostate cancer. PSA levels drastically decreased – no need for the operation.
- *Steven* – 10+ sessions: Glioblastoma (brain cancer), tumour gone, reduced to fluid.
- *Elaine* – 10+ sessions: Lung cancer, given 6–12 months to

live. Tumour disappeared completely. Reappeared several months later, much smaller mass.
- *Sam* – 1 session: Terminal ovarian cancer… at the point of dying. Suddenly talking/eating/drinking/walking.

Are you telling me that if you had the cure for cancer you'd still be sitting here, in this room? I had a moment where I shot out of my body to the other side of the conference room and saw myself sitting there, small and insignificant, bristling with the dirty secret of those hastily written notes resting on my lap. The gauntlet had been thrown down for no other person in the room but me, so it seemed. Was I delusional about my abilities, or crazy for not standing up and announcing them? Would the audience be any less in awe of my journey than the story of this man and his luxury cars and fabulous homes in many countries? If he woke up the next day and discovered that he could detect invisible energetic forces in the ether, that he could manipulate those forces to transform living molecules and affect health and healing – was there a chance he would impress himself? *"Fuck, yes!"* This was my moment. That had been my cue. But the urge to raise my hand was swamped by a fearful instinct to remain silent and seated. Who was I kidding?

I recounted my cancer 'miracles'. It wasn't difficult to explain away each one of the apparent 'healings' that had taken place. Chenelle's breast lump had been significant enough for her GP to refer her to an oncologist. After two sessions with me, yes, the lump seemed to have come to the surface, and had then disappeared. But what if her GP's diagnosis of malignancy had been wrong in the first place? And Robert, though his PSA levels had indeed decreased to the point where his prostate operation had been considered no longer necessary, a year later he died suddenly and unexpectedly of a heart attack. The same was true of Sam. She may have 'miraculously' recovered to the point of leaving her hospital bed to return home, but she too was no longer around to sing my praises. As for Steven and Elaine's tumours dramatically going into remission, it's quite possible that their improvement had nothing to do with me. In addition to receiving healing, they had both undergone extensive chemotherapy treatment.[21] Also, both their tumours later reappeared. Steven, sadly, died 2.5 years after his diagnosis, 18 months after his first session with me. Elaine followed, also passing 2.5 years after her diagnosis, and 2 years 2 months after her first session with me.

A few years ago when I was relatively new to healing, my younger daughter was experiencing difficulties concentrating on her work at school and her older sister suggested that I take her to a clinic in Central London to see a consultant clinical psychologist, an eminent scientist of 40+ years who specialises in the field of 'neuropsychophysiology'. Dr Parkinson's procedure involves attaching electrodes to various parts of the head that are linked to an impressive series of machines that measure the activity of the cerebral cortex. The conclusion of the tests was that my daughter was deemed to have a 'bright brain' and strong levels of lo-beta, associated with 'good academic performance'. However, she also displayed an excessive slow and fast wave brain pattern that prevented her from showing her potential. As I watched the bar charts build and collapse and the lines of coloured frequencies stretch and concertina on the multiple machine monitors, a thought occurred to me.

I explained to the eminent doctor that I was a healer and that it might be interesting to see whether I could affect my daughter's brain wave patterns in any way. This suggestion obviously appealed to Dr Parkinson's scientific mind. She adjusted the machine dials and studied the screen with interest as I placed my hand either side of my daughter's head and 'played' with the electromagnetism of her aura. Soon the display of lines and charts were moving in various directions. After a thoughtful pause, Dr Parkinson explained that I was indeed having a positive effect on my daughter's brain wave patterns. I was amazed, but also a little disappointed by the low-key delivery of the doctor's verdict. She seemed unfazed by what had just happened (perhaps she was accustomed to healers turning up and making this kind of request). She later described the outcome of our little experiment to my older daughter, adding that she had her doubts that the healing benefits my younger daughter had received would 'hold'. Nevertheless, for me, this was real confirmation that whatever was emanating from the palms of my hands was having an actual effect in the physical world.

I returned my attention to our guru. His promise was that he could make each and every one of us a millionaire – if we believed in him enough; if we were sufficiently determined to adopt his business model; follow his ten infallible steps; invest a few thousand pounds in his programme. Yet so far, in his attempts to convince, he'd said nothing I hadn't heard many times over from multiple sources. As a mere audience member, I may have lacked his Aussie millions, but I could at least claim many satisfied clients to attest to my own credentials. So, why wasn't I the one up there, addressing my own audience? Of course I knew why. It had everything to do with that huge wall that I had erected between myself and the image of myself. Unlike me, this fearless 5-foot motivator had constructed a giant public persona on the basis of pumping his self-worth to the multitudes. His passionate self-belief had earned him every part of his success. I, on the other hand, couldn't convince even myself of my own accomplishments. Had my track record included indisputable cures among my cancer clients, I would still be searching for a way to discredit that proof. No wonder I was afraid to stand up, to rise to the challenge of publicly claiming my worth. This time it had nothing to do with being shy. After so many years, despite the many incredible results, despite the evidence of Dr Parkinson's machines, despite the personal gratitude of scores of people relieved of pain and suffering, despite the verifiable case studies and mostly unsolicited testimonials, I was still struggling to decide whether or not I deserved to be *Great*. My mind began to take me on a long journey into the past, a version of my life flashing before me. I remembered those earlier times when it wasn't always like this, when I was accustomed to chasing success on shimmering waves of anticipation and excitement; when doubts played a minor role in my determination to work long and hard towards a single goal; when every defeat was translated as necessary lessons to be learned on the fast-track to victory. I was broadcasting my *intention* to be a winner, and the universe was mirroring that intent right back at me...

... When I co-established Hi-Time as a vehicle to promote my early stage work, in no sense could I have been described as a theatregoer. On the other hand, the two talented people with whom I had teamed up, one a lighting designer and the other a director, were creative graduates who lived and breathed theatre. But it soon became apparent to me that though my partners knew so much more than I – they also arguably knew too much. We had meagre resources to establish a theatre company, which meant that begging, borrowing and scrounging favours would be the order of the day. I was up for that. Pumped and ready to do whatever it took, I once decided to contact a well-known actress to ask whether she would take the lead in one of my plays, unpaid, of course. I was pulled up by my partners. No way could this lady be approached in such a direct manner, I was told, there was a certain protocol to observe. What was I thinking? At first I flinched from what I took to be the chastising, even mocking tones of my partners, and was stung by my own youthful exuberance and naivety. But I soon saw the folly of blindly accepting 'the way things are', and my attitude became fixed. I didn't want to hear another thing about 'the rules'. What was the use in being knowledgeable about restrictions if that knowledge prevented one from getting exactly what one wanted? From that moment, I made a conscious decision to disregard the status quo of the theatre world and continue operating in semi-ignorance. I was in my flow and, the way I saw it, obstacles were simply tests to judge how badly one wanted to succeed. The actress in question turned down my offer of little or no money in return for her professional services. However, she did feature in some of my later work and became, and still remains, a firm friend.

A couple of years later, I was working on my sitcom, *Us Girls*. The experience was truly a baptism by fire, and throughout I encountered a succession of seemingly insurmountable problems. From developing story ideas, to writing the scripts, to casting the actors, to the actual filming of the episodes, each step of the way was fraught with issues and difficulties that I could never have conceived, being totally new to all aspects of working in the media. And the challenges, far from letting up after the first series when we disastrously had to release our lead actress, only grew. Whilst writing Series 2, I was still holding down a part-time job at NML, and it was during this time my daughter underwent major surgery that included a week in intensive care. Without ever having formally learned the art and technique of writing, I had few resources to fall back on. I was struggling, flying by the seat of my pants, near breaking point. Somehow, though, with some help from the writer Sharon Foster, I managed to survive the immense stress of the situation and get all six scripts to completion. At the BBC rehearsal facilities in North Acton, beyond exhausted, I realised that I could not sustain the intense method of working I'd grown accustomed to. That's when the phone rang. It was my agent. I heard the bubble of excitement in her voice as she enquired whether I was sitting down. Pausing for a dramatic millisecond, she spilled the surprise news that she'd secured me a gig on a national soap! This was big news indeed. *Us Girls II* was coming to an end and there had been no suggestion of another series. The experience had been amazing: being a valuable contributor at the BBC; the publicity around the series; the invitations to do's where I could mingle with the likes of Dawn French, Lenny Henry, Richard Curtis and the best-selling crime novelist, Martina Cole, but there were no assurances that my 15 minutes of fame would continue. And here I was being offered writer's heaven on a plate. A soap would mean regular work, financial security and a national profile. My answer was instantaneous.

"No. I'm not ready," I told my agent.

To her flabbergasted ears it must have sounded like career suicide. And who could blame her if she did think this? She hadn't been privy to my eye-opening discovery during the painful process of the sitcom that I knew zilch about TV writing, and even less about the industry. As my agent was no doubt picking herself up off the floor, I was already looking ahead to all the essential reading, courses and workshops in which I would need to immerse myself. Far from shrinking from the incredible news or suffering from a lack of self-belief, I was choosing a longer path that would ultimately lead to becoming a mature and professional writer. It somehow never entered my consciousness that the offer could not be repeated or that I should fear losing it. And sure enough, six months later, after my journey into the worlds of acclaimed scriptwriting masters such as Syd Field, Jurgen Wolffe and Robert McKee, the universe returned to knock once more on my door. That magical earth-angel script editor, Heather Peace, having switched genres from sitcoms to soaps, popped up again. Would I like to attend a meeting to discuss the possibility of becoming a regular soap writer, she asked. This time there was no hesitation. "Yes!" I shrieked, as though this was a first-time-ever proposal. And so began my long-term tenure on the programme, during which time it became apparent that the groundwork I had laid by committing to studying my craft ensured my own survival in the sink-or-swim waters of the soap-writing world. If I had leapt at the earlier opportunity purely out of fear, I'm certain I would have lasted no more than one or two episodes – the fate of numerous writers who came on board, many of them professionals from radio and the stage. As it was, I held the position of team writer for ten respectable years.

After that dynamic decade, however, the soap world was behind me and I found myself cut off not only from my scriptwriting colleagues, but from a significant source of income. Around another ten years later, following a long period of bewilderment, ups and downs and financial struggle, no one was more surprised than I when my path led me to becoming an established healer. Over time, I acquired a website, various practitioner accreditations, a steadily increasing client list, a meetup group, amazing testimonials, and the ability to speak to small groups. But I had once again reached an impasse in my life. There was a feeling of dissatisfaction, a distinct *knowing* that I was being called to take the plunge into something far deeper. I wasn't afraid, just defeated by not being able to determine that next step. That's what I kept telling myself, as I remained in a stuck place, rigid with uncertainty. Something was about to give – and it did, in a single unannounced moment. From carrying on with life as normal, I was suddenly unable to stand, sit, kneel, crouch, step or lie down without triggering a bout of excruciating seizures in my lower back. An X-ray diagnosed degeneration of the lumbar 5: ankylosing spondylitis. A crippling back condition would be devastating news for anyone, but it was especially so for me, someone who had become very proficient at depending on No. 1. I was a do-er, a giver, and less frequently a receiver. Now I was being forced into a position of depending on everyone around me, for everything. I had no choice but to relax my belief that no one could do any of it exactly like me, and to surrender to the unbelievably generous assistance I was being offered – from being dressed, to being driven, to being shopped and cooked for, to sympathetic company, to even being helped across the road. Accepting 24/7 help was a strange and uncomfortable first experience for me, like using a muscle that I'd forgotten I had been born with. Through lack of use that muscle had become stiff, deoxygenated, self-conscious and painful to move. In my powerless state I was to make two discoveries about myself: 1) behind my bold declarations of self-sufficiency I harboured a quaking hidden fear; 2) there was a lesson to be learned that had been showing up time and time again in my life. With my head down, existing, surviving, I hadn't been able to see any of this. Now the scales, very slowly, were beginning to fall from my eyes.

The hospital prescribed painkillers, anti-inflammatories and bed rest. I failed to see how this strategy alone would address the long-term problem of a degenerating spinal disc, so I sought and tried many healers. But none could help and, the pain being so great, neither could I help myself with self-healing. Then, through my friend Nathalie, I discovered Iwin, a wise and wonderfully talented Chinese acupuncturist. She explained that I'd accumulated an excess of cold energy (*chi*) as a result of failing to protect myself from the negative energies of my clients. As someone for whom healing had arrived as an intuitive force and not something I'd studied, I had never learned the rituals of self-protection. Neither did I necessarily believe in them. Iwin, however, a healer herself, advised that these rituals were essential if I wasn't to deplete my own energies and expose myself to problems. I began to see that she might be right – in a way. Though I still don't subscribe to the idea of 'fear-based' protection, Iwin opened my eyes to the fearful way in which I was viewing the world. In order to maintain the amazing results and glowing client testimonials I'd been getting, I had indeed become accustomed to using reserves of my own energy. Later, with hindsight, it would become apparent that an underlying trust issue was causing me to try too hard, believing that unless I gave *everything* to every client, I would fail each time. Once, feeling personally responsible, I worked on a client for *four* long hours and didn't stop until her painfully curled arthritic fingers were able to uncurl free of pain. Though I was witnessing its magic every day through each miraculous healing, I was distrusting that the same abundant flow of universal energy that surrounds and supports us all could also be a reflection of the effortlessness, the boundlessness, the magnificence of my own true power. The truth was, despite achieving incredible personal change, I was resisting my fullest potential, and my lower back was bearing the brunt. No wonder the alternative therapists I contacted were unable to help me.

One day I got in touch with a guy with a reputation for being a healer and EFT practitioner. The constant pain I was suffering was pointing to my 'stuckness' and I needed someone experienced enough to help guide me through my own wilful unconscious denial. This much I knew. My therapeutic saviour, Arram Kong, turned up. But rather than take my hand to tap my acupressure points, he instructed me to "just lie there" as he searched in a purple bag and brought out a newfangled light machine. My first reaction was annoyance. I had booked a specific therapy and I was in so much agony I wasn't in the mood to be experimented upon. But the surprise was on me. Several minutes after the device was placed on my adrenals, I released an unexpected and spontaneous sigh. In no time I noticed my breathing becoming deeper, more regular. I could feel my entire body gently lengthening... unwinding... relaxing. I even started to drift off a little, forgetting my constant vigil for the incessant pain. Half an hour later, I was able to ease myself off the massage couch with barely any assistance and walk around the room, pain-free for the first time in two solid weeks of agony. The pain-mask I'd been wearing cracked as I broke into a smile of utter disbelief. Cold laser technology had entered my life – and its timing could not have been more perfect. The next day, however, like a punch in the lower back, the pain returned in full. But I knew that something amazing had happened and I made the instant decision to buy my own laser. Armed with this laser, I got into the habit of using it each day to sink into *zero-point*, the infinite, electromagnetic field that surrounds and permeates everything. We express this field as the point of 'no thought': when we witness events without feelings or emotions, detached from outcome, being entirely in the moment, resonating with our Highest Essence. Zero-point felt like a delicious sea of calm and tranquillity that allowed me to float above all the minor everyday undercurrents of disappointment, annoyance and irritation, and to go with the *flow* of life. It was this *flow* that became my healing force. From this place I was able to *allow* the process of self-repair.

Forgiveness and acceptance of the past played an important part, including mentally releasing that 13-year-old from her vow of isolation and fierce independence in her perception of being unsupported. Yes, that old onion of my motherless childhood was peeling away yet another liberating layer of onion skin. Despite the numerous opportunities being presented to me (the ultimate was meeting Robert during this period and refusing his help), the lesson that I was failing to recognise was this: in life there are many chances to receive, to accept support, and one must be gracious and open to them. If we are blind to that support, we also become blind to the blessings and joys of life that are everyday and in everything. Resentment, blame and judgement then start creeping into our way of seeing things. Eventually, these unserving emotions settle as subtle cellular contractions in the body, depriving that particular area of oxygen and life-giving energy. Over the years, as more disappointments are experienced, attracted by a restricted way of viewing the world, these energy-sapping emotions gradually weaken that targeted (vulnerable) part of our body – in my case, my lower back. The writer and publisher Louise Hay (*Heal Your Body / You Can Heal Your Life*) has taught us that the body constantly speaks to us through discomfort, pain and disease, in the language of metaphors. So, for example, communication and self-expression issues manifest in the throat; feelings of over-responsibility and burden settle in the shoulders; anger issues and suppression of bile relates to problems with the liver and gall bladder; a perception of lack of support (particularly financial) manifests in the lower back, and so on. My stubborn, crippling back condition had indeed been speaking to me, directing me to address the fact that I was still playing small by distrusting the one infinite source of support – the universe. The pain of ankylosing spondylitis finally forced me to unbend and go in the direction of flow, at which point, thankfully, my disc issue finally resolved. Today I am pain-free and have never had a recurrence of those agonising symptoms.

Richard complained of having had a back pain for the past few days. It was a muscular discomfort in the middle of his back towards the right. When I scanned his field (*aura*) I detected interference, not in the back area, but in the region of his right shoulder. He was organising a charity event at the time, and he'd shared how he was feeling burdened by the responsibility. I asked him to concentrate on the back pain and let me know the very first image that floated to his mind. What he saw was an image of himself rushing around, against the clock, frantically attempting to get everything done. Immediately he winced from a flare-up of the pain. At the same time as he had been describing the image, I was sensing in my right palm the interference that was being directly generated by his thoughts. It took less than ten minutes of 'clearing' movements with my hand to change the vibration of his electromagnetic field from a dense lower frequency to a higher frequency. When he got up, the back pain had completely gone.

... I came back to the present, sitting among the wealth creation audience. It was so clear to me. I had fallen into the habit of denying my own greatness, forgetting the lessons of my journey. Unless I returned to acceptance and ease, the same, or another, part of my body would again start 'speaking' to me. When I got home I was still mulling over these thoughts when I became drawn to the vision board that hangs on my kitchen wall. I'd created it about nine months earlier to illustrate the points I would be making at one of my women's meetups. A vision board is both a visual representation and reminder of your wishes, your *intentions* for the future. There are no rules when creating something like this. It can be in the form of a scrapbook or even a shoebox to which, over time, you add your collection of magazine or newspaper clippings – whatever focuses your *intent*. Mine is a framed A3 with a selection of miniaturised Google images arranged in an artistic fashion. The resulting collage represents the three main areas of my intended future life: healing, writing and travelling. So, for example, among the many images there is one of a stack of published books; the notice for a book launch; people lining up for a book signing event; a comedy script; a gleaming writing award; and a 'Comedy Show' sign. There is also a picture of a healing room; a hotel suite that has the look of a healing space; a group of people at a conference; a charity organisation's happy, smiling children. Then there is a picture of a soaring plane; a luxurious first-class flight cabin; scenes from locations in Australia, New Orleans and along the Italian coast. I used to visit the board regularly to remind myself of how my life was flowing, but I had since grown out of the habit. Now was the time to return to the belief that it was within my power to create my own world. Soon after reacquainting myself with the board and paying it regular attention, I attended a Healing Codes workshop and woke up the very next morning with the idea and contents for an *entire* book on the subject of the cold laser technology I had recently discovered. Though it took a further few months to take that first hastily scribbled but detailed outline to final draft, that initial spark of inspiration eventually manifested into what has become a steadily selling self-publication on Amazon.[22]

At the workshop the lovely facilitator Halina Hampson asked the audience for a volunteer, someone with an emotional or physical issue. I'm usually quite reticent in such settings, but this time my hand shot up. Even so, someone raised theirs before me. But it was obviously meant to be, as I was the one chosen. I sat in the hot seat and referred to my residual back pain. Halina was clearly about to eject me for another delegate as my discomfort of 2 out of 10 was hardly worth the bother. I quickly added that the emotional reaction to the pain, i.e. frustration, was a high 8. Satisfied with this, Halina asked me to enter my heart and see what image came up. I saw an illuminated road. It instantly occurred to me that the symbol signified my journey. The road was empty – and I was meant to be on it! A great sadness suddenly filled my heart (Halina, a psychic, said she saw thorns around my heart). After the healing I tried to bring up the original sad feeling associated with the image but there was nothing. I felt light and energetic, and the pain in my back seemed to have gone. When I sat down and crossed my leg I noticed that there wasn't the usual accompanying hip ache.

Since that time when I was reacquainted with my vision board, I have had the enormous privilege of travelling first-class return to Australia where I stayed in Sydney for several days before travelling on to Byron Bay on the Gold Coast. There, I visited the quirky, hippy town of Nimbin and posed for a photograph in the exact same location that is an image on my board! Some months later, by an incredible fluke (though we know by now that there is no such thing) I spoke with a neighbour and through a serendipitous series of events ended up submitting a shelved comedy script to the long-established forum, *Player-Playwrights*, founded by *Birds of a Feather* writers Maurice Gran and Laurence Marks. My script was enacted by a team of professional actors in front of an audience, and several months later I was presented with the organisation's *Comedy Writer of the Year* award. During the summer of 2013, a young lady visiting the UK from LA had a healing session with me and subsequently told me that the experience was so powerful it had transformed her life. Her elated testimonial led to a trip to California where I gave healing to a number of her show business acquaintances, and where I stayed in a West Hollywood hotel suite, complete with treatment couch. Later still in the year, I had the privilege of going on a surprise all-expenses-paid trip to the Italian island of Capri where I made friends with two gutsy young ladies, one American, one French. Some weeks later, the couple visited our family in London and attended one of my meetups. The outcome of that visit is that I have an open invitation to visit *New Orleans* as both a houseguest and to run a women's workshop. These two ladies' connections to a global charity also led to my being invited to Cannes to deliver a healing process during a World Peace Night sponsored by the Michael Jackson Family Foundation. At the airport I was picked up in a stretch limo and shared a ride with Joe Jackson to the Radisson Blu Hotel where I also met Mandla Mandela (Mandela's grandson and tribal successor) who, over breakfast, shared jokes and showed me photos of his recent trip to Kenya. Then came the little miracle of this book in your hands being accepted for publication...

There are many other pictures on my vision board symbolising my future intentions (such as the one of Oprah Winfrey, whom I seriously intend to meet in person one day – *there's* big of me!), but I mention the specific examples above because *every single one* of my aspirations represented by those various cut/paste Google images manifested in reality soon after I began to take notice of the board. How amazing is that? Sure, events haven't always materialised exactly the way I imagined (filming of a YouTube series based on my comedy script took off wonderfully then foundered, though who knows where this little venture will eventually take me?), but they have often blossomed in other bountiful ways that I could never have possibly foreseen (I overcame my resistance to a neighbour who seemed 'too much like hard work', and it resulted in the most beautiful impactful friendship, three months before his sudden and tragic death). This is what happens when we stop denying our value to the world and quit opposing what is here for us. Convincing ourselves that we are unworthy, comparing ourselves unfavourably to others, blaming ourselves, doubting our abilities, and giving in to impatience and feelings of failure are some of the ways in which we create a constant state of struggle that keeps us separate and unfulfilled. Whatever it is we are resisting in ourselves (*'I'm too X'*; *'I'm not Y enough'*) will only persist the more we feed it with our attention. After energy, our human form is composed mostly of water. These two elements – energy and water – represent the essence of the human spirit – freedom and motion. When we fall into the rhythm and flow of the universe, we come into harmony with, and acceptance of, our own inimitable being. We start to recognise and appreciate that in this *entire* world, actually, there is only one mould bearing our impression; there is not a *single* person on this planet with the capability of making our unique contribution. For this reason alone, you might want to consider trusting that the magical currents of life, with all their ebbs and dips and crashing waves, will eventually take you to the level of your highest – the reason why you are here, after all.

In the following *Allowing Handbook* I share some of my magical tools and techniques. However deeply you find yourself wading through the turgid brown stuff, these resources are designed to assist you in allowing the flow of miracles into your every-second and your everyday.

Chapter 11

Homecoming

We are all just walking each other Home.
Ram Dass

I have attended far too many funerals recently, sitting in the back pews of cold stone churches listening to grieving friends and relatives pouring out their hearts in remembrance of their loved ones. For those of us who are left behind, it is the easiest thing in the world to see through the blemished character of that person who once lived, to the deep inner sanctum of their soul. Laid to rest are the usual criticisms, judgements, disappointments that would have clouded our vision and compassion were the departed still with us. With their passing, we are finally liberated to salute and appreciate unconditionally the divinity, the preciousness of a single life, however imperfectly it may have been lived. In the radiant passage of grief we recognise that no one is called to be superhuman; no one is responsible for single-handedly saving the world or another person. Our sole task is to shine our light, however dim or faltering, so that others by example may learn to shine theirs. Together, in this way, we all help to illuminate the path, in particular the darkest corners of our fears and suffering. At our journey's end those who knew us when we walked among them understand that no life is too insignificant, too unpardonable, to be showered with forgiveness and acceptance.

So why wait for the solemn occasion of a eulogy reading? Why not express gratitude to those who, at this very moment, are touching and transforming our homecoming, sometimes without even their own awareness, sometimes with no more intervention than their mere presence? Why not honour them, now, with the knowledge of their contribution to our existence, a gift that may inspire their own light to glow even brighter? This chapter is my own living acknowledgement of those on this earthly plane to whom I am forever indebted for my life of spiritual growth; to my angels and soul family members, who have all played and continue to play their part beautifully in assisting me on my homeward journey.

Donald Davies – who gifted me with my first spiritual book and ignited a passion that has sustained me ever since. When I lost that precious out-of-print copy I didn't rest until I tracked down a hard-to-find, second-hand replacement. That's how dear it is to me, as are you, generous and valued friend. *Thank you.*

Dr John Nicholson – who supported me in so many unimagined ways during my early years of self-discovery, and who extended my education by teaching me the value of taking no prisoners in the rugged pursuit of personal excellence. *Thank you.*

Vyanne Hanlan – whose bravery, courage and fighting spirit has shown me what it is to be a warrior and a seeker in the most divine sense. Keep well, keep going, stay blessed, and *Thank you.*

Newton and **Tarrant** – for graduating, despite the odds, from that School of Hard Knocks with your hard-won successes; and for finding the time, through small acts of kindness and recognition, to prove to me that you still care. *Thank you.*

Jasmine – for going before me and cushioning my landing in this once-bewildering world and whose flawless sacrifices enabled me to achieve success and become the person that I am today. You are precious and will one day realise your full worth. *Thank you.*

Joely – who saw me before I saw her and chose me; and whose love continually tests that underdeveloped part of me that needs to forgive more, relax more, criticise less. *Thank you.*

Maxwell – whose beauty and joyous energy is there to remind us all that life is the best excuse for a party, to live fully without hesitation, apology or regret. *Thank you.*

Naomie – who was born a Buddha, a shining example, and whose grace continually throws a light on my human imperfections in order that I might remember who I am yet to Become. *Thank you.*

Richard – my soulmate, my defender, my love, who helped me to rediscover trust and who introduced me to the beauty and stillness in nature. You were waiting for me long before I ever found you. *Thank you.*

And to those teachers, mentors and guides whose inspiration caused this book to explode into being. There are many, but especially:

Oprah Winfrey – my early role model, my separated-at-birth big sister. You stole so many of my working hours, and I loved you for it. *Thank you.*

Kirtana and **Deva Premal** – your music still touches my soul with its magic, its call to that place within us that feels like home. *Thank you.*

Anthony Robbins – your juice, your energy, your passion blessed me in those moments when hope was not so bountiful. *Thank you.*

Brandon Bays – you brought my attention to my 'just-in-case' suitcase. Through you, I learned that there's no better time to open it up and to flaunt its contents, all of it, right here, right now. *Thank you.*

This list does not exclude all the other countless and unnamed beautiful souls who have walked into, beside, and passed through my life (you know who you are); the many of you who are continuing to support and nourish me with friendship, laughter, kind words, delicious cake, and by just being there. The roll call of names and deeds of kindness would fill the pages of another entire book, I am that blessed. I love and am in gratitude to you all, dear friends and companions new and old.

I apologise to those I've judged harshly in the past. You, too, are walking home and entitled to your wonderful barefooted journey through this, the time of your life.

If you cannot do Great things, do small things in a Great way.
Napoleon Hill

Has my story inspired you? I hope so. I hope it has moved you in such a way that you will begin looking at your own narrative as one worth telling. I hope you will realise that your journey in becoming who you are today is no less heroic than the journey of a 5-year-old child squeezing an overripe banana in excited antic-ipation of a dream to come. Whether you acknowledge this fact or not, you and I were born heroes. We came into this world perfect, seeing perfection through perfect eyes. Yet as we travelled along rocky roads, often choked with thorny growth, we began to lose sight of our own completeness. Perhaps the particular impasse on your journey was the unforgettable pain of your parents' divorce. Or, maybe it was the birth of your baby brother or sister that caused you to believe you were no longer special or wanted. Or maybe the veil of darkness fell when you were abused by a trusted adult. No matter what the experience, when we are robbed of the *Light*, too young to know that we can still reach for it and reignite it again in our hearts, we are the same lost soul, fearing for our own survival. Whatever the story that has brought you here today, reading these words, it is a story about your quest to regain what has never left you. I am here to tell you that even in your deepest, darkest moments, the spark was never extinguished. You just didn't know how to trust deep enough that you were not alone. Until we wake up, that is our human prerogative – to make the mistake of believing that our individual stories set us apart. Blinded by the details, we fail to see that each and every one of us recounts the same tales of forgetfulness, the same dreams of remembering; dreams in which we have the power to be anything, do anything, become anyone. Dreams that prompt us to recall that we are here, not as walking flesh, but as spiritual beings inhabiting a human experience. Trapped inside the pain, the limitations and the illusion of this human body, it's easy to forget who and what we truly are. We are *Light* itself. The magic of *Light*.

Months before I was due to try my luck submitting the opening chapters of this book to various publishers, I admitted to my dear friend Hetty that I felt like a fraud. I was convinced that there was at least one last big turning on my road that I needed to take in order to justify proclaiming this memoir. I was looking at all the boxes still to be ticked on my life's journey: I wasn't a major player on the healing circuit; I certainly wasn't earning the money associated with being a renowned healer; I couldn't command a huge audience that might want to listen to anything I'd have to say; I wasn't travelling the world helping the children I so desperately wanted to make a difference to; I hadn't set up *Space-for-Grace*, that healing/spiritual community I had so long envisioned; I was pretty much invisible and unheard of to the majority of people on this planet. I can still hear Hetty Larkai's broken shriek over the iPhone as it lost, then regained, its signal.

"How much more proof do you *need*, Carmen?"

This was her reaction after I had told her about my latest healing success. Her outright indignation on my behalf caused me to jolt upright, to take notice of the message contained in this very book: *Wake up! You are in your own magnificence, right Here, right Now!*

Testimonial:

On Friday in the cold and dark early hours of the morning, I slowly made my way to the Urgent Care Centre at the Whittington Hospital. Since Wednesday I had been slowly losing the mobility in my right arm, the pain becoming more and more unbearable. Having hardly slept and in a fit of tears and desperation, I decided that I needed to seek medical help. A couple of hours later, I left the Whittington with a considerable amount of very strong painkillers and a diagnosis. I had been told that I had a 'Frozen Shoulder', something that could happen to anyone at any time. It sounded so harmless but meant that I was going to spend the next month in excruciating pain and with no more than 30 degrees of movement in my right hand and that I could expect stiffness in the arm for the foreseeable future (and possibly the need for an operation). I was told to head home by the doctor, that I could do nothing more than rest, ice the shoulder, keep it elevated and take the painkillers I had been prescribed. How was I going to be able to work and live with this diagnosis?

After explaining the diagnosis and expected recovery to Carmen, a determined look came over her face: "Months," she said and shook her head. Carmen treated me for two sessions and advised me to tap on the pain myself in between. It sounds so simple when I write it down but the last 36 hours have shown me that there is so much more to healing than conventional medicine. I started the first session by hardly being able to move my arm, I was in constant pain and, though I was hiding it, absolutely terrified of what this diagnosis meant for me. Even knowing that Carmen had helped so many people I was still sceptical: what if this doesn't work for me? At the end of the second session, as I lifted my arm up towards the ceiling, I could have cried with joy. Instead, the biggest smile broke out over my face. In just over 24 hours I had gone from hopeless to hope-filled.

I have not only been healed by Carmen but I have been given a gift: the knowledge and belief that I can heal myself. To me that is a priceless thing. I go forward from this knowing that Carmen will be there should I need her, but that I now have the tools to continue this voyage of healing. That the emotional baggage I carry, that the aches and pains I experience are not just something I have to live with. That for me and for you there is a different way of life out there, if you can find the courage to find and take it. So starts my new journey: to stop smoking and more importantly to not let my life be ruled by my fears. B.T.

[a few days later...] *My arm is wonderful and that is the complete truth. The residual soreness has now almost completely gone. I have full movement and no twinges at all. I am still in complete awe, to be honest.*

So, I end this chapter of my life with no apologies at all. Witnessing my mother's pain and anguish at an early age was the perfect catalyst that brought me to an understanding of my purpose on this earth. It is to help alleviate the pain and suffering of others – on whatever level that may be, whether mental, emotional, physical or spiritual – by pointing the way towards the *Light*. Whilst living my purpose, I am not perfect. There is more work to be done, for sure. And, yes, there is every chance that tomorrow I may wake up and, yet again, mistake this enticing illusion for reality. But I promise you, that state won't last for very long. When you've come this far into the journey, there's absolutely no appeal in returning to the shadows. For there will always be someone awakened by my story; there will always be another's story (perhaps your own) to jog me back into alignment. And that is all it will take for me, once again, to meet the magic of the day shouting into the *Light*, *"I am magnificent! I am magnificent, just as I Am!"*

And so are you, too. Please don't forget that.

In memory of **Kevin Thomas McKellar**. During the brief span of our friendship you were a breathtaking shining example of unflawed, unconditional love. For that alone, *I Thank You.*

> *God may not be there when you want him, but he is always on time.*
> **Terrell Owens**

Part II

Life starts to change for the better when you realise you just might be wrong about everything.
Prince Ea

This Handbook is infused with Love and Magic.
Bask in both.

Sh*t Happens, Magic Follows

Allowing Handbook

Introduction

And the day came when the risk to remain tight in a bud was more painful than the risk it took to blossom.
Anais Nin

Be still. Notice what you are feeling. Notice where in the body you are feeling that feeling. Is it a welcome feeling? Is it comfortable? Benign? Does it support who and what you are in this moment? Or does the feeling disturb your peace? Does it trip you up? Cause you to question your worth in this world? Is it difficult to remember the last time you felt light, happy, *connected*?

Life. It happens to all of us, no exceptions – when, in truth, it could actually happen *for* us. I am a healer, and I like to think of myself as awakened, but that doesn't make me superhuman or infallible to the snares and traps of this existence. Each morning I still remind myself that it is up to me to choose how I perceive or respond to any situation; that it is always possible to rise above it all; that I can refuse to buy into the illusion that this (this pain; this idea; this situation; this belief) is all there is. But I'm human. Sometimes I forget, sometimes I'm caught up in the day before I've had a chance to think my first thought. In large part, this is my reason for writing this book, to document a reminder of the immense power that we all possess. For these are the important facts of our life that we must never forget: We are a product of our conditioning. We view life through the filter of this conditioning. But this conditioning that causes the feelings that we experience in the mind and body – pleasant or unpleasant, welcome or unwelcome – is *not* who we are. This conditioning is often the dam, the brake, the roadblock, that prevents us from recognising and claiming the magic just beyond our immediate reach that is here for us in every moment, should we choose to stretch towards it. When the brown stuff hits the proverbial fan, it's entirely our own prerogative to decide what to do next. We can either respond the way we are accustomed to responding – left-brain leading, problem-solving, defending, denying, protecting, guarding, shrinking, fearing, giving up. Or we can clear the sleep from our eyes and recognise the substance on that fan for what it really is – an unexpected opportunity, a calling to start afresh, to find a new footing on a completely different path; to look beyond the standard formula for happiness and welcome the magic that will elevate us to our next level.

This Handbook is a summary of the major teachings that I have gathered and developed on my long journey signposted towards enlightenment and freedom. Each one of these powerful tools, tips and techniques will help you to shift your perspective and change your response the next time you come up against a hard place. Remember: you can either remain a reactive being in what you choose to see as a harsh environment, battling your way through the odds stacked against you with fists, flesh and brawn; or you can surrender to the assistance of universal magic that exists to guide us gently back to growth, happiness, peace and hope.

How To Use This Handbook:
I have already lost touch with a couple of people I used to be.
Joan Didion

- Read from beginning to end, before returning to the beginning again. There is a lot of information and many different concepts to absorb, some of which may be entirely new to you.
- You will notice that the first part of this Handbook contains what I regard as the sixteen magical elements of this universe (*Magic!*). These fundamentals can positively

transform your perception of the outer world and bring peace and harmony to your inner existence.

- In the second part of this Handbook I have listed seventeen different scenarios – particular issues (*The Brown Stuff*) that may resonate with where you are today. Within each of the different sections you will find tips and techniques that are designed to help you shift or resolve your difficulties. There are also indicators to return to the first half of the Handbook where you will be reminded of the magic elements that exist to rescue you from the brown stuff and transform your life.

- Reread those sections that cause you the most resistance. Give yourself permission to try any of the associated exercises with an open mind.

- Spend as much time as you *need* with each section. It may take you an hour, a day, a week to fully absorb, digest and action a particular exercise. In many cases you will be overcoming strong resistance to ingrained thoughts, beliefs and habits. Give yourself all the space and time your mental processes demand to learn this new emotional language. *Don't rush!*

- Consider this Handbook as a wise and non-judgemental companion. It's easy to become weighed down by life's problems and to forget that each of us has the ability to shift ourselves out of a helpless or hopeless state into another more beneficial state. During such times, this Handbook will be a faithful friend to remind you of your magic, your true power, and to guide you in the direction of personal freedom.

- You will discover that every problem you perceive as unique to you is, in fact, interrelated with everyone you know. As exceptional as we each are, we are all part of the *One*. By the same token, the solutions available to us are interconnected with the same magical values of peace,

love, compassion, truth, harmony, openness, understanding, acceptance and forgiveness. You will discover
these themes throughout this Handbook.

Magic!

Brown Stuff

Here Comes The... *Magic!*

Energy

Everything in life is vibration.
Albert Einstein

Magic is energy. Energy is a magical force. It is all around us and permeates everyone and everything. Energy was present long before the universe ever existed. Energy cannot be defined, it cannot be created and it can never be destroyed. Call it *Chi*, *Prana*, *Ki*, *Holy Spirit*, *Life Force*... Energy is who and what we are, from this life, to the next, and the next.

Feeling Energy: Stop for a moment. Be patient and relaxed. Rub your hands briskly together for half a minute or so. Now, hold them a hand's span apart, palms-facing. Close your eyes. Engage your senses. Notice what you notice. Do you sense a little pressure between your palms? Some tingling, maybe? Electricity, perhaps? Resistance? Heat? Tension? Heaviness? Play with the space between your palms by slowly and gently pulling your hands apart and drawing them closer together, without touching. The sensations you are feeling are *subtle energy*. Depending on your sensitivity, you will feel this energy to a greater or lesser extent.

Connecting With Energy: Adopt the habit, the moment you wake up, of spending just 3 minutes making the *intention* to connect with the energy around you. Sit upright and open your palms. Fall into the rhythm of your breath. Consider the infinite power of the universe that surrounds you. Give yourself permission to make-believe. Imagine taking a USB and plugging yourself into the portal of the universe. Feel the subtle tingle of energy in your field.

Sixth Sense

The world is full of magic things, patiently waiting for our senses to grow sharper.
WB Yeats

Our brain, via our five physical senses (sight, hearing, touch, smell, taste), collects information about the external world to construct the reality that surrounds us. Were we to fully exploit these five basic senses, however, we would discover that there is a world beyond; that the creation of magic is possible, not through the logical processes of thinking, analysing and rationalising, but by accessing the inner, metaphysical and higher dimensions[23] of our mysterious, though no less real sixth sense. We would come to realise that we somehow know things without knowing how we know. How? Well, just like invisible radio waves, extra information is being broadcast to us all the time in the form of subtle frequencies. When we learn the art of being *still*, in the moment, and relax our five physical senses with the *intention* of tuning into what comes, we are able to connect to the world of the unseen, unheard and unfelt of the magical dimension. There is a welcome familiarity about this world that, contrary to superstition and some religions, is not at all frightening or weird. How could it be? It's where we come from. It's where we will return to. It's our *Source*. Our origin.

I was once the back passenger in a car. Sitting in the front was Dr Eric Pearl, the world-renowned healer (that's a whole other story!). I was suddenly captivated by the most unusual smell that at first I thought had wafted in through the open window. I was about to comment, but then decided to keep quiet as I was surprised and confused by the experience. It's not often you encounter a smell that you cannot identify. The closest I can come to describing it, even after all this time, is the scent of the colour purple. I now believe that that perfume was emanating from the spirit world and that it had something to do with Dr Pearl.

I've also mentioned before that numerous clients of mine have commented on the scent of flowers during their sessions. These are examples of clairalience. The very first time I visited the healer Seka Nikolic and instantly and absolutely knew that healing was an ability that we are all capable of, I was in the realm of claircognizance. My clairsentience is my most developed sixth sense; I seem to be able to read all manner of information in a person and in their field.

The Subconscious

The mind. A beautiful servant. A dangerous master.
Osho

Our subconscious is watching over us 24/7, regulating all our automatic bodily functions that keep us alive such as our breathing and the beating of our hearts. It stores all our beliefs, memories of the past and impressions of the world around us; as well as controlling our emotions (to the point where we feel emotions – anxiety, fear, shame – we wouldn't voluntarily choose to feel). Even during sleep and in our dreams, our subconscious continues weaving information and meaning into our lives. While the subconscious is the *operating system* that the conscious mind is not fully aware of, the unconscious can be likened to a heavily fortressed invisible vault from which our *guardian*, the subconscious, has the power to withdraw protected (forgotten, repressed, denied) information to present to the conscious mind, but only when it considers it safe to do so.

The conscious mind is under the illusion that it is running the show. But it is only when conscious decisions are backed by the subconscious that our commands are unquestioningly executed as though our existence depended upon it. Our subconscious secretly holds the majority of our beliefs about the world – most of which we inherited in childhood from parents, educators, peers, the church, the media and life's direct experiences. Many of us do not question most of our taken-for-granted beliefs, and the subconscious will *act* on anything and everything, whether or not our belief makes sense (a house spider is as life threatening as a tarantula); whether the situation before us is real (an actual spider); or imagined (thought of a spider). Our beliefs are directly responsible for our general feelings (good or bad), and whatever we feel is made *physical* by our subconscious' connection to the central nervous system. So, no matter how much we try to rationalise that the picture of a spider will do us no harm, our contrary belief will cause automatic feelings of anxiety that will be expressed as, say, butterflies in the stomach.

The majority of our decision-making is driven by the subconscious, and without its agreement, it is unfeasible that the conscious mind alone will achieve our goals. However, when the subconscious and the conscious are fully aligned we become an unstoppable force in the creation of magic.

Example:
Sara is borderline obese and would (*consciously*) like to lose weight but is finding it impossible. Beneath an outward appearance of confidence she secretly suffers from anxiety. She has been controlled by a (*subconscious*) belief that it is not safe to be slim and attractive. Through therapeutic intervention Sara unearths a repressed (*unconscious*) memory of sexual abuse. During the healing session, Sara acknowledges the subconscious belief that had kept her 'safe' during childhood. Her subconscious is reprogrammed to accept that as an empowered adult it is safe to be slim and attract the attention of men. Sara's conscious mind that desires to lose

weight is now supported by the subconscious. Via the body's natural biochemical processes, the subconscious is now able to relay this slim-is-safe information to the fat cells. All of which results in a happier, slimmer Sara.

Exercise:

- Think about some of the everyday beliefs you hold – about yourself; about your life; about your country; about the world; about your place in society.
- Notice which of these beliefs make you feel either peaceful or anxious.
- How many of these beliefs are actually your own?
- How many of these beliefs are unquestioned, automatic and taken-for-granted?
- Can you attribute where some of these beliefs originally came from (parents, family, friends, teachers, religious figures, the media, etc)?
- How do you feel when you start to question some of these beliefs?
- Are there some beliefs you would like to change, but fear the consequences?
- Think of one particular belief you hold that is not serving you in life. Test this belief against these questions:
  - Does this belief make you feel peaceful or anxious?
  - Is it actually your own belief?
  - Do you know who or where this belief originally came from?
  - Would you like to change this belief?
  - What would be your new replacement belief?
  - What would be the consequence if you lived your life according to this new belief?

Seven years after the death of my mother, I was coming to a turning point, emerging from a long, dark tunnel of loss and confusion, feeling directionless, motherless. At a conscious level, I knew that I had something to offer the world, but the outer landscape seemed bleak, revealing few opportunities for improvement and self-expression. I was a simmering cauldron of frustration and resentments towards the world, whilst in every corner of what I saw as my hopeless life I was looking for visibility and validation. That loyal servant my subconscious attended to my silent pleading and produced a breast tumour, seemingly in a matter of days, to satisfy both my empty craving for nurturing and my inner desire for attention. When I recognised the immense power of my subconscious, I made a conscious decision to pay more attention to my beliefs about the world (hopelessness) and the uncomfortable feelings caused by those beliefs.

Thoughts

A man is what he thinks about all day long.
Ralph Waldo Emerson

Thoughts intrude upon us 24/7. In the day-to-day, it's impossible to stop thinking. Even when we think we are not thinking, we are thinking unconsciously. Thoughts are powerful. Just take a look around you. Everything that you are able to see, hear, touch, smell and taste began with someone projecting the thought: "I can/shall/will do that." That single *thought* led to the belief that the objective was possible/achievable. That firm *belief* provided the *energy* for action to take place. That *action* taken resulted in the thing now in your presence or possession. Every thought, every idea, finds expression in the environment as a physical *manifestation*, including our health and well-being. So, life's magic is revealed when you pay focused attention to what it is you desire and, conversely, when you practise paying no mind to what it is you don't want. We all create mental pictures all day long. If we can't help creating the thoughts that make up our mind movies, we might as well command ourselves to *choose* only those thoughts that benefit, nurture and empower. Right?

Thoughts 24/7: Spend the next 24 hours being completely aware of your inner chatter and where it leads you:

- Notice whether you dwell mostly in the past, the present or the future.
- How often do you find yourself sifting through, analysing, raking over things that happened minutes, hours, days, weeks, months, years ago – all the could-have/should-have/would-haves?
- How much time do you spend worrying about what might happen in the future – either making plans and contingencies, or feeling like a helpless victim in the face of what might come about?
- What stories do you make up about yourself? Are you under-appreciated, and undervalued? Are you lucky and successful? Are you resentful about being left behind by everyone else getting on in life and not you?

Visualisation / Imagination

I saw the angel in the marble and carved until I set him free.
Michelangelo

Pictures and images are the language of the subconscious. When we visualise something, or see with the mind's eye, the subconscious directs the physical body to respond, whether that thing actually exists in reality or not. An example is the young child whose bladder empties during a nightmare. Another example is Deepak Chopra's story of a man who, when told by his doctor that a black mark was detected on his lung, died within three weeks believing he had cancer. Later, old X-rays of this man were found. They showed that twenty years earlier the same black mark was visible on his lung.

People often confuse visualisation and imagination, and have the notion that what they 'see' behind closed eyes has to be as clear as real life or as vivid as a dream, otherwise they are not achieving either. This is not the case. We are all capable of visualising: we do it every day, thinking ahead, planning, recalling memories, remembering what something looked, tasted, felt, smelt or sounded like. While *visualisation* is retrieving, receiving and detecting information that is already known and present, *imagination* inhabits the world of our make-believe. It takes visualisation one creative step further where we modify, fashion, rearrange, and alter available information into something that doesn't already exist. We can all *visualise* a red apple. We can also *imagine* a blue apple with white spots. Children happily inhabit these realms and, for this reason, some of us wrongly believe that we may have outgrown this ability.

In order to manifest what it is we desire, we first have to put an image of that thing on to our mental screen so that our servant, the subconscious, can act upon it. It's no different to building a house or aiming for a particular destination. Without a plan or drawing of the house; without a detailed map of the journey, we are bound to get lost, confused, reach the wrong address or fail to achieve our objective. When we visualise we are instructing our subconscious with the shape of our desire, the details of our goal. In order to get there, we must first have an idea of where 'there' is.

Front Door Exercise:
- Imagine that you have been asked to describe, in full detail, what your front door looks like. Include information about the construction and fabric of the door: height, width, whether wood, glass, plastic, etc; the colour; any panels or glass panes; the position of the bell or knocker; any visible dents or scratches; whether there is a

number or not, and whether that number is painted, metal, or otherwise, etc.

- Now imagine a different door – one that might appeal to an 8-foot giant with colourful and garish tastes. Describe it in a similarly detailed way to above. Employ your other senses and notice, for example, the *sound* of the door when rapped, whether it is solid or hollow-sounding; the *smell* of the door, perhaps it's fresh paint or it's pineapple(!) scented; the *feel* of the door, whether its texture is smooth, rough or even wavy.

- Were you able to do that? *Visualisation* is nothing more than retrieving information. *Imagination* is simply allowing the mind to play with information in whatever fashion that takes your fancy. No rules apply!

Michael had severely damaged his back in a tragic and unfortunate accident. After eighteen years of struggling with his painful condition, he came to see me. I wanted to find out what subconscious images were triggering his stress response and preventing his body's natural healing. During the visualisation, the scene I expected to arise was the day a grown man had tackled him to the ground, breaking his back. Instead, he recalled his recent MRI scan – the moment he saw the actual devastation of his spine and realised that there was no hope. This resonated with me, as a few years earlier I had been diagnosed with ankylosing spondylitis[24] and I too had been distressed by the sight of the X-rays that showed a disintegrating spinal disc, a bleak prognosis for my future health. In order to begin my own journey of self-healing, I first had to work on erasing the frightening image from my mind. In a similar way, I worked with my client, using visualisation to replace the image of crushed vertebrae with the image of a strong spine and healthy discs. After one session, he said he felt much lighter, and he even managed the stairs to the bathroom without his crutches. There was much more work to be done, for sure, but this subconscious image was the first major stumbling block to him recovering his health. No amount of therapy would succeed if his subconscious was aligned with the image of an irretrievably damaged spine, powerfully suggesting that healing was an impossibility. After only two sessions he noticed such a dramatic difference in his mental outlook, he posted a lengthy and effusive testimonial on Facebook. Excerpt below:

"Carmen clearly has a gift in enabling me/you and many others to release and actually feel the 'bad' energy leave the body. It is incredibly emotional and painful but a blessing and a cleansing of the body's energy... It was the size of a loaf of bread and I felt it reduce to a ball and eventually disappear. It's a bit personal to tell you this bit but it's how it was. It felt like a cold rush over my body centralised into a huge loaf-sized pain at my stomach that basically felt like it was flowing out my ass if I'm honest. Man that feels like it should be embarrassing to say. A breeze of bad energy flowed out my ass. There ya go. Michael Knight"

Intention / Conviction

Be careful what you wish for, it might come true.

Making an intention gives us possession of the magical key to the universe. When we pair intention with conviction we now have the power to use that key to unlock the door to the palace of our dreams. Intention states what it is we *want*; but intention/conviction asserts what it is we are about to *get*. We convince ourselves. We hold an expectation. We have total faith in a particular outcome – regardless of all evidence to the contrary. The moment these two potent mental forces make an alliance you are all set to lift one foot out of the mucky brown stuff. In no time, you are stepping, gathering motion. Motion creates energy / *is* energy. Energy creates matter / *is* matter. Matter is your new reality borne out of intention. But be careful where you place your focus. Be careful what you wish for. The intention/conviction combo is in effect a turbo-charged thought or wish and, as with the consequences of loose thoughts, we must be wary of unintended intentions.

Frame Your Intentions:
In the positive and affirmative:

- *"My shoulder feels relaxed and supple"* rather than *"I no longer want this pain in my body"*
- *"I am the correct weight for my height"* rather than *"I am not a size 20 any more"*
- *"I am confident and ready for this interview"* rather than *"I can't afford to fail this interview"*
- *"I am healthy and whole"* rather than *"I don't want to be sick any longer"*

Why? The mind translates words into images. In the second examples above, the images that the brain will understand are "pain", "size 20", "fail" and "sick". These images will become embedded as instructions for more of the same, as the subconscious cannot interpret "no longer", "not", "can't" or "don't" into images. What you think about, comes about. So, focus on what you want.

In the present tense:

- *"I am healthy"* rather than *"I will be healthy"*
- *"I am slim and energetic"* rather than *"I am going to be slim and energetic"*
- *"I am in the perfect relationship"* rather than *"One day my perfect partner will come into my life"*

Clear, simple language goes directly to the subconscious for the creation of powerful images that can be translated into reality.

The most powerful manifesting command is 'I Am', suggesting to the subconscious that your desire has already been achieved.

*As a young child my client, **R**, fiercely intended to 'punish' her unkind parents by wishing illness upon herself. In her young mind she imagined that being ill would result in her mother and father being tormented by guilt. Her subconscious loyally implemented this order by efficiently creating a mind-body programme. It wasn't until years later, during our session, that my client made the connection between this powerful early intention and her own body turning against itself in an unrelenting autoimmune cycle of ailments and disorders.*

*When **Robert** developed prostate cancer, during one of our sessions I helped him to connect with his subconscious to find out why he had the 'need' to manifest this condition. His subconscious came back with a one-word reply: "Ambition." I had no idea what this might mean, but Robert immediately knew. This particular session was early on during his period of depression and he told me that he felt he was coming to the end of his useful life and that he needed new challenges, new difficulties to overcome in order to feel 'alive' again. In what might be regarded as bizarre logic, his subconscious had created a cancerous growth to satisfy this intention. When Robert replaced this unconscious intention with a more empowering goal, the progress of his cancer halted and regressed, and soon after he surprised himself by discovering that he had a powerful enduring passion for art!*

Perspective

The eye sees only see what the mind is prepared to comprehend.
Henri Bergson

There is a modern parable of two dogs entering a room of mirrors. When they exit the room, one leaves with his tail happily wagging while the other is whimpering, his tail between his legs. What happened? The playful one who entered the mirrored room with a fun attitude saw only pure joy in the reflection of the 'other dogs'; his companion who went in growling saw only aggression and viciousness projected back at him in the form of 'other angry dogs'.

What if the world surrounding you was totally made up and controlled according to what you believe and what you choose to see around you? If you could shift your perspective in this way, how much personal power do you think you would gain? There are countless situations in life that cause knee-jerk reactions such as anger, fear, blame, shame, embarrassment, irritation. We can't seem to help ourselves. For example, how would you react if your boss overlooked you for promotion in favour of someone below you; your neighbour wrongly accused you of scratching his car; you missed your flight to a longed-for holiday destination; you were diagnosed with a serious illness? Would it be the end of the world for you? Evidence that the gods are against you? Confirmation that you were born unlucky? When the brown stuff strikes, it's easy to say "be positive", "look on the bright side", but how do you actually do that? One empowering way of transforming the ups and downs of life is to imagine that you are both the scriptwriter and the lead actor in your own film – your *Life Movie*.

The next time something challenging happens to you, slip on your 3D **Life Movie** lens, observe your movie, and ask yourself:

- For what reason did I create this character, this situation, this conflict?
- What is my audience learning about me, the hero(ine) of

this movie?

- In what way do I need to adjust my hero(ine)'s beliefs or behaviour in order to change this particular scene or even the direction of the entire movie?

Let's put this exercise into (fictional) practice.

Scene 1: Garden: The next door's cat has dumped the brown stuff smack bang in the middle of my lovely lawn – again. I'm furious. I rant, I swear, I hop, I plot to shovel it up and chuck it over the fence on to the neighbour's organic tomato patch.

Then you remember – ahhh, Life Movie! You ask yourself, for what reason would I create: 1) a blasted cat that torments me; 2) unending conflict with the neighbours? Ahhh. Maybe it has something to do with that easy temper of yours, maybe the audience are learning how the little things in life seem to so easily tip you over the edge. Perhaps that explains yesterday's scene...

Scene 2: Doctor's Surgery (Flashback. Yesterday): I've just had my blood pressure taken. The results aren't too good. Doctor writes my regular repeat prescription and warns me that I've got to cut stress out of my life.

You think to yourself, what if my blood pressure is pointing to the cat as a symbol of my out-of-control anger issues, and how I need to take stock of my life? What if I decided to change my beliefs and behaviour? Could I alter the last scenes of this movie so that it doesn't end predictably in an escalation of neighbourly conflict, stress and unhappiness? You think, maybe you could give it a try. You've got nothing to lose except bad relations with next-door and a possible heart attack on the lawn.

Scene 3: Garden: There's crap on the lawn again. As if to mock me, the cat prances and preens at the end of the garden. I can feel my blood boiling... but I force myself to take a deep breath. On the exhale, I surrender to the idea that it's a cat I'm dealing with here! This 4-legged creature has no understanding that 'my' arbitrary patch of dirt and grass is forbidden territory. For the first time, through eyes that are not misted red with rage, I actually notice the cat – its majesty, its pride... how damn cute it is. I think to myself, maybe I could befriend it? Maybe I could see this cat as my responsibility? Maybe I could put out a litter tray? Maybe I could train this moggy to respect my prized lawn?

Scene 4: Garden (3 months later): I'm mowing the lawn, the cat snuggling up against my inner left leg. Lately, we've become best of friends. My neighbours peer over the fence bearing a little boxed gift. They've noticed how attached I've become to their little Gerald and know how much I'll miss him. What? They're moving house! I really should jump for joy, but the neighbours are right, I am actually surprisingly disappointed to hear the news. The cat's been great company and, after a while, it had even stopped relieving itself in my garden.

Scene 5: Doctor's Surgery (2 days later): I've just had the usual blood pressure check. I'm talking to my doctor about the new neighbours who have just moved in. They're non-cat owners. My doctor suggests maybe I should consider getting my own cat – all that loving and stroking seems to have had a positive effect on my blood pressure!

You realise that life was teaching you an important lesson. Don't sweat the small stuff. Anger doesn't have to be your first response to everything. There's always another way, another solution. Now that you've learned the lesson, the cat issue never again shows up in your life. How about that?

Ideas / Intuition / Problem-Solving

*Cease trying to work everything out with your minds. It will get
you nowhere. Live by intuition and inspiration and let your whole
life be Revelation.*
Eileen Caddy

Those flashbulb moments – when deeper thoughts arise that are
above the ordinary – happen to all of us, all the time. In our
normal mundane conscious state, we couldn't think up these
inspired ideas if we tried. They materialise not from the head,
but from the wisdom of the soul – that spark of the divine that
we all are. These powerful moments usually occur when we are
in a passive, drowsy, relaxed state, when our brain waves are in
the slower vibrations of alpha and theta. During this 'hypnotic'
state, the normal resistance of the conscious mind is lowered and
we are more open to internal and external influences and suggestions. Both Einstein and Mark Twain attributed their flashes of
genius to these magical interludes. Just before sleeping, Robert
Louis Stevenson would give tasks to the power of his subconscious mind (which he called "mental brownies") to create ideas
for his books: *"My brownies, God bless them – who do one-half of my
work for me when I am fast asleep, and in all human likelihood do the
rest for me as well when I am wide awake and foolishly suppose that I
do it myself."*

Those twilight moments of contemplation, meditation, and
just before sleep and upon waking, are the best times to exploit
the God-sends that help us find solutions to problems.

Before Going To Sleep...
Make the intention to:

- have a dream about your problem
- have the dream reveal the answer to your problem

- remember the dream or the solution upon waking

NB: *Have a pen and notepad handy by your bed.*

Keep a **Grace Book** for jotting down any sparkling gems of inspiration and golden nuggets of intuition that come from grace. In the jigsaw puzzle of life, you never know when these gifts might come in handy or serve your higher purpose.

Resistance / Allowing

Silence may mean acceptance or the continuation of resistance by other means.
Mason Cooley

We don't always like the circumstances we find ourselves in; we might not appreciate other people's behaviour and how they impact upon us; we may find it difficult to live with our personal flaws, weaknesses and inadequacies. When we encounter difficult situations we often react by judging, criticising, disapproving, condemning, rejecting. One emotion leads to another and before we know it we are caught up in a vortex of torment and bad feelings. We may consciously decide that we are going to ignore, evade or push away the ideas, thoughts, irritations and memories of what it is we don't like, in the belief that this is how to escape the prison of our own negative emotions. But for some reason the anguish only continues. Why?

Resisting that which we find uncomfortable in ourselves and in others only causes us to suffer, both emotionally and physically. By putting up resistance we powerfully fan the flames of our attention upon the very issue we wish to avoid, if not at a conscious level, certainly at a deeper subconscious level. Rather than disappearing, our concerns mushroom, intensify, infiltrate our mind, body and soul. So, how do we shift the clinging brown stuff?

Allowing or *surrendering* to 'what is' is the magic bullet: making the firm decision that we are not going to attempt to change, fix, or make right the situation. Acceptance of our lot may come across as a manifesto for admitting defeat or giving up but, on the contrary, the first step towards finding peace and resolution in any situation is to actively acknowledge and to take responsibility for our own resistance. The second step is to understand that there is usually a good reason why resistance is showing up in our life. By presenting to us the people, situations and things that cause friction in our everyday, the world acts as our mirror, constantly reflecting back at us what it is that requires healing in our soul. When we take this stance it's easy to accept the process of *Allowing*. In so doing, we open up our awareness to the real options available to us to end the suffering and to reclaim our personal freedom.

Take A Deep Breath

- Become present in your physical body
- Bring up an unresolved issue in your life
- Notice how the issue makes you feel
- What emotion comes up (if there is more than one, choose the strongest)?
- Notice where in your body you feel that emotion
- Rate your emotion 0–10 (10 being the worst feeling)

Close Your Eyes

- Take another deep breath
- Relax
- Take a little while focusing on your in-breath and out-breath
- Tell yourself, with conviction: *"I accept this moment; I accept it for what it is"*
- Without any judgement or desire for change, *allowing*

whatever feelings that show up, witness all aspects of your issue – the good, the bad, the indifferent

- Again, pay attention to where suffering is being expressed in your body (e.g. sore throat, backache, headache, etc)
- Observe other subtle reactions of your physical body to it witnessing your issue/situation
- Ask yourself: *"What is the lesson for me in this suffering?"*
- Without analysing or questioning, allow the thoughts on the fringes of your consciousness to emerge
- Notice your body while this is happening
- When you are ready... take another deep breath
- Open your eyes
- Notice how you are feeling emotionally. What is different? What has changed?

NB: *It may help if, while you meditate on the above, you ask someone to gently guide you through the steps.*

Finding Answers Through Your Body

Everything you'll ever need to know is within you; the secrets of the universe are imprinted on the cells of your body.
Dan Millman

How would your life change if you had a magical device that could respond with the utmost truth and integrity in every moment to questions that you want answers to? Phenomenally, right? What if I told you that you absolutely do possess such an instrument? Our *soul* holds the blueprint for why we are here and what we are here to do. The physical body is the *conduit* to the soul, able to convey the answers to questions in a binary yes/no, true/false format. Unfortunately, we have got into the habit of believing that our body is none of our business – until it is poorly, that is. And even then we have learned that we are not our own best custodians, and are in the habit of handing over our physical selves to healthcare professionals.

Our bodies *matter!* We are powerful when we listen to the language of the physical, the hotline to our soul. The communication from our soul is subtle, however, easily drowned out by the 'louder' conversations that are constantly going on around us – our internal fears and worries, other people's opinions, our conditioned perception of what is happening out there in the world, etc. But if you become still enough, you will notice that the electromagnetism (*aura*) that surrounds the body either expands or contracts depending on how 'aligned' or in truth we are with ourselves and our purpose. We sense this expansion as a peaceful, calm, relaxed sensation; whilst contraction, agitation or interference of the electromagnetic waves around us causes feelings of physical discomfort in a number of different ways.

Here's how to **Find Answers To Questions**:
- Get into a relaxed state – concentrate on your breath, become lost in stunning scenery or a beautiful sunset, cuddle a sleeping baby, stroke your furry pet, listen to calming music, whatever induces peace in your body.
- Notice the subtleties of your body in this state. What does peace feel like? Where do you feel it? In your head? Heart? Everywhere? Remember that feeling.
- Now, hear yourself firmly repeating in your mind one of the following supportive statements:
  Yes! Yes! Yes!
  Love! Love! Love!
  My name is [your name]!
- Notice how the even-ness of peace is either maintained, deepened or heightened. You may even feel some tingling or excitement.
- Now hear yourself firmly repeating in your mind one of the following non-supportive statements:

No! No! No!

Hate! Hate! Hate!

My name is [a name that is obviously not yours]!

- Notice the subtle changes to that peace in your body. You might feel heaviness, tension, agitation, butterflies, tightness, pain or discomfort in particular parts or all over your body.
- Return to calm by internally stating one of the earlier supportive statements. Feel the even-ness return.
- You now have a yes/no true/false barometer. From this state of calm find answers to questions such as: *Is this the right job for me?; Can I trust this person/situation?; Am I ready to make this move?; Is this emotion I'm feeling related to X (name the person)?* And so on. A 'yes' answer will maintain the feeling of peace; whilst a 'no' answer will cause interference in your field.

NB: Truth is always in the moment. What is true in this moment might not necessarily be true in the next hour or day or week, depending on changes in your circumstances.

NB: Also useful – look into the art of kinesiology or 'muscle testing'.

Gratitude

Trade your expectation for appreciation and the world changes instantly.

Anthony Robbins

Scarcity and lack is a state of mind. The more we feast on that state, expecting more of it through our thoughts and the things we say, the universe will grant us our wish and continue to serve up the same menu of unsupporting situations. We are an electromagnetic frequency station. The signals that we broadcast are the same signals we receive. If our thoughts and beliefs are tuned into a particular frequency, we will attract *like* frequencies. The more we tune into the frequency of love and abundance, the more we magnetise matching qualities into our lives. If we continually show appreciation for what we have, however little that may be, we are, in effect, broadcasting the frequency of abundance. No matter what your circumstances, there is always something to be grateful for, there are always blessings to be counted.

Glass Half Full

- How do you normally see the world? Is your glass half-empty or half full?
- Are you accustomed to complaining, or giving thanks?
- What is there to appreciate in your life right now?
- Who do you need to thank today? For what?
- What are the unappreciated *gifts* in the problems and challenges that you are facing?
- Find the blessings in disguise in all areas of your life – friends, family, health, finances, work. Target one person, one situation, one area at a time.
- Practise catching yourself thinking a glass-half-empty (unsupportive) thought and turning it into a glass-half-full (supportive) thought. It's been said that it takes approximately 30 days to establish a habit. Have fun practising!
- Copy Oprah's example and keep a **Gratitude Journal**. Each day write down five things you are grateful for – from the laughter of your children, to the view of your garden, to a beautiful song you've just heard, to the ripeness of a mango.

The first time I returned to Jamaica in my early 20s, I was a single-

parent university student. I had lived frugally and worked hard during the previous years in order to make the trip. I tracked down an estranged half-uncle on my mother's side. He appeared shrunken and much older than his 50+ years, the dark, care-worn folds of his leathery skin a result of the lean and tough times he'd evidently witnessed. I squirmed beneath the scrutiny of those sallow, bloodshot eyes fixed upon me, the young privileged one from England. The suffering and envy in that gaze refused to release me until I had experienced a little of the pain that it had endured. "Have you ever gone to bed on an empty stomach," my uncle's voice trembled, "knowing that the cupboard is bare and in the morning there will be nothing, nothing at all to eat?"

In that moment I felt the sharpest pang of hunger deep in the pit of my stomach. It was unimaginable to think that anything or anyone could prevent me from immediately relieving that sudden scraped-out discomfort. My options ran through my mind: I'd buy something; ask for something; borrow something; exchange something; be given something. In those ponderous seconds I confronted a glaring truth about myself: real hunger was an experience I had been spared my entire life. Hearing my uncle's despair struck a chord more visceral and compelling than any of my parents' rantings of 'starving Biafrans' when we children used to toy with the food on our plate. Since that day, I have an unconscious gratitude programme that activates each time I raise a morsel to my mouth.

I pull damp clothes out of the washing machine and I'm overcome with a flash of gratitude, remembering the Friday nights of my childhood – my mother bent double over the bathtub brimming with the week's dirty washing for a family of six. An assortment of colours submerged in cold grey water.

I'm assailed by another flash as I hold a glass tumbler beneath the gushing tap, watching it overflow with clean, clear, running water. I'm recalling the Facebook image of an emaciated Sudanese man.

He's stooped on haunches, scooping infested ditch water with the cradle of his bony hands.

Forgiveness

He that cannot forgive others breaks the bridge over which he must pass, for every man has need to be forgiven.
Thomas Fuller

Who can put their hand up and say they have never, in some degree, at some point in their lives, cheated, lied, caused pain and suffering to others? Often when we condemn another person, our psyche recognises something in that person and their actions that is a mirror of ourselves. Effectively, we are not only condemning other people's transgressions against us, at a deeper level we are having difficulty forgiving ourselves for our own wrongdoing. But there's worse.

If you have a grudge against someone, if there's unresolved conflict in a relationship, if you can't move on from a certain tense situation, how might the story of that clash affect you personally? It influences you at every level – emotionally, mentally, physically, spiritually – through anxiety, indigestion, hurt feelings, bad breath, endless thoughts, sleepless nights. The way to find relief from these damaging effects is to first forgive yourself: for holding on to the past; for being unable to let go and move on. Self-forgiveness will clear the dense energy that is keeping you in a bad place. When your thoughts, beliefs and judgements about another person are liberated, you will gain your own freedom as you finally detach from that person or situation.

- Think of a situation in your life where you are **Unable To Forgive** the other person(s).
- Notice what emotion comes up when you think of that

story – Anger? Resentment? Sadness? Futility? Shame? Hopelessness? Rejection? Etc.

- Where in the body do you 'feel' that emotion – e.g. tightness in the chest; lump in the throat; heaviness in the heart; pain in the lower back, etc.
- Be totally honest, and think of the part (even if it is only small) you may have played in the story.
- Forgive yourself totally for your part. Let go. Relax.
- Imagine how you might begin to forgive that person.
- Write a **Forgiveness Letter** – in the first person: *"I'm so sorry, I have been holding a grudge for so long... etc."*
- Sit in front of the mirror and read the letter aloud as if your reflection is the other person.
- Think of the story again.
- Notice the magic of your body transformed (you may need to read the story again, with more empathy, to heal deep feelings).

Make It Happen!

If you don't like something, change it. If you can't change it, change your attitude.
Maya Angelou

Use this process for any dream, desires or ambition that you would like to see materialise.

- Reserve some quiet time to **Imagine** the future you want. What will this future look like? What are you doing/saying? Who are you with? What can you hear/smell/taste/touch/see in this world? Imagine a perfect 24 hours in your new life, right from the moment you wake up. Keep returning to this visualisation in your meditations, during your daydreams, before going to bed, upon waking – whenever you remember. Bathe in the glow of the excitement and anticipation. *Enjoy* the process of making it up.

- Start **Planning**. Buy a notebook dedicated to designing what your dream is going to look like. *For example, my friend, an IT guy, confessed his long held dream of creating and owning an arts complex. I suggested that he might consider the following questions: what kind of performances would I like to showcase; what type of building would I be looking for; in what area; how many people would make up my team; what would my initial budget be; how much would the rent cost; what about additional expenses; what would I call the complex; what kind of logo would I design; what would my website look like?* Lose yourself in the process, really getting into all the fine details. Be as absorbed as a child at play. In this way, you are sending messages to the subconscious (remember, it doesn't know the difference) that the world you are imagining is actual, is real. It's the energy of passion, pleasure and excitement that incites magic and brings dreams into being.

- **Set Your Intention** to receive all that you have planned / are planning.

- **Then Let Go.** By doing so, acting as though our intention has already been achieved, we are demonstrating implicit trust in the universe, allowing the creative force of magic to manifest.

- Letting go does not mean *do nothing*. Continue to **Work Towards** what you want, in the knowledge that the universe will deliver to your detailed specification – or better. For example, in the case of my friend, it will mean discovering what is new and up-and-coming in the world outside of his safe, cosy front room. Nothing will materialise unless you research and activate the very things you say you want to build your life around. If you desire a new house but don't have the funds, get on an estate agent's list, actively view properties and whet your appetite with what's about to come into your life (that's what I did). *A client of mine wanted to be more sexual and in touch with her body. I suggested that she visit dress shops she would usually pass by, and try on clothes that she wouldn't normally dare to wear – fake it till you feel it.* If you want to see yourself as financially abundant, go to an expensive hotel, sit in the lobby and order whatever you can afford, even if that's just an exorbitantly priced bottle of water or cup of coffee. Get accustomed to feeling as though you belong in that environment. *When I left university I did something similar. I was unemployed, and craved a life that was full of buzz and creativity but I didn't know what that was. So I got into the habit of visiting Central London at every opportunity. I'd sit outside a cafe nursing a cup of tea, watching the world go by, pretending that I had a place among the lively hustle and bustle around me. Soon after this, I was in the world of theatre and creative writing.*

- Now, here comes the magic. Start **Noticing** those pebbles of encouragement, however small or 'insignificant', that the universe begins dropping on your path. You might see a performance that inspires you to think "that's the kind of show I'd like to showcase"; you might coincidentally bump into someone who gives you the exact information you are seeking; you might see a billboard, a TV programme or a newspaper article that echoes the world that you are aspiring to – take all of this as a sign that the universe is responding to your desires.

- **Keep Going!** Despite the weather, the daily news, global projections, your friends' cynicism, your own occasional lapses of self-belief. It is at the exact moment when you're about to give in that the universe will sweep you up and take you along your path. Sometimes the path may not be exactly the one you had in mind, but none of your original efforts would have been wasted. Everything that you have done to get to where you are will have been just perfect for your journey. Time and hindsight will show you this.

Meditation

In our stillness... we are at peace in our life. Stillness saturates us in the Presence of God.
E'yen A. Gardner

We are all familiar with the necessity for, and the benefits of physical exercise. But did you know that meditation is every bit as important for mental harmony, emotional equilibrium, and maintaining the flow of our vital energies? In stillness, the mind transcends all concepts, enabling us to embrace all of life's contradictions that would normally bring fear, confusion and insecurity. In this space there is no right, no wrong; no good, no bad; no 'shoulds' and no 'have tos'; and the body is able to nourish and renew itself.

Paradoxically, those of us who already practise meditation will know that when life becomes difficult it's all too easy to convince ourselves that we're too busy / too stressed / too panicked to meditate. This is a gentle reminder to recognise that when you're in these tense states is exactly when you most need the no-mind of meditation.

If you don't already meditate, sometimes the practice is made to sound more complicated than it is. People imagine, as I used to, that meditation is something unreachable, some divine state that takes years of mastery and the adoption of special postures. No such thing. As with any practice, you can go deeper into the more advanced levels, but the basic steps will get you to where you need to be. The most difficult requirement is persistence and commitment.*

Ten Simple Steps To Meditating

1. Wear loose clothing.
2. Find a quiet place without distractions.
3. Get into a relaxing position that suits you.
4. Close your eyes.
5. Notice the areas in your body that are clenched, and gently tense and release.
6. Begin by concentrating on your in-breath and out-breath.
7. Thoughts will enter your mind**. Welcome them without encouraging them.
8. Imagine your mind as an empty room with a window at either end.
9. Allow all thoughts to flow through one window, and out through the other.
10. Keep returning to your breathing.

NB:

Some days will be harder than others to achieve a meditative state. Persevere. Keep it up daily, even for just ten minutes. Regular practice matters – otherwise it is easy to get discouraged or out of the habit. You will know when you get there.

**It's normal for the mind to begin churning the moment you start to meditate, creating all sorts of reminders, debates, recollections and general chitter-chatter. The first few times it might be useful to have a pen and paper handy to spend ten minutes dumping any persistent thoughts on to paper before settling back into the meditation.*

EFT

EFT is at the forefront of the new healing movement.
Candace Pert

The magic of EFT (Emotional Freedom Technique)[25] cannot be overestimated. It has an extremely important place in this Handbook. There is not one single emotional, physical, mental or spiritual difficulty outlined here that cannot be addressed or relieved by its practice. EFT involves tapping specific acupressure points on the fingers, head and body whilst affirmations are voiced either aloud or silently. This calms the stress response and rewires the brain to react differently to its usual triggers in the environment. The technique is quick, safe, extraordinarily easy to learn and can be used in any kind of situation for anyone, including babies, children and animals. It is simply the most effective self-help tool out there and I would strongly recommend that you research the many websites and web pages devoted to teaching its basic principles.

EFT Resources:
- www.Emofree.com – **Gary Craig's** website (videos, testimonials, resources, training)
- www.EFTuniverse.com (videos, testimonials, resources, training)
- YouTube – search for 'EFT' and you will find many tap-along videos. Two are **Magnus Tapping** and **FasterEFT**. Search for **Nick Ortner** or **Jessica Ortner** *or the web for many more pages on the subject.*
- *The Tapping Solution: A Revolutionary System for Stress-Free Living* – book by **Nick Ortner**
- *Try It On Everything* – book by **Patricia Carrington**
- *The Healing Power of EFT and Energy Psychology: Revolutionary Methods for Dramatic Personal Change* – book by **David Feinstein, Donna Eden, Gary Craig**
- Search Amazon for many more books on the subject.

Daily Reconnections To Magic

I am realistic. I expect miracles.
Dr Wayne Dyer

Each Morning *anticipate* your day:
- What do I want to achieve?
- How do I want my day to be?

Each Night *review* your day:
- What lessons have I learned?
- What could I do better next time?
- What is there to be grateful for?
- Forgive yourself for everything.

By now, you should feel confidently armed with sufficient magic to deal with the unpleasant brown muck that life has a habit of throwing at us. So...

Here Comes The... *Brown Stuff!*

I Don't Know How To Give / Receive Love

Love is the energy of life.
Robert Browning

Love is the currency of the universe. Our mind, body and soul demand love in order to feel whole, integrated, at peace. Sometimes the act of giving and receiving love isn't as easy as it ought to be. When we are afraid of love, a way of falling into its embrace is to apply the principles of compassion and forgiveness – to ourselves; learning that we are worthy of love without the precondition of being or doing something first.

Examine the daily thoughts that crop up in your mind. Would you nourish a beloved child with these thoughts? Or would you forgive that child and show compassion, no matter what? Honour yourself as your own beloved child. Release yourself from whatever happened in the past, even yesterday. Those 'mistakes' and regrets are the stepping stones of experiences that brought you to where you are now – reading this book and seeking the *Light*. When you begin to love yourself, two things happen: you expand your capacity for giving love to others, and you raise your own standards for what you regard as acceptable behaviour from others, opening up your heart and mind to receiving the full quota of the love that you deserve. The next time someone pays you a compliment or gives you a gift for no particular reason, receive it with an open heart. Know that you deserve it as much as you deserve your own life.

Love, Compassion, Forgiveness
- Sit in front of the mirror, look your reflection in both eyes and say, *"I love you. I adore you. I forgive you."* How does

this make you feel? Where do you feel that feeling? Practise this every day until you can say the words without flinching, squirming, feeling undeserving or self-conscious.

- Catch yourself criticising or judging yourself unfairly. Replace each negative with a statement of approval and unconditional love. (Continue whether you believe it/feel it or not. Practice makes feelings.)

For example:
My hips look fat in this
I look attractive and desirable in whatever I wear

I hate myself for thinking that thought
That thought is not who I am, I'm releasing my guilt for thinking it

I wish I was as clever as him/her
I love and appreciate my own unique qualities and abilities

- Each time a negative thought pops into your mind, immediately hear yourself give the command, *"Cancel!"*
- Wear an elastic band as a bracelet for a day. Snap the band against your wrist whenever a judgemental or critical thought occurs. Notice how many painful reminders you receive throughout the day.

Recap: Resistance/Allowing

I Don't Know How To Find Joy In My Life

I don't think of all the misery, but of the beauty that still remains.
Anne Frank

When was the last time something good happened to you,

however small? How did you react? With gratitude or with judgement? Going with the flow or holding back? Did you even notice fortune smiling upon you, or were you hurrying on to the next thing? Study the pattern in your life. When things are going well, are you comparing the moment to something or someone else? Are you waiting for something catastrophic to happen to snatch away the happiness? Become aware of any unconscious conditioning where your main focus is on what is lacking and scarce in your life. When we acknowledge our mental programming, we can begin appreciating the simple things that make us happy; opening ourselves up to wider abundance and the goodness that life has to offer.

Don't set yourself impossibly high standards. Who do you know who is *really* happy, all of the time? Don't fall for the mask that most of us hide behind. Even the most enlightened of us have to consciously remind ourselves that happiness is always here for us, if we choose it. Maybe happiness wouldn't be so elusive if we all agreed to reject the fake media images of perfection that are designed to feed on our obsessions. We could have a universal Quit Day: quit pretending we're not allowed to be confused/depressed/sad; quit downloading those neurotic programmes that we inherited mostly in childhood that continue into adulthood; quit being who or what we think we're supposed to be, or told to be, and just BE.

Perfection and Failure:

Have no fear of perfection. You'll never reach it.
Salvador Dali

- How many times do you hear yourself saying: *"This isn't good enough"; "This isn't the right moment"; "The next time will be better"; "I'm not ready yet"; "That's not my best"?*
- In the quest to be perfect, failure is inevitable. You will

never attain perfection in a way that appeals to everyone, so why aim for the impossible?

- Accept that your 'flaws' and 'imperfections' are part of the uniqueness of who you are. If there is no other like you, how can imperfection exist?
- Happiness and joy are found in the recognition that you are the most perfect specimen of You.

Make the intention to stop deferring happiness

- Find an excuse for joy in your life – right now. Perhaps you can enjoy feeling the sun's warm rays on your bare skin; a clean refreshing gulp of pure water; the way a particular item of clothing blends with your eyes/your complexion; watching the innocence of a child lost in play?
- Really appreciate the moment for what it is.
- Ask yourself, what if, in the next moment, I could allow myself to be open to even *more* joy?
- Keep a 'Good Things' jar. Fill it with notes about good things, however small, that happen to you over time. When life starts getting you down, empty out the jar and enjoy the notes.

- *Recap:* Intention/Conviction
- *Recap:* Gratitude
- *Recap:* Resistance/Allowing

Who Am I Supposed To Be?

If it doesn't challenge you it won't change you. Use every challenge as an opportunity to stretch yourself and become better.
Zig Ziglar

I can't answer that question for you, the answer lies within yourself. We have become so accustomed to shielding ourselves from the scary truth of our own potential, we are literally afraid to breathe, never mind speak our truth. In order to survive alongside our fears, we split ourselves into two – our *physical self* that exists out there in the world; and our *potential self* whose presence we continually deny out of fear that it might engulf us with its demands that we live our life in greatness. We know we need to change in some way, but the challenge seems beyond us, so we stuff down this uncomfortable truth, bury our potential self, and carry on with the day-to-day. What we fail to realise is that every single moment gives us a fresh chance to take up the challenge of personal change; to discover who we truly are here to be.

The very first step towards finding our own truth and integrating our two selves is to acknowledge the blocks that keep them apart. Notice the *words* you yearn to say but bite back out of fear of feeling small, vulnerable, exposed; those emotions you admire in others but stop your own self from expressing because you might appear weak or lacking in self-control; the moments when feelings rise up inside of you but you push them down before they surface and reveal you are not who you present to the world; the times when it doesn't feel safe to utter sentiments such as "I love you", "I miss you", "I'm sorry", "I'm scared".

It's time for us to acknowledge our deep inner truths by confronting the thoughts, feelings and emotions that we are holding back. Deep truths are persistent. The more we suppress them, the more they have a habit of leaking out, showing up in different mental and physical manifestations – the stutter, the nervous twitch, the pacing, the awkward movements, the frantic manner, the red flushes, the headache, the impatience, the irritation, the fast temper, etc. When we dive into our doubts and worries; when we test the brown stuff by saying aloud what we fear most, we get a taste of our own freedom. We realise how much life has been passing us by; the time that we have wasted, waiting to exhale.

- **Dare Yourself** to find a situation where you can voice any of the following statements. If the thought of saying a particular sentiment to a particular person makes you feel uncomfortable, that is the right challenge for you:
  - *I love you*
  - *I miss you*
  - *I'm sorry*
  - *I'm scared*
  - *It's my fault*
  - *Please forgive me*
- Go deeper into the narrative to discover the true nature of your personal block. For example:
  - *"I love you and it makes me scared to say it because I don't feel good enough for you"*
  - *"I'm scared of the future because I can't cope with what life demands of me"*
  - *"It's my fault, but if I admit this you might hold me responsible and I will have to face up to my actions"*
- Once we shine a light on to our deepest fears, we clear the way of those obstacles to seeing our purpose and our future.

- *Recap:* Visualisation/Imagination
- *Recap:* Resistance/Allowing

I Want To Change But I Find It Impossible

Start where you are, use what you have, do what you can.
Arthur Ashe

In every moment there is the opportunity to change your vibrations by doing something different. To change your *life*, however, requires doing something different *every single day*. Don't wait for conditions or circumstances to miraculously resolve in order for your feeling to change. There is no learning in this strategy. First change your *reaction* to the condition or situation as it exists now. At first, expect change to feel strange, uncomfortable, scary. During this period you may feel a strong urge to give up and run back to your comfort zone. Recognise that what you are going through is a period of transition. Congratulate yourself for having the courage and the faith to hang in there.

- **Make Changes** by consciously examining your old ways of seeing and doing things in the world. If those old habits don't serve you, choose to do things differently or not at all.
- If you've just returned from a holiday or a break away from your routines, this is the perfect opportunity to examine your life with new eyes.
- What single thing are you prepared to start, to give up, to change, to stop altogether, every single day, starting today?

I'm going to... reduce my smoking by half; notice when I'm biting my nails and stop; take one less sugar in my coffee; wake up half an hour earlier to do some gentle exercises; eat my 5-a-day every day; keep a diary; say "I love you" morning and night to my partner; wear something nice that makes me feel good about myself; meditate for at least ten minutes every day; spend 50% less time on social media; quit listening to the TV news; read something inspiring daily; switch to organic dairy produce; write a section of my book every day, no matter how little, etc.

- Make the intention that *today* is the day for change.
- Find friends and mentors who will support you. Emulate those whose example teaches you how to aim higher.
- Keep the faith. It's been said that it takes approximately 30 days to change a habit.

Why Me?

Take all the manure that has been thrown at you and use it as fertiliser.
Eartha Kitt

As you read these words, know that this moment right now is perfect, that there could never be a better moment for you. You might be suffering so much you are beyond pleading with the heavens: *"What did I ever do to deserve this?"* Even so, this is not some pithy sentiment intended to look good on paper; the truth is that everything happens for a reason, and the reason is *You.* There are lessons in everything that is unfolding right now in your life, if only you would know that. What if you could take a chance and break away from old ways of seeing by appreciating your situation through different eyes? What if you could accept that these difficult times just might be a sign of how advanced you are as a student of this life? You've passed elementary with flying colours – now here comes the superior brown stuff that will take you to your next level. *"But I never asked for this!"* I hear you scream. Perhaps not. Not in a way that you would under-stand whilst you're knee deep in the brown stuff, but when the clouds part and the magic appears, that's when it will all make perfect sense. Or would you rather take a different view? You could decide that everything and everyone is against you; that there isn't and never has been any kind of mercy or support from anyone in your life; that you have been utterly rejected and abandoned by the so-called universe. You have free will, the prerogative to view life through whichever lens you choose. But ask yourself: which perspective makes me feel better about myself; which gives me the hope and the strength to carry on and overcome my challenges?

In order to grow fully into whom we are meant to be, we get to experience both sides of what life has to offer – the *yin* and the *yang*. It's how we recognise happy by knowing sad; how we are able to distinguish the dark because of our experience of the light. The muck that is thrown at us can be our very salvation, the lucky misfortune that is the key to turning our life around. The lesson might not be evident right now, but one day in the near or distant future it will all become clear. Your greatest gift could turn out to have begun with your worst nightmare, your deepest challenge. And let's not forget, how we get through the brown stuff might just be the lesson itself.

- *Recap:* Perspective
- *Recap:* Resistance/Allowing
- *Recap:* Gratitude

A few years ago I wrote a self-development book that failed to get published. I lost heart sending out my manuscript and suffered a lot of pain and frustration, especially as the disappointment came immediately after the long, drawn-out saga of my first novel being (repeatedly) rejected. Why me? I asked. I had worked so hard and sacrificed so much. It seemed so unfair. But where am I today? I'm looking back on both those experiences and appreciating exactly why I didn't get what I thought I wanted at that time. In terms of the novel, my 5-year-long protracted drama of writing and rewrites, raised and dashed hopes, and absolute 'failure', brought me to my dark night of the soul. It was this total breakdown that directly led to the life-changing discovery of my healing abilities, from which I have never looked back. Regarding the subsequent self-help book, at the time I didn't have an iota of the real-life experiences to draw upon that I do now. Yet, the labour I put into that book was by no means a waste of my time and efforts. Far from it. Though I wasn't ready then, and didn't recognise that I wasn't ready, I was nonetheless building towards this day. Today. This book in your hands draws upon the foundations of that earlier manuscript, but surpasses it in accomplishment. The publisher who turned me down back then, magically, unwittingly, is the same publisher who took me on this time. The universe works in ways to serve our highest, our best interests. Keep that knowledge in mind, and keep going!

I Can't See The End Of This Suffering

Suffering is necessary until you realise it is unnecessary.
Eckhart Tolle

Sometimes it's hard to see the way out of a dismal tunnel, or to imagine grief or worry coming to an end. Give a number to your feelings on a 0–10 scale, 10 being the worst feeling. Decide how long you intend to give yourself to get over your present difficulties. Remember, it's your choice, it's your script – you are in control of your own *Life Movie*. The Long Road begins with a decision. Where do you want to be in, say, three months? Feeling clearer in your mind? Less heavy in the heart? More hopeful of the future? When you make your decision, mark that *end date* in your calendar. Also mark today's date as your *start date*. This gives you power over a situation that may seem entirely out of your control at this time. Now, instead of living out your pain and suffering unendingly day-by-day, you will literally be magnetising towards healing and the prospect of a resolution. Remember: Have an idea of what your future will look like, but don't become overly attached to an exact outcome. The universe may have different, better, plans for you – always in keeping with your highest.

Calendar For Change

- Write the following information on today's date of your calendar:
  - What is the situation that is causing me to suffer?
  - What is the emotion (anger, hate, shame, blame, anxiety, fear, numbness, etc) that I am feeling?
  - Where in my body do I feel that emotion?
  - How do I rate the emotion on a 0–10 scale?
  - How long will I give myself to continue experiencing this pain/suffering (end date)?
  - At the end of this period, how do I want to feel?
- Now mark your end date on the calendar.
- Let go of any expectations. Get on with your life, and resist the temptation to obsess about the end date.

- *Recap:* Intention/Conviction
- *Recap:* Resistance/Allowing
- *Recap:* Meditation

I'm Fearful Of So Many Things Right Now

Forget Everything And Run versus: Face Everything And Rise.

Feeling fear is natural. We fear public speaking, flying, heights, the dark, intimacy, death, failure, rejection, commitment, creepy crawlies. But it is when fear keeps us from taking the next step, from fully embracing our potential, that it's time to question its presence; time to liberate ourselves from past experiences of impotence and old stories of personal unworthiness. The rewards of facing up to our fears can be immense, life-changing. Think of the exhilaration of a first-time skydive, the sense of achievement completing a marathon, the relief and accomplishment of overcoming our nerves and getting up on stage and delivering a speech. When we face our fears, on the other side we are always greeted by an experience of magic.

- When you are overwhelmed with fear, go to a quiet space and put your hand on your heart. Really **Feel The Fear**. Notice where you feel it in the body.
- Visualise a big oak tree with many branches. Imagine the branches heavy with each of your fears as you say them aloud: *"I'm afraid I can't pay my tax bill; I'm nervous about making that phone call; I'm tense about my test results; I'm scared we'll lose our home; I'm anxious my kids won't get the school of their choice; I'm terrified of facing another day... etc."* Keep going until you're emptied, and include these extra branches: *"Fears I might have forgotten"*, *"Fears I can't remember"*, *"Fears I'm too scared to admit to myself"*, *"Fears I might be reminded of later"*.
- Say to yourself: *"I release all the feelings of hopelessness, helplessness, panic, lack of control, rejection, abandonment. I make peace with my worst fears. I forgive myself. It's safe to let it all go, right now."*
- Now imagine the tree being pulled up by the roots. See it crash to the ground. Watch the branches and leaves wither into dust.
- Notice fresh green shoots emerging from the earth, growing into a new oak tree.
- Say to yourself: *"I'm in control now. I'm so powerful. I bless those thoughts, beliefs and judgements I created in the past, and I now choose better ones."*
- Imagine that new oak tree with branches that bear the weight of your new desires, dreams and ambitions. Say aloud what these are: *"I have a healthy balance in my bank account; my children are happy at school; I have a new job that fulfils me; I feel safe to be alive in this world, etc."*

- *Recap:* Resistance/Allowing

- *Recap:* Finding Answers Through Your Body
- *Recap:* Meditation

Towards the completion of this book I was at an Inspire'd event during which various speakers took to the platform to talk about a variety of topics related to their personal experience. A few minutes before the interval the host announced a 'Wild Card' slot where a member of the audience would be invited up on stage to share a story of their own. I immediately felt nervous, as if the invite was targeted specifically at me. I tuned into my body and quietly thought to myself, "I'm going to talk." My body released the tension and felt calm. I could do it. It was the right thing to do. I then said to myself, "No, I can't. I'm not going to talk." My agitation returned. My body was obviously steering me in the direction that would most benefit me. As soon as the host finished speaking I approached her and told her that I would like to be the Wild Card. Unlike the guest speakers, I had nothing prepared, so this really was going to be a test of my fears. But at least I had until the end of the presentations to calm my nerves and think about my subject. Imagine my surprise when straight after the break the host called me up on stage! I could have bluffed my way through, hiding my quaking nerves and feigning confidence but, instead, I decided to share my truth with the audience by confessing my terror of public speaking. Immediately, my admission was met with claps, cheers and shouts of encouragement. This wonderful response, and all the prior work that I'd done on myself, helped boost my spirits and melted my nerves. It wasn't long before I was in my stride. Fifteen minutes flew past, during which I realised that I actually enjoyed the experience of being the centre of everyone's attention. In the past I would certainly have interpreted the silence of the audience as criticism and judgement, but this time I knew that everyone was listening attentively to my story about Sam and how I began my journey of healing. I named my talk "The Day My Life Changed – Forever."[26] When I stepped off the stage to enthusiastic applause, I knew that my life was forever changing, and that change felt really good.

I'm Feeling Really, Really Low

Admit to the bad days, the impossible nights. Listen to the insights of those who have been there, but have come back.
Shane Koyczan

You don't have to be in the deepest, darkest, unrecognisable pit to be acquainted with the state of depression. Depression often lurks beneath the radar of so many other euphemisms – deep sadness, unhappiness, fear, guilt, low self-esteem, not feeling on top form, not coping very well, etc. Depression is a sign that for too long you have been putting on a brave face, elevating others' needs before your own, repressing your feelings, afraid to ask for help, pushing yourself beyond your limits, beating yourself up for not being superhuman.

Play Detective to get to the heart of your depression:
- What is the frequency of your depression? Do you feel low most of the time, or only sometimes?
- What triggers the depressed state? Is it a particular thought? When you are in a certain location? Do you feel OK until you see somebody or hear someone say something?
- If you had to teach an alien how to 'do' depression, how would you describe the process? E.g. go to bed, cover your head and shut out the world; sit in front of the TV and numb out; descend into a darkness of deep sadness; withdraw inside and beat yourself up or call yourself names; constantly think suicidal thoughts; feel exhausted and totally empty; shop or eat or drink excessively and mindlessly; obsess about pornography, etc.

- Close your eyes, go deep, and answer these questions:
    - *Where* exactly do I feel depression in my body?
    - How does depression *feel* (e.g. a heavy weight on the shoulders, a dull pain in the heart, a hollowing in the chest or stomach)?
    - Does it have a *colour*?
    - What kind of *shape* is it?
    - What kind of *tone* or *texture*?
    - Does it have a *voice*?
    - Is that voice *sad, angry* or *fearful*?
    - What is that voice *saying*?
- Allow yourself to sit in that sensation of depression, noticing the familiar urges to push it down or to run away.
- Accept the uncomfortable feelings, embrace them, all the while observing as if you are that alien who is interested in knowing what this experience is like.
- Be aware of any mental, physical or emotional changes, whatever those changes are. Keep going until the original feeling transforms into something lighter, more bearable.

Go deeper. Ask yourself:
- What do I get out of staying depressed? If I got better, how would I lose out? For example: I'd no longer be the centre of attention; I'd be treated differently by friends and family; I'd be expected to start getting on with my life; I'd lose all the support I've become accustomed to; Everyone who cares for me would go back to their own lives; I'd be lonely and have no one to talk to; I'd have to face up to how much of my life I've wasted.
- Is the depression a mask for other emotions such as anger, sadness, guilt or fear? What am I angry/sad/guilty about? What do I fear?
- What particular activities make me come alive? We are all born with a purpose. This purpose is expressed in our

passion, our innate creativity. When we are not fulfilling our purpose the effect is of dampening our life force. What desires am I suppressing at the cost of my own energy and vitality?

- Am I being physical enough? Alone too much? Don't forget the restorative powers of movement – being in nature, walking, exercising, doing stuff that you love. And if you're not too deep in the pits of despair, simply assisting another person who has greater needs – without disregarding your own – can be extremely therapeutic.

- *Recap:* Energy
- *Recap:* Resistance/Allowing
- *Recap:* Gratitude
- *Recap:* Meditation

I'm Feeling Like A Failure

Sometimes you win, sometimes you learn.
John C. Maxwell

Are you feeling like a loser right now? Are you stuck in a rut of underachieving? Does success seem out of your reach / something that happens only to other people? Do you feel worthless and envious of others' good fortunes? If you're mired in this kind of brown stuff, it's an indication that your perception is due for a major overhaul. Forget the excuses, explanations, justifications, it's time for *action*. The first thing to recognise is the fear and self-judgement that is holding you back.

Truthfully answer the question: **Do I deserve** success – Yes or No?

- If the answer is No, recap these sections:

- *Recap:* Subconscious
- *Recap:* Perspective

Now examine any **unconscious beliefs**. Do any of these fears resonate?:

- If I became successful people and friends might stop liking me – no one actually likes a winner.
- Successful people can often be so ugly, ruthless and untrustworthy – I don't want to be one of them.
- It will be such hard work maintaining success – is it actually worth the effort, the hassle?
- What if I lose touch with reality? I prefer to remain the down-to-earth person that I am.
- There'll be so much stress and challenges – am I up to it? Do I want to make the sacrifices?
- When you're successful, everyone wants a piece of you – I'd rather be private, invisible, low-key.
- What if the worst happens – I become successful and then fail?:
  - I will feel even worse than I do now
  - I'll let everyone down, including myself
  - I'll be a bad person
  - I would lose respect, status, trust
  - I'll be a loser
  - I could risk my possessions, self-worth, friends
  - People will laugh at me
- In your mind you are possibly seeing success as a hazardous business, one you're terrified of failing at. In order to pursue your desires, dreams, ambitions you first have to be willing to take risks, make mistakes. Using the mantra (a repeated word or statement that helps quiet the mind and take you deeper into the subconscious) below, work on your fearful mindset until you begin to see failure in its true light:

"Right now, I'm failing because I haven't started succeeding. The moment I take my first action step, whatever that is, I'm immediately a success."

- *Recap:* Gratitude
- *Recap:* Make It Happen!

I'm Feeling Stuck, Scared, Fearful Of The Future

You can close your eyes to what you don't want to see, but you can't close your heart to the things you don't want to feel.
Johnny Depp

When we are in this place we have a habit of suppressing or running away from what it is we are feeling. We do this by numbing or distracting ourselves with anything from TV, social media, the Internet, holidays, drama and arguments, to alcohol, smoking, shopping, sex and drugs. But the solution to all our problems lies in the very discomfort we are trying to flee. We cannot heal, we cannot move to the next level, when we are stuck in an emotion we are not allowing ourselves to feel. Instead of fearing fear, why not take a chance and try a different strategy? Befriend it, embrace it, *feel* it. Stop judging and condemning yourself. Realise that there is nothing wrong with being fearful.

Accept that Fear is:
- *Natural.* It's just another emotion, all part of being human
- *Important.* It exists to keep us safe from danger
- *Inescapable.* We will always experience it, in varying degrees

The real problem with fear is when the trauma or drama has played out (*the boyfriend has left; the parents have divorced; that school presentation flop is yesterday's news*) but we remain stuck in the same old emotions of powerlessness, hopelessness, helplessness, rejection, abandonment. When the story has passed and there is no longer any real or actual threat, fear is usually tied up with having a particular agenda of how things should be/should have been: *I should have another boyfriend by now, what's wrong with me?; I'll hate it if Dad remarries, he ought to be here for me, he should never have divorced Mum; I'd love to be able to present my arguments but until I'm flawless I won't risk the humiliation.*

It's important to maintain our passion and our desires (*I want to be with someone; I want parental love; I want to be the best*), but **learn to let go of the pain and suffering of having to manifest outcomes in a specific way**. Trust that the universe will meet you wherever you wish to end up. However, stay open to the idea that the scenery might not be exactly as you imagine or expect, but that the results will always accord with your highest. In this knowledge – relax.

Be grateful when a fearful emotion surfaces, this is a sure sign that it is **Time For The Emotion To Be Released**:

- Don't judge yourself for having feelings
- Don't label your feelings good or bad, right or wrong
- Give yourself permission to ride out the emotional tidal waves that are bound to surface every now and then
- Feel what you feel and allow it to *pass*

- *Recap:* Thoughts
- *Recap:* Perspective
- *Recap:* Resistance/Allowing
- *Recap:* Gratitude
- *Recap:* Meditation

I'm Tense And Overwrought All The Time

When we give ourselves the chance to let go of all our tension, the body's natural capacity to heal itself can begin to work.
Nhat Hanh

Everyone has their particular stress points, those places in the body where we hold on to anger and fear. Mine are my throat and finger joints. Where are yours? Typical areas where we habitually clench, flinch, constrict and stiffen are the throat, neck, shoulders, jaw, fingers, stomach, lower back, knees. We are no different to Pavlov's dog salivating at the sound of the dinner bell. We react to triggers in the environment that are consciously and unconsciously setting off our automatic nervous responses all the time. Noticing the habits of your body is the first step towards reducing the level and impact of stress in your life.

As you continue through the day, see how many times you
Catch Yourself Tensing
• Note the area and make a point of consciously *stopping*
• Breathe into those areas
• Allow yourself to let go, *relax*
• Smile (fake it till you feel it)!

Our general attitude to life can affect the **Daily Tensions** we experience. Are you the type who:
• Holds continuous mental arguments?
• Complains a lot?
• Blames and points the finger?
• Talks about people doing things to you?
• Is always waiting for disaster to happen?
• Frequently discusses what's wrong in the world (from the news to the weather to the economy)?
• Is attracted to drama and disaster (personal, social or

fictional)?
- Feels like life's victim?

- *Recap:* Thoughts
- *Recap:* Resistance/Allowing
- *Recap:* Gratitude
- *Recap:* Meditation

I'm Caught In A Cycle Of Anger

Holding on to anger is like drinking poison and expecting the other person to die.
Gautama Buddha

Recognise that you are in exactly the right place, right now – paying *attention* to your feelings of anger. Anger can be a positive and healthy emotion that, if properly focused, equips us with the energy and motivation to respond to injustices in the world. But when we express anger to punish or harm others we can end up harming ourselves. We smoulder with resentments, brood on the past, or run vengeful scenarios in the mind. Meanwhile, day-by-day other irritations build upon the original wrongdoing until a backlog of draining emotions threatens to send us over the edge. Blood vessels constrict, blood pressure rises, and flow to the heart is restricted, leading to susceptibility to possible strokes, heart attacks and other stress-related ailments.

The next step is to *own* your anger. Realise that you alone are creating everything in your *Life Movie*, including what you are angry about. The ego right now is itching to disagree with this statement and put the blame on everyone else and everything that is out there. But when we feed the ego's need to be right, we only continue the struggle with ourselves. Anger is a flame that will consume us, whilst the apparent cause continues to burn. Override the ego's need to be in control – *I'm right, the other person is wrong.* Break the ties with personal pain and suffering by refusing to play the role of victim of your story. *Ask yourself:* what is the feeling behind the anger that I don't want to feel; what is the loss that I will suffer if I let go of the anger? The answer might not come right away, but if you hold this space, understanding will arrive with some amazing results. You may realise that underneath the anger lies unresolved, unexpressed sadness, grief, fear or loss. This is the beginning of your freedom from this potentially caustic emotion.

Respond Rather Than React To Anger

In the midst of an argument, own the moment, rather than allowing the emotion of anger to own you. Practise and learn this drill until it becomes a habit:

- *Pause* – resist the knee-jerk need to be right, to have the last word, to control the argument
- *Breathe* – in the midst of anger we often forget to breathe; breathing slows down our reaction, gives us time, releases pressure on the heart, brings us to centre
- *Count to Ten* – by the time you get to ten, the flames of anger will have subsided, reducing the risk of personal attack, regrettable action, an escalation of the story
- *Retreat* – take yourself somewhere to calm down. Dim the lights and lie in a darkened room, play relaxing music, meditate, exercise, go for a run or slow walk in nature
- *Be Aware* – examine the trigger points that led to your anger; congratulate yourself for how you responded; forgive yourself if your response could have been better; aim to improve on your drill for next time

- *Recap:* Perspective
- *Recap:* Resistance/Allowing
- *Recap:* Meditation

I'm In A Bad Place And I Don't Know How To Escape

Rock Bottom became the solid foundation on which I built my life.
JK Rowling

Whatever is happening in your life, no matter how dire right now, hear yourself say: *"Stop!"* In the stillness that follows give yourself permission to *accept* the situation for what it is. This doesn't mean you have to like what is happening. You are simply breaking the spell that says that life has to continue in exactly the same way. You are allowing yourself to end struggling *against* what is happening. Notice the tension or rigidity in your body – this is exactly where your struggle is manifesting. Relax those areas. Let go. Once you are in a place of acceptance, you have created an opening through which magic can now make its appearance. The above quote by JK Rowling echoes the sentiment that when we believe that our entire world is falling apart, actually, it may be the beginning of things falling into place. Stay open to the possibility of the unexpected.

There is also another possibility – that you are your own jailor and unaware of it. Unconscious acts of self-sabotage sometimes keep us holding on to what hurts; locking us into an endless cycle of the same-old same-old.

Think of your issue and honestly ask yourself – is there a reason why **I Don't Want Things To Change**? Perhaps:
- I get to be right
- They get to be wrong
- It would pain me if they were let off the hook
- I might need to start proving myself
- I'd be exposed / scrutinised / have to face the music
- I won't be special / noticed / get the attention I deserve any more
- I'd rather the suffering I know than an unknown suffering

- It terrifies me to leave my comfort zone

- *Recap:* Perspective
- *Recap:* Ideas/Intuition/Problem-Solving
- *Recap:* Resistance/Allowing
- *Recap:* Finding Answers Through Your Body
- *Recap:* Meditation

I Feel Emotional Pain

Pay attention to why you are choked up... It's the butterfly in your own cocoon. It wants out.
Steve Chandler

See emotional pain as a cry for freedom. Hurt, jealousy, pride, self-pity and other sore emotions are blocking the body's flow of energy and seeking release. Needing to be right creates its own pain. During or after an argument, take the time to step back and examine your personal role in the story. See the argument from the other party's perspective. This will help you to shift from a rigid stance of *'I'm right'* to a more relaxed attitude of *'I accept'* that can magically open up possibilities. The other person may be wrong from your standpoint, but from their own logic, they can equally be 'right'.

Emotional Pain:
- Accept that you might not be able to change another person's viewpoint, but you do have the power to change how you *respond* to that viewpoint. In this altered perspective lies your own liberation.

Ask yourself:
- Am I holding a grudge against someone?
- Do I need to forgive someone or release the past?

- Do I need to accept someone or a situation?
- Am I being too hard on myself?
- Am I the one who needs to be forgiven – by me?

- *Recap:* Perspective
- *Recap:* Resistance/Allowing
- *Recap:* Forgiveness
- *Recap:* Meditation

I'm Experiencing Physical Pain / Discomfort

Much of your pain is the bitter potion by which the physician within you heals your sick self.
Khalil Gibran

Study the pain with the curiosity of a child, the detailed interest of a forensic scientist. Close your eyes and ask yourself these questions: Where is it? How deep is it? How frequent? What 'colour'? What 'shape'? Is it dull, sharp, pounding, intermittent, spreading, contracted, hot, cold? By staying with and *noticing* the pain in this way, you are owning it rather than allowing yourself to become its helpless victim.

Create Healing Images *using the power of visualisation:*
- A bottle brush clearing a narrow space to relieve constriction / congestion
- A plunge into an ice-cold stream to bring down a high temperature
- A flame burning away a growth
- A dial gradually going down the numbers to reduce the intensity of suffering
- A warm hand stroking and comforting a racing heart
- Unscrewing and gradually loosening the metal vice of a migraine headache

Be inventive and come up with your own healing images!

- *Recap:* Visualisation/Imagination
- *Recap:* Intention/Conviction
- *Recap:* Resistance/Allowing
- *Recap:* Meditation

I'm Suffering From An Illness

Illness doesn't make you less of what you were. You are still you.
Tony Snow

Know that in every moment your body is perfect just as it is. You are not your disease or your condition. So, give yourself a break and permission to dispense with the 'ill person' label. Next, tune into the energy of your physical body by making friends with it. Learn its subtle rhythms and conversations. What might it be telling you? What negative thoughts, beliefs or judgements are feeding the illness? No chronic disease develops overnight – everything physical first began as a thought that became a belief. Chronic illness is usually an indication of a rigid unconscious belief held for a long time.

The *placebo effect* is your ally. Its existence has been known by the medical establishment since the 1950s – that the mind can heal the body through thoughts and beliefs. The placebo is a sugar pill or distilled water that the patient believes to be real medicine and it has led to countless people being cured of seemingly incurable diseases, including many documented cases of cancer remissions. Sometimes the doctor him/herself is the placebo. Have you noticed how minor issues like colds start to get better the moment you book that surgery visit? The opposite, *nocebo effect*, is when the mind believes that something bad is going to happen in the body, and that expectation then becomes manifest. Doctors can have the hexing power of the nocebo, for example, when they make pronouncements such as: "You have an incurable illness; you'll need to take that medicine for the rest of your life; you have a 5% chance of survival; you have six months to live." The subconscious accepts these messages and creates programmes that lead to changes in the body, for better or for worse.

The body is a natural and powerful self-repair mechanism – healing, maintaining, and growing. Among the activities that help bring the body into a state of balance are: massage, yoga, tai chi, qi gong, meditation, exercise, intimacy, cuddles, laughter, listening to music, petting animals, dancing, going out with friends, being in nature, doing what you love. Are any of these a feature of your life right now? Assist your body to help itself by engaging in as many of these activities as you can.

Seek out and **Banish Areas Of Negativity** in your everyday:

- Start by accepting where you are now – fully and completely. This doesn't mean giving up on the idea of ever getting better. It means totally acknowledging and making peace with the situation that you are in, in every moment. It means relaxing any mental denial or physical resistance to your condition.
- Don't make yourself feel any more hopeless by blaming yourself. Depersonalise your condition by seeing it for what it really is – energy trapped and needing to flow; a part of your soul communicating that it is yearning to be free.
- Energy cannot flow while you're wallowing in negativity. Replace all talk of 'illness' with talk of 'health and well-being to come'. This is not denying the reality of your situation, rather, it is you making a powerful statement of your arrow of *Intent*.
- Research cases of people with your condition who have found ways of healing themselves and beating the odds. A single exception is proof that miracles are available to all

of us.

- Reprogramme your mind to override any unconscious 'need' for your illness:
    - Visualise your end desire (see yourself as whole and without your condition)
    - Imagine how being in this state would *feel*
    - Give thanks for the healing to come – and let go of expectations
    - Repeat this daily mantra (or similar) for several minutes just before sleeping and first thing upon waking. Do it with feeling: *"I am already whole. I am completely free of the need for this pain / condition."*
- Avoid getting into involved conversations with people who insist on discussing illness in helpless, defeatist terms and who see you as a victim of your condition.
- Seek the company of others who regard illness as an opportunity to heal by moving on from previous rigidly-held beliefs about life, wholeness, the world.

Talk To The Affected Area Of Your Body:
- *Ask:*
    - What *emotion* is it that you are trying to help me *not* to feel?
    - Which *story* is it that you are holding on to?
    - Who do I need to *forgive* to begin to heal myself?
- Make reassurances as though this hurt part of your body were a friend in need of support and encouragement. For example: *"Heart, it's time to learn that there's really nothing to be afraid of. I'm here for you. I'll protect you. We can work on this together. So, there's no need to gallop at the least thing. There's no need to try to run away from me. We can do this. Trust me."*

- *Recap:* Thoughts

- *Recap:* Resistance/Allowing
- *Recap:* Forgiveness
- *Recap:* Finding Answers Through Your Body
- *Recap:* Meditation
- *Recap:* Calendar for Change (page 259)

I Can't Let Go, I Can't Forgive

Nothing in the universe can stop you from letting go and starting over.
Guy Finley

Why do we find forgiveness such a challenge? Because often our righteous beliefs tell us that letting go is a sign of personal weakness. We believe that forgiving means caving in to a person, allowing that person to get away with doing wrong. We believe that that person needs to be taught a lesson; that enemies don't deserve our forgiveness. We believe this stance gives us power. Conversely, looking at forgiveness in this way plays into the hands of our transgressor. That person gets to control how we feel and how we see ourself – angry, a victim. On the other hand, the moment we recognise that forgiveness is never about the other person – it's always about us – we regain control and empowerment.

Another major reason for becoming stuck and unable to let go is because we believe that forgiveness equates with having to have unreasonable tolerance for others. Let go of that belief. The fact is, sometimes people's behaviour can be unpardonable. In these instances, it is reasonable for us not to condone an action that is bad or unacceptable. What we do excuse, however, is that part of the person that is struggling with a shortage of personal resources. These inadequate resources can be anything from self-love, self-worth, education, experience, maturity or empathy, to issues relating to mental or emotional capacity due to historical or family dysfunctions or deficiencies. Each one of us can only *do* better when we have reached the stage in our lives when we know *how* to do better. That person who has done wrong acted as a result of certain limiting beliefs and emotions, in exactly the same way that we continue to wrestle with our own failings. Leaving unacceptable behaviour aside, forgive that part of your transgressor that is still struggling to get there, and free yourself from personal suffering.

Fallacy Of Forgiveness:

I have to be face-to-face with the person in order to forgive them.

I have to accept that person back into my life.

That person will end up feeling good whilst I will be left with unresolved feelings of being soft, lenient, a loser, taken advantage of.

The magic of forgiveness only benefits the person who is being forgiven.

Truth About Forgiveness:

Forgiveness doesn't have to be done in the presence of anyone.

Forgiveness doesn't necessarily have to lead to reconciliation.

Forgiveness is what you do to cleanse your *own* toxic emotions, heal your *own* physical body, and set your *own* soul free.

Forgiveness is what takes you out of the smelly stuff and into the magic of peace, freedom and happiness.

- *Recap:* Thoughts
- *Recap:* Perspective
- *Recap:* Resistance/Allowing

- *Recap:* Forgiveness

Some years ago I was working on a TV programme. I was brought in as the lead writer but found myself among a group of creatives who knew one another and were very cliquey. I was professional and courteous at all times, but for some reason I was seen as a threat and treated as an outsider. I had the option of either speaking up about the subtle treatment I was receiving and risk being ostracised even further, or proceeding according to the saying "Change the things you can, accept the things you can't; have the wisdom to know the difference". So, I bottled up my grievances and stoically endured the situation. During those difficult meetings an ache grew in my lower back and increasingly I found it uncomfortable to sit, so I would stand and pace during the meetings. One weekend I was on the Kent coast with the family and the pain got so bad my partner pulled up directly outside a massage parlour so that I could crawl from the car straight on to the masseuse's table for work on my stiffened muscles. By this time I was feeling a certain amount of antipathy towards the group and really didn't look forward to the meetings which, in my opinion, dragged on unnecessarily, unprofessionally and unproductively.

I realised that I was holding these tense feelings in my back, and that it was in my own best interests to do something about it. When I got home, I found a quiet moment, relaxed into a meditative state and began visualising. I saw myself surrounded by the unfriendly group and looked each person in the eye. I then asked the question, "What are you so afraid of that would make me appear such a threat to you?" I stayed with each person in turn, till the answer to my question was revealed and I was filled with enough compassion and forgiveness to see past each individual's reactive fears. I repeated this process until I had forgiven everyone. I finished by imagining the group as miniature people standing on the palm of my hand, surrounded by Light. I opened my heart and sent each person genuine love before blowing them off my hand and into the Light.

The next morning I woke up, my back pain had miraculously gone!

I was so overjoyed that at the very next meeting I demonstrated to the group how, from being bent with pain, I could now touch my toes without any discomfort whatsoever. After that day, the atmosphere noticeably improved and I even started to enjoy myself. By releasing through forgiveness, I was no longer burdened by the group's projected fears or by the weight of my own animosities that had been resting in my lower back.

The aim of these exercises is to achieve emotional rebalance at the same time as supporting your need for whatever medical treatment is required.

The above suggestions do *not* replace professional medical advice.

Emancipate yourself from mental slavery, none but our self can free our minds.
Bob Marley

A friend came to visit and talked about how desperately unhappy she was in her marriage. She mused that she had realised ten years ago that she had to end it, but did nothing. She was now 50 years old and regretting that she had wasted a further ten years of her life. When I suggested that perhaps a first step towards a new future might be to hold the mental attitude that she was 'available' to attract other men into her life, her rather affronted response was, "But I'm still married!" When I asked whether there was any chance of the marriage surviving, she firmly said no, and recounted all the reasons why her husband was not the right man for her, never would be and never had been. She heard herself saying all of this yet she was blind to both the contradiction of her response, and the prison of fidelity she had chosen for herself. It reminded me of how elephants are trained in some parts of the world not to stray. For a period they are tethered by rope to a sturdy structure like a concrete post or a large tree. Over time, the elephant learns that it is hopeless to try to escape. In the end, all that is required to control the movements of a giant beast is a rope secured to some part of its body with the other end casually fastened to something as flimsy as a plastic chair. Even in the confines of her own mind, my friend couldn't allow the universe to present her with the man of her dreams. This is an example of how we unconsciously allow old habits and routines to block us from receiving what we truly deserve in life. Until we make the change mentally, a plastic chair, or a sheet of paper bearing an official stamp, is all it will take to imprison us in a world of pain, suffering, boredom and misery.

When all is said and done, the only person with the power to change their life is the person looking back in the mirror. Sometimes it will take a personal tragedy for transformation to come about – that moment when we are brave/beaten/exhausted/defeated enough to draw a line in the sand and declare that our old life is behind us and our new life is beginning right here, right now. My wish for you is that your own personal change will not require a disaster. I'm hoping that the information in this Handbook will be enough of an invitation for you to free yourself from the same old mental slavery and to begin trusting the process of transformation. You have nothing to lose by opening up to the magic that exists in the universe – trusting what it might bring into your life and where it could take you. There is always another way through the brown stuff that life repeatedly throws at all of us, and this might just be the way for you. If you *allow it*.

Notes

1. General Post Office
2. **LD** – your consciousness remains in your body; you have an awareness of being awake whilst in the dream state i.e. wide awake in a dream.
3. **OB** – your consciousness separates from the physical reality of your body; you have a real experience in the astral plane. People who experience Near Death (NDE) describe OB events.
4. Nathalie's chicken soup stall was a popular fixture at the local Farmer's Market for a year until she branched out into other areas of earning an independent living. Mark would be very proud of his businesswoman wife!
5. Freud popularised the three theoretical levels of the mind – conscious, subconscious and unconscious. Today these concepts are used differently by various writers, psychiatrists and psychologists. When I refer to the unconscious and subconscious I am describing different levels of awareness, where the conscious mind is fully aware. Information in the unconscious is the most deeply buried and less accessible to the conscious mind, whereas information in the subconscious can be more readily brought to the surface of the conscious mind. But as the subconscious is in constant communication between the conscious and the unconscious, I sometimes use unconscious and subconscious interchangeably.
6. *"There is a set of three nerves which connect the base of the spine to the brain. When Kundalini awakens, it rises through the central nerve to the brain, which causes what seems like an explosion in the brain, since the dormant areas begin to blossom like flowers. All happenings in the spiritual life and all outstanding works in any walk of life – poetry, painting, writing, music, war, science, art,*

philosophy, etc – are related to the awakening of Kundalini. It is the creative energy, the energy of self-expression." Center for the New Age Newsletter (Vol 3, Issue 9, 2003)

7. *Dead Proud* ed by Ann Considine, Robyn Slovo; The Women's Press, 1987

8. *Naomi's Secret*; Heinemann, 1990

9. *The Big Red Trouble*; Heinemann, 1991

10. *The Moving Mystery*; Orchard, 1996

11. *Charlie's New School*; Orchard, 1996

12. By remarkable coincidence, Andrea and I had lived in the same street in Finsbury Park around the same time during the 1980s. Whilst I worked in television, she worked in the film industry; later we both attended the City Lit to acquire novel-writing skills; and much later, still, I was involved as a Voice Coach on the TV production of her award-winning novel, *Small Island*.

13. According to Hungarian biologist **Mihály Csíkszentmihályi**, millions of bits of information and stimuli impact your senses and nervous system every single second. Your mind must filter most of it out of your conscious awareness in order for you to:
    - not be overwhelmed constantly;
    - be able to cope with that amount of information;
    - have the freedom to think and act consciously in such an environment.

14. About eighteen months later, I returned to Seka, this time with my son about a condition (recurring cold sores on his top lip) that I knew the doctors would want to treat topically without investigating the root cause, and that I believed stemmed from something more fundamental, a blockage of energy. After only one session he, too, showed amazing results.

15. In the context of this story and the healing of others, I use the word 'healing' loosely. We naturally heal ourselves. Those of

us who call ourselves 'healers' are simply enabling others to generate or kick-start their own innate ability to self-heal.

16. Emotional Freedom Technique (EFT) – sometimes referred to as 'acupuncture without needles'. A self-help tool using light tapping on acupressure points accompanied by affirmations to break the connection between certain thoughts/beliefs that trigger negative emotional and physical responses.

17. Neuro Linguistic Programming (NLP) – a process that makes the connection between language and behaviour patterns to enable an individual to achieve goals in life.

18. During the healing that took place in his hotel room, Bobby described how, despite my not actually touching him, he could distinctly feel the energy, as though his poorly right foot was being squeezed by both my hands. He described the sensation as "unbelievable". The following year when I next saw him, Bobby thanked me for the healing, commenting that it had added an extra five years to his life.

19. During his time in the concentration camp, the Austrian Holocaust survivor and neurologist/psychiatrist Viktor Frankl decided that no one had the power make him think what he didn't want to. *"The one thing you can't take away from me is the way I choose to respond to what you do to me. The last of one's freedoms is to choose one's attitude in any given circumstance."*

20. This is an actual scenario that had caused one of my clients untold stress for many years, leading to OCD tendencies and, which, until her subconscious offered it up, she'd had no conscious memory of!

21. Recently a lady diagnosed nine months previously with breast cancer, who had already decided to forego chemo and conventional treatment in favour of alternative methods, decided to come and see me. Two weeks after a single healing session, she wrote: *"Good news! Today I had an ultrasound. When I was first diagnosed in November 2013 my lump*

was 2.5cm. An ultrasound in April indicated it had gone up to 3cm. In June I had a 'manual' examination and the doctor told me it was 4cm! Today it's 2.8cm!!! Yeah! Thank you so much. I loved your treatment and am eager to have another session with you."

22. *Cold Laser Technology and Frequency Healing* – by Carmen Harris

23. The clear or 'clair' senses of these dimensions are: clairvoyance (*seeing*), clairsentience (*feeling*), clairaudience (*hearing*), clairgustance (*tasting*), clairalience (*smelling*) and claircognizance (*knowing*).

24. I recount the full story in the memoir section of this book.

25. EFT is a self-help technique based on another technique called Thought Field Therapy (TFT) that was devised by a psychologist called Roger Callahan. Gary Craig, an engineer, was a student of Callahan and simplified TFT into EFT.

26. I recount this story in the memoir section of this book.

BOOKS

O is a symbol of the world, of oneness and unity; this eye represents knowledge and insight. We publish titles on general spirituality and living a spiritual life. We aim to inform and help you on your own journey in this life.

Visit our website: http://www.o-books.com

Find us on Facebook:
https://www.facebook.com/OBooks

Follow us on Twitter: @obooks